BALLAD OF THE ANARCHIST BANDITS

BALLAD OF THE ANARCHIST BANDITS

THE CRIME SPREE THAT GRIPPED BELLE ÉPOQUE PARIS

JOHN MERRIMAN

NATION
BOOKS
New York

Nation Books
116 East 16th Street, 8th Floor New York, NY 10003
http://www.publicaffairsbooks.com/nation-books
@NationBooks
Printed in the United States of America
First Edition: October 2017

Published by Nation Books, an imprint of Perseus Books, LLC, a subsidiary of Hachette
Book Group, Inc.
Nation Books is a co-publishing venture of the Nation Institute and the Perseus Books.
The Hachette Speakers Bureau provides a wide range of authors for speaking events. To
find out more, go to www.hachettespeakersbureau.com or call (866) 376-6591.
The publisher is not responsible for websites (or their content) that are not owned by the
publisher.

Print book interior design by Amnet Systems Private Limited.

Library of Congress Control Number: 2017951124

ISBN: 978-1-56858-988-6 (hardcover)
ISBN: 978-1-56858-989-3 (e-book)

LSC-C

10 9 8 7 6 5 4 3 2 1

For Peter McPhee

CONTENTS

CONTENTS

PROLOGUE

At 8:45 in the morning on December 21, 1911, in Paris, Ernest Caby, a thirty-two-year-old employee of the Société Générale wearing the uniform of the bank and a blue bicorn hat with a tricolor cocarde, stepped off the tramway at its stop at Carrefour Damrémont-Ordener in the eighteenth arrondissement beyond Montmartre. The stop stood about one hundred yards from the branch office of that bank at 146 rue Ordener at the corner of Cité Nollez. Over his left shoulder, Caby carried a cloth sack, and in his hand, another. This morning, it was filled with 5,266 francs in silver. In his left hand he carried 318,772 francs in *titres* (securities), some of which were negotiable. Inside his coat was an envelope containing twenty thousand francs in bank notes and five thousand francs in cash.

Passersby in the busy morning hour in a neighborhood of modest means gaped at a Delaunay-Belleville parked near the bank, some approaching the luxury automobile to have a closer look. Alfred Peemans, a bank official, walked out the door of the Société Générale to meet Caby as he approached the bank, and together they headed toward the bank. When they reached the corner of the Cité Nollez, near the front door of the bank, a man stepped out of the luxury car holding a revolver in his left hand. From just a few feet away, he shot

The automobile used in the robbery.

The holdup at the Société Générale, rue
Ordener, Paris. The courier Ernest Caby is
shot by one of the bandits.

Caby point-blank in the chest, and then shot him twice more. The courier collapsed at the base of a tree.

Peemans was unharmed and ran into the bank, shouting, "They are attacking our courier!" Several bank employees followed Peemans out into the street in time to see the man fire a fourth shot, which lodged near Caby's spine. The gunman then grabbed one of Caby's bags; another man grabbed a second sack. Both men jumped back into the waiting car, leaving Caby lying in a pool of blood.

Two municipal policemen (*gardiens de la paix*) arrived from different directions and moved toward the automobile, but they were met by a barrage of shots fired from inside the Delaunay-Belleville as it sped off. A bus arrived, blocking the street at the corner of the rue du Cloys, and a tram was crossing the road, but the driver of the speeding automobile skillfully avoided both and turned onto rue Montcalm and then onto rue Vauvenargues and headed out of Paris via the porte de Clichy. No one managed to stop them before they made their escape.

News of the holdup and shooting at the Société Générale exploded in Paris. Although it was the first holdup in France using an automobile, it confirmed public worries about the use of automobiles in burglaries to elude the police. In this case the thieves were better armed and better equipped than the authorities. The police had very few automobiles at their disposal. Caby, who survived, was the only casualty, but the holdup was an embarrassment for the police.[1]

From his office on the Île de la Cité, Louis Lépine, who had been the prefect of police since 1893, moved quickly to coordinate the massive police operation intended to find the bandits. Born in Lyon in 1846 into a family of modest origin, Lépine had quickly given up law for administration, serving in Saint-Étienne as prefect of the Loire. The Prefecture of Police of Paris had been created in 1800 and charged "with all that concerns the police," in the widest possible sense. Louis Lépine's post was therefore an important position in the hierarchy of power in France. This position enabled him, as it had his predecessors, to intervene arbitrarily, forcefully, and sometimes secretly on the edge of illegality in the investigation of crimes, ordering arrests and searches as he pleased, dipping into an enormous drawer of secret funds that enabled him to pay off informers and police spies. Lépine knew how to manipulate the municipal council of Paris; he had staked his reputation on his ability to prevail in negotiations with anyone who might check his power. He imagined himself to be "the king of Paris," or the commander "by divine right," imposing military discipline on "his" agents, "his" brigades, and "his" administration. As he sat behind his large desk—with his mustache and short beard, invariably wearing a dark suit and tie, matched by a black top hat when he went out—Lépine had no idea who might have carried out the audacious attack on the courier who worked for Société Générale. But his attention soon turned to the possibility that anarchists were involved.

The next morning, in their small apartment in plebeian Belleville, Victor Kibaltchiche, the Brussels-born anarchist son of Russian émigrés, and his companion Rirette Maîtrejean, a fellow anarchist who had come to Paris from her village in central France, read in the newspapers about the dramatic, bloody theft and getaway. Victor immediately thought of someone who might have done it: a certain Jules Bonnot, whom Victor and Rirette had recently met in anarchist circles—"He is crazy enough to have done that!" Victor and Rirette read the descriptions of the perpetrators. For her part, Rirette doubted that a man whom eyewitnesses described as being small with a thin mustache could have been Bonnot. Victor disagreed. And another accomplice had been described as "seeming very young, not very big, wearing a martingale raincoat, a melon-shaped hat, binocles, and with a face of baby-like rose complexion." Victor immediately recognized Raymond Callemin, once a close friend from his youth in Brussels. Eyewitness accounts led Victor to believe that another Belgian, a violent anarchist named Octave Garnier, was one of the four—or five—men whom passersby had seen in the car. Victor and Rirette realized that although they had had absolutely nothing to do with the holdup, completely disagreed with such violent acts, and had long since distanced themselves from this small faction of anarchists, this could be bad for them. They were already known to the authorities because of the anarchist paper they ran, *L'Anarchie*. The police had been on to them for years, waiting for an opportunity to silence them. And Victor and Rirette knew that if Callemin, Garnier, and Bonnot were behind the brazen holdup, there would be more violent attacks in Paris.[2]

PART ONE

Chapter 1

"THE GOOD OLD DAYS" IN PARIS

In the first decade of the twentieth century, foreign-language guidebooks saluted the sheer beauty of Paris. One touring book described Paris as "the beautiful city . . . , which for ages has been recognized as the chief capital of Europe." Parisian newspapers celebrated the permanent spectacle of Baron Georges Haussmann's *grands boulevards*, centers of conspicuous consumption that had been created when the city was remade in the 1850s and 1860s. The iron balconies along Paris's boulevards symbolized the Second Industrial Revolution, a transformation characterized by steel, iron, and—increasingly—electricity.[1] Guidebooks emphasized the boulevards and their grand cafés, not the city's soaring Gothic churches. The Third French Republic (first proclaimed in 1870 and lasting until 1940) celebrated the city as a showcase of a "happy modernity."[2] This would be the capital of the wealthy—not the unlit, crowded streets of plebeian Paris, or the tiny apartments that impoverished people like Victor Kibaltchiche and Rirette Maîtrejean called home.

In 1910, the Catholic writer Charles Péguy exclaimed that "civilization has changed more in the past 30 years than it has since the time of Christ."[3] French society seemed to be speeding up, accelerating rapidly, if not spinning out of control—and nowhere was this more true than in Paris. Inventions such as the wireless telegraph, telephone, elevators, electric-powered amusement park rides, and then subways had become part of modern life, particularly city life.

A few decades after Haussmann's boulevards changed the city, Paris was altered yet again: by 1900, three hundred fifty thousand electric lamps brought light to the city. It was at this time that the term *Ville Lumière* began to appear in tourist guides for Paris. The Grand Palais, the Petit Palais, the Gare d'Orsay, and the Pont Alexandre III were completed for the occasion when Paris celebrated . . . being Paris. In 1900, fifty million people went to see the Exposition Universelle, which saluted electric lighting with the Palais de l'Électricité. The first Métro line opened up for the occasion in July of that year, its cars carrying visitors along the Seine to the Exposition Universelle that celebrated France and its soaring capital. By 1913, six lines were in operation.[4]

Electricity turned hotels and department stores into what the great novelist Émile Zola aptly called the "cathedrals of modernity"—where advances in glass technology made possible dazzling window displays to attract clients who had money to spend.[5]

When we think today of the Paris in the early years of the twentieth century, great artistic, musical, architectural, and literary accomplishments first come to mind. Avant-garde artists embellished the reputation of Paris as the "capital of art."[6] Like their Impressionist predecessors, the Neo-Impressionists Georges Seurat and Paul Signac; the Post-Impressionists Vincent Van Gogh, Paul Cézanne, and Paul Gauguin; and the Fauvistes Henri Matisse and André Derain reacted in their own ways against tradition, conformity, and "official" art. They came to Paris—and especially to Montmartre, the butte overlooking the capital, whose cabarets and cafés also "represented a new aesthetic," as historian Roger Shattuck put it. The Cubism of Georges Braque and Pablo Picasso reflected the sense of movement and even speed that modern Paris exuded.[7]

Avant-garde music thrived, too. Claude Debussy's expressive piano pieces were so innovative that they were to music what the Impressionists had been to painting.[8] The composer Maurice Ravel combined respect for traditional influences with innovative tempos reflecting the dynamism of the period. Erik Satie's brilliant compositions and humor—including "Three Pieces in the Shape of a Pear"—also reflected the originality of French culture at the turn of the century.[9]

Art Nouveau emerged as an adventurous new style in Paris, as well as in Brussels and Barcelona. It flourished in architecture, graphic art, interior design, furniture, vases, and other household items, and it served as an imaginative response to the geometric, straight lines of the style represented by the *grands boulevards*. Yet Art Nouveau's free-flowing lines and vegetable- and plant-like curves generated hostile responses from some who denigrated it as "noodle art." Even Hector Guimard's "dragonfly" entrances to the Métro, now iconic, at the time had strident critics.[10]

Artists and tourists weren't the only ones who descended on the growing capital city, the population of which rose from 2,345,000 in 1896 to 2,763,000 ten years later. Paris was an endless beehive of activity. On an average day, 60,000 vehicles, 70,000 horses, and 400,000 brave pedestrians crossed the place de l'Opéra, in front of Charles Garnier's magnificent gilded "wedding cake." About one hundred fifty people were killed and twelve thousand hurt each year, taken out by horses, omnibuses (which moved at eight miles an hour), trams (ten miles an hour), and, then, automobiles.[11]

Automobiles were without question one of the symbols of the new age. The first automobile appeared on the roads of France in 1893. The country produced 1,850 automobiles in 1896, 24,000 in 1898, 34,000 in 1909, and 43,000 in 1913. The first regular autobus line began in 1904, linking Saint-Germain-des-Prés to Montmartre.

The guidebooks never mentioned the *quartiers populaires*, or the impoverished suburbs of Paris, where most of the workers who ran the trams, built the popular new cars, and cleaned the city lived. Moreover, guides for visitors presented Paris as a pacified city, with insurrections, revolutions, and the Paris Commune of 1871 in the distant past.[12]

Following France's humiliating defeat in the Franco-Prussian War (1870–1871), ordinary Parisians had proclaimed their freedom from the provisional government that had been set up in Versailles, from which the kings had ruled during the Ancien Régime. After little more than two months, the Paris Commune was overrun by the troops of Adolphe Thiers, the president of the provisional French government. During the state-supported terror that ensued, which became known as "Bloody Week," May 21–28, 1871, as many as fifteen thousand Parisians were killed, many summarily executed.[13]

But that was more than three decades earlier and, at least for wealthy Parisians, easily forgotten. Now, writers described Paris as the "capital of pleasure." For Parisians of means, the years of the *fin de siècle* and the first decade of the twentieth century were "the good old days." Vast sums of money now easily made up for blue blood. The "high bourgeoisie," as they were sometimes known, including many *nouveaux riches*, had largely supplanted the old aristocracy. The term *high life* emerged from this period.[14] The upper classes lived very well indeed, benefitting from the growth of the French economy that would last until 1914. Three years earlier, the census had identified 19.5 percent of Parisians as "employers"—including master artisans and thousands of people who did piecework in their rooms who were strangely classified as "patrons." Another 21.4 percent were classified as white-collar workers, the percentage of which had increased by more than 2 percent since 1886. Finally, 59.3 percent were classified as "manual workers."[15]

Wealthy Parisians dressed, spoke, and lived differently than ordinary people, so much so that even religion became a marker of class divides. The Catholic Church was far more likely to play a role in the lives of the upper classes than it played in the increasingly dechristianized *quartiers populaires* in northeastern Paris and the suburbs, even after the 1905 law on the Separation of Church and State ended government funding for religious organizations and made all churches and other religious buildings national or communal property. Elite marriages, baptisms, and funerals took place in the Church of the Madeleine in the eighth arrondissement. Protestants, too, were counted among the wealthiest Parisians.

As poet and playwright Guillaume Apollinaire put it, the French capital let loose "a fantasy both nostalgic and modernist." For the wealthy, the fin de siècle and the first decade of the twentieth century were a time of dreams: "Everything pointed in that direction: women's clothing, household decorations, sovereign kitsch, and the ambitions of the magnificent symbolist poets. We were in a crucible, in a factory taken over by madness. Everything was possible and everything could suddenly occur."[16]

Upper-class amusements came at an increasingly steep price. Being able to afford an evening at the opera at the Palais Garnier signaled one's arrival in the Paris of luxury, closely identified with the prestige of France, privilege, and central and particularly western Paris. Going up and down the opera house's enormous marble double stairways lit by incredible chandeliers, *le tout Paris* (the Parisian bourgeois financial oligarchy) attended lavish operatic performances and the masked balls that captured the prevalent sense of operatic illusion.[17]

Fancy theaters also were closely identified with privilege. A few years earlier, an architect had noted that the theater was "a place of luxury. . . . The public loves lavish displays." This was now even more the case. Seats for a performance at the Folies-Bergère or Le Lido near the Champs-Élysées went for four to five francs—a day's salary for a worker—with standing room for three francs.[18] This was the Paris of the aging actress Sarah Bernhardt, who would make her "farewell" tour of the United States in 1913 at age sixty-nine.[19]

Other remarkable technological advances further transformed Paris into the world's center of pleasure. The cinema became the rage. The first paying performance was in December 1895, put on by Louis Lumière in the basement of the Grand Café on boulevard des Capucines. That year, the first advertisements appeared on screen— for chocolate, beer, hats, and corsets. In 1907, the Cirque d'Hiver on boulevard du Temple and the Hippodrome de Vincennes were transformed into movie theaters. In 1909, the *Pathé Journal* brought weekly news to the screen. In 1911, the Gaumont Palace opened its doors, becoming the largest movie theater in the world with three thousand four hundred seats. By 1913, annual receipts for films had reached nine million francs in Paris. Parisians had their choice of 121 theaters and 260 cinemas.[20]

The magnates of the "great bourgeoisie" hobnobbed with counts and countesses at fancy balls and receptions and at the horse races at Longchamp. They carried their passion for luxury to the spas that dotted the country. They took vacations on the Normandy coast, on the French Riviera, and at Biarritz. Men belonged to exclusive clubs, such as the Jockey Club near the place de la Concorde. They frequented restaurants such as Fouquet's, which in 1899 had opened its doors on the Champs-Élysées, its scarlet banquettes and high prices symbolizing luxurious privilege. Maxim's restaurant, on the rue Royale, near the Madeleine, offered a wine list of twenty-four pages and 842 vintages. "The City of Light" celebrated the theatrical dimensions of the ever-visible leisure of wealthy Parisians as they strutted and preened, assisted by bowing valets, drivers, waiters, and sommeliers attending to every whim of the privileged.[21]

A spate of publications presented Parisian women as ever ready for amorous encounters. *Les cocottes*, also known as *les grandes horizontales*, came to be identified with the pleasures of Paris, the "modern Babylon."[22] Nothing reflected their decadence, or entrenched class differences, more than the emergence of *haute couture* fashion as a Parisian—indeed French—trademark, at least for foreign consumption. Women closely followed changes in fashion, with voluminous garments and long dresses gradually giving way to narrower and somewhat shorter skirts at the same time that the "bastille" of the corset was slowly collapsing. Hats designed by Coco Chanel sprouted feathers. Women coveted François Coty's perfumes.[23] Men dressed themselves in black bourgeois uniforms right out of Honoré Daumier's caricatures, inevitably complete with top hats.

The *grands salons* of Paris still functioned during the Republic, hosted by various princesses and marquises, including Napoleon's niece,

Princess Mathilde Bonaparte—at least until in 1904, when she passed away. (She was famously unaffected by political shifts. At one gathering, she remarked, "The French Revolution? Why, without it I'd be selling oranges on the streets of Ajaccio."[24]) In the faubourg Saint-Germain, aristocratic remnants and *grandes dames* of the *haute bourgeoisie* received visitors almost every day, standing as determined rivals with those whom they considered craven imitators in the "little wars" of the salons. Political differences were still present, but nothing like the impassioned days when Captain Alfred Dreyfus, who was Jewish, was condemned or found innocent in the lavish town houses of aristocratic families during the "Affair," which lasted from 1894 until 1906. These practices trickled down to some degree. Middle-class women often also received female guests of their social class in the afternoon.[25]

If many in the bourgeoisie aped the aristocratic ideal of not working at all, workers and peasants existed only to provide services for them. Wealthy women managed large households (with their lavish, increasingly ornate interiors), which in effect meant overseeing the help. Governesses and domestic servants tended to their children. Shopkeepers and department-store clerks were there to attend to their shopping needs. Sheer wealth, maintained or augmented by inheritance and timely dowries, created considerable social differences with the various groups of "lesser" bourgeoisie drawn from the worlds of commerce, government service, and education.[26]

The motto of the Third Republic may have been "liberty, fraternity, equality," but the term *equality* amounted to a charade. Bankers, industrialists, financiers, speculators, magistrates, wealthy notaries and lawyers, and high government officials—the *grande bourgeoisie*— ruled the roost. Paris was an imposing center of banking, commerce, manufacturing, and government. The French bourgeoisie lived "three times blessed" because of the economic, social, and political power that was all concentrated in their hands. The French elite benefited from ridiculously low direct taxes on their wealth. Some profited from investment in colonial enterprises, from Russian and

Spanish railroads, or simply from buildings they owned in Paris or elsewhere. Regardless of industry, the upper ranks of the bourgeoisie were able to easily add to their fortunes.[27]

Even political change was more a charade than a reality. For more than the first two decades of the existence of France's Third Republic, conservative republicans dominated. In 1898, the so-called Radical Republic came to power. But this changed very little. French Radicals were socially moderate, opposing both the Socialists and the Monarchists. Most Radicals were confirmed anticlericals who vociferously opposed any institutional role for the Catholic Church in the Republic. However, the Radical Republic appeared to be nothing more than a continuation of previous regimes, in which a small percentage of men of great means got their way as coalitions and governments came and went. When Alexandre Millerand became minister of labor and the first Socialist in a ministry in 1899, he found himself sitting at the same table during cabinet meetings with General Gaston Galliffet, one of the orchestrators of massacres during Bloody Week in May 1871.

The Third Republic has aptly been called *La République des Copains* ("The Republic of Pals"). The Chamber of Deputies, which included representatives of a variety of political opinions, was essentially a club of like-minded men. Many were subject to corruption, spending as much as necessary to be elected with promises and wine. The vast majority of deputies were drawn from the upper classes: wealthy property owners, *rentiers*, bankers, lawyers, doctors, and so on. Thirty to forty percent of deputies emerged from the *grande bourgeoisie*. Only a couple of workers and peasants were elected to the Chamber of Deputies. Deputies shared a collective psychology. They married women from the same social class. They *tu-toied* each other in the corridors, salons, and café of the Chamber of Deputies. Ministries came and went as if through a revolving door, but the personnel of the Republic remained essentially the same.[28]

Given that the Third Republic's founding fathers had constituted executive authority to remain extremely weak—for fear of

"Caesarism," given the heritage of two emperors Napoleon—the Chamber of Deputies essentially ran France along with an extremely centralized administrative, judicial, and military apparatus organized from Paris. The Chamber of Deputies, elected by universal male suffrage, invariably acted on behalf of the wealthy—only in 1914 would it finally approve a tax on revenue. The Senate, whose members were elected indirectly by those elected to the Chamber of Deputies, members of regional councils in each *département*, and municipal officials, was even more conservative, reflecting rural influence.[29] All this contributed to a sense, at least among the Third Republic's critics, of inefficiency and stagnation.[30]

Parisian newspapers, which might have served as a check on the actions of the powerful, were instead largely complicit. The mass press had burgeoned during the big scandals of the Panama Canal Affair, when it became known in 1892 that members of the Chamber of Deputies had accepted bribes from the Panama Canal Company to facilitate a loan. The company had gone bankrupt in 1889. By the twentieth century, however, if France, like old Gaul, was divided into three parts ("estates")—executive, legislative, and judicial authorities—the press had arguably become the fourth, receiving tips from politicians and influencing votes in the Chamber of Deputies. Printing machines (linotypes), developed in the United States in the 1890s, dramatically increased print runs and expanded the power of the press.

Newspapers in the French capital published a total of six million copies a day. In 1912, *Le Petit Parisien* published an astounding 1,295,000 copies a day, *Le Journal* 995,000, *Le Matin* 647,000 *L'Éclair* 135,000, and *L'Excelsior* 110,000. Victor Kibaltchiche's *L'Anarchie* used the same technologies, and while it had a much smaller print run, it was one of the few staunchly oppositionist newspapers Parisians could find.[31]

As Victor Kibaltchiche would quickly discover after arriving in Paris in late 1908, life was anything but rosy for most French workers. They suffered and protested the subdivision of crafts, increased mechanization, the decline of apprenticeship, the increase in piece rates, speedups, and the beginnings of scientific management in large factories. Bosses adopted new strategies to increase profits while undercutting the autonomy of skilled craftsmen, whose resistance to these changes became legendary. Anarchists, who wanted to destroy states, closely identified capitalism and large-scale industrialization with increasingly centralized governments that protected the interests of the wealthy. Many workers and other ordinary people, frustrated with the corruption of the Third Republic and the avarice of their bosses, came to agree with the anarchists.

Unlike anything else, the automobile became a marker of wealth—and the speedup of French society—in the new century. The first Tour de France, the grueling bicycle race that stretches across France, held in 1903, popularized automobiles. The vehicles, which closely followed the cyclists during the race, made people think of new ways of getting around—so much so that suddenly every member of the elite wanted a car. Yet the enormous cost of purchasing and running an automobile also underscored the gap between Parisians of means and everybody else, especially in the new, scientifically managed car factories.

Scientific management, or Taylorism (named after the American engineer Frederick Taylor), offered employers and foremen a means of measuring the performance of assembly-line workers by applying scientific techniques to mass production. Taylorism speedups were particularly prominent in the production of automobiles; Louis Renault had already begun to employ some of Taylorism's techniques. A visitor to a factory in Philadelphia, Pennsylvania, noted that almost all of the workers employed by an owner who had become enamored with techniques of scientific management were quite young. When asked where the older workers were, the owner hesitated and then replied, "Have a cigar, and while we smoke we can visit the cemetery."

Chapter 2

VICTOR KIBALTCHICHE

Un monde sans évasion possible (A world with no possible escape)
—Victor Serge

The fast-paced lives enjoyed by the wealthiest Parisians stood in stark contrast to the abject poverty of so many of the inhabitants of the French capital. This latter group included the young Victor Kibaltchiche, who arrived in Paris in late 1908 with almost nothing.

Paris attracted tens of thousands of transplants like Victor during the first decade of the twentieth century. Some came seeking work; others were looking for an opportunity to get involved in growing antiestablishment movements. Victor would spend only six years in Paris, a relatively brief stop in a life defined by exile and impermanence.

Victor Kibaltchiche was born in Brussels on December 30, 1890, the son of Russian exiles from the tsarist Russian Empire. His father, Léon Ivanovitch Kibaltchiche, the son of a small-town Orthodox priest, had been a junior officer in the imperial guard. He sympathized with Narodnaya Volya (the People's Will), a secret radical socialist organization within the army whose members believed that violent attacks against the state could spark a massive, successful peasant insurrection. On March 1, 1881, members of Narodnaya Volya

The young Victor Kibaltchiche.
Note the Russian-style shirt.

assassinated Tsar Alexander II. Victor's uncle, Nicolai Kibaltchiche, a chemist and member of the Central Committee of Narodnya Volya, was among those arrested and subsequently hanged. When police uncovered the group, Victor's father, Léon, hid in the gardens of a monastery in Kiev and then managed to swim across the Austro-Hungarian border as Russian guards fired at him.

Victor's mother, Vera Pederowska, was from a poor family of Polish nobles. Her father was a military officer. She went to Geneva to study, where she met Léon Kibaltchiche, who was also studying in that classic city of political refuge. Proletarianized intellectuals with virtually no money, they traveled as best they could from Geneva to Paris, where Léon continued his medical studies and read widely in geology and other natural sciences. They moved to London and finally to Brussels, in search of books to read and enough to eat.

Thus it was by chance that Victor was born in Brussels. In every dank one-room—or at best two-room—apartment in which the family lived, illustrations of Russian revolutionaries martyred by the tsarist regime graced the walls. As political refugees, Victor's parents had lost their Russian citizenship. Victor never attended school because the family moved around so much and because his father detested state-run schools—"stupid bourgeois education provided to the poor." His father and mother taught him to read in French, Russian, and English with the help of old, cheap editions of Shakespeare, Molière, Lermontov, and Chekhov that could be found in flea markets in the Belgian capital. His father instructed Victor in history, geography, and the natural sciences. He took his young son to libraries and museums, where Victor developed the habit of taking notes on what he read or observed. When Victor was twelve, his father asked him, "What is life?" His son first replied that he did not yet know, but then added, "You will think, you will struggle, you will be hungry." Victor Kibaltchiche's youth and subsequent life would be like that. He would later add, "You will fight back."[1]

Life was indeed a struggle for the family. When they went briefly to England hoping for better things, they ate wheat that Léon gathered on the edge of a field near Dover. In Whitechapel, Victor contracted—but survived—meningitis. In a mining suburb of Liège, in Belgium, where Léon had apparently found some work, the family lived above a small restaurant. They fell asleep as enticing smells of *moules frites*—nothing more Belgian than that—rose up from the restaurant of the same name, but which they could not afford except on occasion when the landlord extended them a little credit. Once in a while, the restaurant owner's son traded them a bit of sugar in exchange for stamps from Russia or other odds and ends. Victor developed the habit of nourishing himself on sugared coffee into which he dipped a piece of dry bread. His brother Raoul, two years younger and dangerously ill, literally wasted away in a dark room. Victor told him stories, wiped his forehead with ice, and gently lied that he would soon be better. Raoul died in 1891, barely nine years old, of tuberculosis, but also of hunger and, as Victor remembered, of "misery." Victor and his father carried Raoul's body to the cemetery at Ucel, the small town where they were living at the time.[2]

When what was left of the family moved to Charleroi, Victor called a large house capped by a crafted gable "Raoul's house." He never forgot the faces of children condemned to hunger—above all, that of his younger brother. He was not even a teenager yet, but Victor had already begun to ask himself what was the value of surviving, if not to help those who were at risk of being unable to hold on.[3]

In 1903, the Kibaltchiche family again settled in Brussels in the grim faubourg of Ixelles, the population of which had risen to almost sixty thousand people, up from forty-four thousand a decade earlier. Victor's father often got by pawning the few possessions the family had, buying them back when things were a little better. This was the way it was for poor families. At times, Léon depended on usurers to have any money at all. The family ate well enough the first ten days of any month, not well at all the second ten days, and insufficiently the last ten days. For Victor, these memories were "stuck in his soul as nails in a chair." His father regularly carried a little box under his arm when he left home to try to get hold of some bread on credit. Successful or not in his quest for food, he plunged into an atlas of human anatomy or books on geology when he returned.

For Victor, words like *bread, hunger, money, no money, work, credit, rent*, and *landlord* took on "an extremely concrete sense," although things got a little better when his father found work at the University of Brussels.[4]

One day when he was twelve, Victor, dressed in a Russian-style shirt with red and mauve checks and carrying a single cabbage, was walking up a street in Ixelles. On the sidewalk across the street, he noticed a short, bespectacled boy about his age staring at him with condescension. Victor, never one to shy away, headed in the boy's direction, mocking his antagonist's glasses, and the two exchanged shoves before the other boy asked him if he wanted to hang out with him. Victor agreed, and the two became friends.

The other boy was Raymond Callemin, the myopic son of a small, illiterate, alcoholic shoemaker of considerable temper, Napoléon

Raymond Callemin.

Callemin, who "lived sitting on his stool, leaning at the window over miserable old shoes on a provincial street of Ixelles." Raymond's mother had died young, and Raymond grew up in the streets of Brussels, left to his own devices and enduring the prostitution of his sister, age fifteen. Their late mother's father provided some stability, which allowed Raymond to earn his *brevet*, the certificate of primary schooling. Callemin later claimed that in those days he attended the theater at least once a week. Raymond was placed as an apprentice in a sculpture workshop and then became an apprentice typographer.[5]

In those days Victor, who was only thirteen years old, was like Raymond: living by himself much of the time and in need of friendship. Victor's parents traveled often and then became estranged, splitting up when he was fifteen.[6] His mother, "completely worn out by endless difficulties and sometimes abject misery, as well as serious crises of hysteria," decided to return to Russia, in principle to fight against the tsarist regime by creating free schools. She died of tuberculosis in 1907. Victor's father took up with another woman. Victor moved out of the household and into a small room by himself.

Victor and Raymond quickly became inseparable. They read the same books and discussed them at length. The adolescents absorbed Émile Zola's 1898 novel *Paris*, the story of anarchists in the French capital. Raymond particularly enjoyed reading Auguste Comte, one of the founders of sociology. They also read Alfred Musset and Victor Hugo.

Victor and Raymond found a quiet place for reflection on the roof of Brussels's enormous Palace of Justice, reaching the rooftop by passing various signs telling them "No entry." The massive structure was, as Victor remembered it, "a veritable country of steel, zinc, and stone, geometrically uneven, with dangerous fall-offs." They compared the Palace of Justice to the ancient Assyrian constructions they had read about in a book.

Far below them stretched the Belgian capital. The Palace of Justice stood on the same level as Brussels's upper town of grand boulevards and the elegant hotels of the Avenue Louise. It stood proudly above the impoverished neighborhoods of la Marolle, with its "smelly, narrow streets, with laundry hanging everywhere, full of gangs of little brats, amid the shouts coming from the *estaminets* and the two human rivers that are the rue Blaes and the rue Haute." Since the Middle Ages, the same population had "stagnated there, subject to the same injustice, in the same masonry, without possible escape." Completing the picture, the prison for women, a transformed monastic establishment, was wedged between the Palace of Justice and the lower town. Victor and Raymond could barely hear the clacking of the *sabots* as the prisoners walked back and forth in a courtyard during their brief daily release from their cells far below. From the roof, Victor and Raymond watched one day as a well-dressed lawyer arrived in a fancy carriage, "full of self-importance, carrying a small briefcase full of papers assessing laws and crimes." They burst out laughing, "Ah! What misery, what misery, this existence!"

Victor and Raymond were joined in their adventures by Jean de Boe, an orphan from Anderlecht who worked for a typographer and lived with his washerwoman grandmother—he stole to provide modestly for her—near the filthy waters of the Seine River, and by a tall, very pale boy named Luce who worked in a department store and would soon die of tuberculosis, that murderous working-class disease. Sunday was the only day off for the small group of friends, but they had no money to do much of anything but wander among the throngs in Brussels's crowded streets, "young, scrawny wolves, who had the pride of reflection (*la pensée*)." They were, as Victor remembered, "a band of adolescents closer than brothers." Their bond was solidified by their daily struggles. Victor later noted, "In short, life seemed to offer us nothing more than ugly slavery."[7]

Jean de Boe evoked such lives in his aptly titled poem "*Misère*":

From the first moment, in the cradle of the conquerors,
In the sad shadow of their glory,
I wove my pathetic rags
And made my bed in the black mud.

. . .

Here I am, misery, see
What I drag along with me,
The raggedy cortege
Made of hunger, vice, and hate.

. . .

I am the misery that grows,
And which will one day take the palace.
I will avenge the shame,
Of the vile shadow in which I grovel.[8]

Victor became an apprentice photographer, earning ten francs a month—virtually nothing—for which he worked ten hours a day, not including the hour and a half he could take for lunch and the hour of travel each way to get to work. He moved on to similar jobs, including that of an office clerk and a technician for central heating. Employers proposed apprenticeships, but without any pay at all. The best that Victor could find, for the equivalent of eight dollars a month, was a position assisting an elderly businessman who owned mines in Norway and Algeria. Life for a poor adolescent was like that.

The little group of friends had less time for their Sunday strolls, and they began to grow apart. But Raymond and Victor remained close, even when they disagreed about how to face the life of poverty that stretched before them. Raymond was determined to escape "the poisonous corruption that was bosses, their workers, bourgeois, magistrates, police, and others, all these people disgusted me." He first stole at age seventeen, receiving a short jail sentence. Raymond's partner in the minor crime—another friend, not Victor—received a suspended sentence. Raymond had defiantly questioned anyone's right to judge him. His father's anger meant little to him, and in fact made him "*plus révolté.*"

Raymond still found time to fall in love. He had become attracted to a young Russian student, Macha, whom he met at the Biblio-thèque Royale. Raymond remembered: "With her I spent the happiest hours of my life. The intimacy of two young people talking together about the goodness of humanity, building idyllic castles in the air, was something so sweet and good. I can still picture the poor, neat little garret where she lived, the tiny table over which our heads always touched and our hair mingled, as we felt each others' hot breath; our hands never stopped meeting, and our cheeks brushed lightly, and in this way we experienced pleasures that were sweet and entirely innocent." But the young woman returned to Russia, leaving Raymond heartbroken. He composed poems with her in mind. "Oh! To be handsome! Oh! To be strong!" he wrote over and over.[9]

Raymond went back to work, first as a butcher's assistant, then in a bakery, and then in another meat shop. Lying about his age, he worked sixteen hours or more a day for seventy or eighty francs a week. When he asked for a day off, his boss became angry and fired him. Raymond then found a low-paying job assisting mechanics, but without relevant skills, there seemed little hope for him in this line of work. He worked on roads, again for pitiful wages. He hated that workers were completely subjugated to the authority of their bosses, and he also was appalled by the number of workers he saw drowning in alcohol and smelling of tobacco. He participated in one brief strike and was arrested. Two more subsequent arrests brought several more months in jail. Participation in another strike and in a brawl earned him six days in prison.[10] Raymond would not so easily submit to the ugly slavery to which he and Victor seemed condemned.

At age fifteen, Victor had an easier time holding jobs than Raymond, and he rarely got caught up in the brawls that landed his friend in jail. But he too was frustrated by his circumstances, and he found himself contemplating the political situation in distant tsarist Russia, the country of his family's origin. As the stirring news of the Revolution of 1905 arrived, Victor learned of strikes, mutinies, and executions. The revolution brought the grudging establishment by Tsar Nicholas II of an Assembly, or Duma, although it had little power. Perhaps with the Russian example in mind, a year later Victor helped found the Fédération Bruxelloise des Jeunes Gardes Social-istes in Ixelles, an antiparliamentary organization under the influence of the French radical socialist and antimilitarist Gustave Hervé.[11]

While most other young men their age talked about bicycles or women, Victor remembered: "We were chaste, awaiting better of ourselves and our fate." Although they fervently believed that soci-ety could be transformed, Victor and Raymond both soon lost all faith in socialism, which seemed increasingly reformist and tediously doctrinaire. Socialist leaders told their faithful followers, according to Victor, "March along slowly and in rows of four and believe in ME." Demonstrators almost inevitably ended up drinking at *estaminets*, bringing good business to their wily owners. Elections seemed only to prop up corrupt states and the interests of the wealthy. There seemed to be nothing combative about reform socialism, and Victor and Raymond increasingly believed it would never work. They laughed at Socialist leaders, but their laughter was bitter. Victor real-ized, "Corruption (*la combine*) is always there and everywhere."

Victor did manage to make connections with some local officials, but these men were just as complacent as he had feared. He obtained an appointment with a municipal councilman, who invited him to his elegant residence, which indicated to the young visitor that the politician "was slowly making himself rich." Victor tried to engage the man in the realm of ideas; this proved impossible, and Victor left in disgust.

How, Victor wondered, could one create a just society that was both "ardent and pure"? In recent decades, states had consolidated their power, turning cities into garrison towns. Victor did not want to compromise, but Socialist politics in Brussels seemed to offer *only* compromise, not revolution. What would become of his desire to fight, his desire for justice, his intense will to get away from the city and away from a life "without possible escape"? Victor and Raymond's goal remained absolute freedom—nothing else would do.[12]

Victor contemplated what to do with his life. Should he become a lawyer, like the proud men he had watched from above as a young boy, striding confidently into the Palace of Justice? He began studies in law at the Université Nouvelle—which had broken away from the Université libre de Bruxelles and had attracted many radical students—but then gave them up. Victor concluded that lawyers were there "to invoke the laws of the rich which are unjust by definition." Should he become a doctor, caring for the wealthy while advising from afar those living with tuberculosis in poor neighborhoods? All he could offer the poor, he knew, was encouragement to eat well, to seek fresh air, and to rest—none of which was possible for desperately poor workers. Or should he become an architect and build comfortable residences for the wealthy? If he had been the son of a bourgeois professor, he might have taken one of those paths, seduced by "the theory that progress would come along slowly from one century to the next." Victor told his father that he did not want to continue his studies. By then, he had moved out of his father's house and into a small furnished room of his own. When his father asked what he wanted to do, he replied, "I will work. I will study without undertaking studies." Victor did not dare say: "You are vanquished, I see it very well. I will try to have more strength, or more fortune. There is no alternative." Like his father, beaten down by struggle, he was committed to fighting all his life against the injustices he saw around him. Victor hoped to have more strength, or more luck.[13]

Victor determined that anarchism was the only way to carry out this fight and he became a committed anarchist. "Society remains the enemy of all individuality," he wrote. "The individual must struggle against Society, against imposed social duties."[14] Many French and Belgians looked to the revolutionary socialist Jules Guesde for inspiration. But Guesde believed that revolution would lead to an all-powerful state, albeit one that would look after the interests of ordinary people. Another state, although potentially of a different kind, was not what anarchists had in mind. At the age of eighteen, Raymond also became an anarchist, vowing to "defend himself until death." The state, he concluded, must be destroyed.[15]

Victor and Raymond became vocal anarchists immediately. Their first target was consumer cooperatives, which were increasingly common in Belgium and France but afforded workers only about two percent in savings. When Victor and Raymond distributed anarchist tracts outside cooperatives, directors angrily called them "vagabonds." Next they condemned Émile Vandervelde, a young Belgian Socialist leader, who in 1907 supported Belgium's annexation of the Congo, the chamber of horrors perpetuated by King Leopold II. Victor and his friends shouted their opposition at meetings of the Belgian Labor Party in Brussels and then stormed out.[16]

Victor and Raymond concluded that workers were not ready to rise up, and they required education in the possibilities of anarchism. Two years earlier the pair had read a brochure by Peter Kropotkin, *Aux jeunes gens*, and it had clearly influenced them. Kropotkin asked young people to look around themselves, look into their consciences, and understand that their duty "is to put yourself on the side of the exploited and to work for the destruction of an unacceptable regime."[17]

In 1907, Victor and Raymond visited an anarchist community in the forest of Soignes in Stockel, just southeast of Brussels—"a free environment" ("*un milieu libre*"). A table near the entrance was strewn with anarchist pamphlets and brochures. A saucer near the reading material held this small sign: "Take what you want and leave what you can." A path led to a white house that appeared amid the foliage. Above the door was a sign that read, "Do what you want." In this seemingly ideal setting lived printers, gardeners, a shoemaker, a painter, and others, some with their spouses or female companions and children. Such communities were intended to show that people could live in egalitarian harmony without the intrusion of state authority or the concept of property; by their very existence, the communities could serve as a form of propaganda. Victor and Raymond, overwhelmed by the setting and by the idea of anarchism, suddenly stood up and broke into verse: "Stand up, you who are sleeping. . . . It is the Angel of Liberty, It is the Giant Light!" Not long thereafter, the owner of the land kicked the anarchists out, forcing the group to relocate to Boitsfort, which was a little closer to Brussels but still in a rural setting. Russian, French, and Swiss anarchists joined the small number of Belgians.[18]

Anarchist communities, stretched for resources, usually did not last very long. Some fell apart over disputes and jealousies, which was eventually the case for the community in Boitsfort. But this did not undermine Victor's confidence in an anarchist future in which such groups would proliferate, if only at first to provide a setting that would show anarchism "under a truer light, with its ideal of peace, life, and peaceful labor." Such communities would stand, in Victor's words, as "the first cells of the new society."[19]

The anarchists who floated in and out of Boitsfort included several violent revolutionaries, among them a Russian chemist known as Alexander Sokolov (his real name was Vladimir Hartenstein) from Odessa who had arrived in Belgium via Buenos Aires, not an amazing trajectory in a time of fast and sturdy steamships. Victor described him as "a man of firm will, formed in Russia by inhuman struggle . . . he came out of the storm, and the storm remained in him." It was Sokolov's belief that in order to wage "social war . . . one needs good laboratories." He had set up his "perfect laboratory" a few steps from the Bibliothèque Royale in central Brussels. Aware the police were on to him, Sokolov fled to Ghent, locking himself in a rented room, readying two loaded pistols. When police stormed in, he wounded two officers before being shot dead. In the subsequent trial, Victor and Raymond were summoned as witnesses, although not accomplices. They used the occasion to defend Sokolov; the Russian anarchist had given his life, in Victor's words, "to awaken the oppressed."[20]

The vast majority of anarchists rejected such attacks. After all, such activities gave anarchism a bad name. Moreover, any revolution that would destroy the state seemed distant, and its outcome seemed uncertain. Victor became an "individualist" anarchist: rejecting theoretical assurances that the day of revolution was near, and instead believing that people had to be transformed one by one, in order to create "new values."[21] The revolution could come later.

When he was eighteen, Victor began to contribute articles to a four-page anarchist newspaper called *Communiste*, and then to its successor, *Le Révolté: Organ of Anarchist Propaganda*. He had a knack for writing, and it gave him a venue to work out and refine his ideas about individualist anarchism.

Victor could not find sufficient work in Brussels, even as a badly paid typographer, because of the anarchist propaganda he was writing. He and Raymond "felt like we were in empty space." Moreover, Victor's status as a refugee and his involvement, however distant, in the Sokolov affair made him vulnerable to expulsion from Belgium.[22]

In 1908, Victor decided to leave Brussels and seek work elsewhere. He carried with him only ten francs, a second shirt, and several notebooks. At the train station, he ran into his father and told him he would be going to Lille for two weeks. He never saw him again. In the quartier of Fives-Lille, he rented an attic room in a miners' residence (*coron*) for two and a half francs a week, payable in advance. Victor needed a job, and quickly. Mine work in the region seemed a possibility, but a miner warned the frail Victor that he would not last two hours there. Three days into his stay, he had only four francs left. Bread, a kilo of green pears, and a glass of milk, purchased on credit from his understanding landlady, left him twenty-five centimes for the day. The soles of his shoes betrayed him, and not having enough to eat left him dizzy and sitting on benches in a park, dreaming of soup with some meat in it. A chance encounter brought work for a photographer in Armentières, twelve miles from Lille, for four francs a day—for Victor a fortune. He left the *coron* each morning at the same time as the miners in their leather helmets in the chilly fog of the Nord. When he returned home at night, he read *L'Humanité*, a socialist paper edited by the reformist socialist leader Jean Jaurès. Through thin walls he could hear his neighbor beating his wife, who through her tears sounded as though she was pleading for more abuse. It was dispiriting, to say the least. How could the lives of such people be improved? How could they be brought to understand that a better life could be found?

Victor had exhausted the employment opportunities in and around Lille. His next stop would be Paris in November or December 1908. Like arrivals in the French capital from the provinces, who went to the quartiers of their countrymen upon their arrival in the big city, anarchists knew where to go to find a welcome.[23] Soon after reaching Paris in late 1908, Victor headed for rue du Chevalier de la Barre in the eighteenth arrondissement on Montmartre, where the anarchist newspaper *L'Anarchie*, begun by Albert Libertad in 1905, was published. The offices of the newspaper had quickly become a center of anarchist organization and police suspicion.

Raymond Callemin had also become a militant, with the fanaticism and energy of a convert. And so he, too, almost inevitably ended up in Paris, although not for very long. After briefly working as a "*homme sandwich*" (passing out fliers for a clothing store) in order to earn enough money to buy a decent pair of shoes, fed up with city life and "all those loudmouths," and wanting to avoid military service, Callemin hit the road in search of fresh air and the countryside, working odd jobs and doing harvest work. He finally reached Switzerland. Callemin had avoided military service in Belgium by refusing to report as required in 1910 and going back and forth over the border as needed. That summer he spent a short time in jail following a brawl. On one trip on the train, he had only a ticket for a previous stop—having spent what little he had to buy something to eat—and jumped off in Valenciennes in the Nord. A railroad official chased him and then kindly let him go. He worked in Valenciennes for a short time, but was let go; later, he remembered that "frontier" bosses were among the worst. He committed two burglaries there, and then he was on his way back to Belgium, to Charleroi, where he met up with anarchists, carried out more burglaries, and again was jailed. He was barely twenty years old. Upon his release, Raymond Callemin returned to Paris.[24]

Chapter 3

ANOTHER PARIS: "MISERY IS EVERYWHERE"

Anarchists like Victor Kibaltchiche immediately felt at home in the overcrowded, largely plebeian quartiers of the northeastern part of Paris and in the grim working-class suburbs north of the city. In this, Montmartre played a special role. And that is where Victor Kibaltchiche went upon arriving in Paris.

More than three decades before Victor first arrived there, the Butte Montmartre had a rendezvous with history. It was there that the Paris Commune had begun on March 18, 1871, when ordinary Parisians prevented troops sent by Adolphe Thiers from taking the cannons of the National Guard from the butte. On the rue du Chevalier de la Barre (then the rue des Rosiers), the crowd executed Generals Claude Lecomte and Jacques Clément-Thomas and took control of first the butte and then all of Paris. The victory was short-lived. When the Commune fell during "Bloody Week" in May 1871, the French army targeted Montmartre in particular for reprisals, including summary executions—during the "tricolor terror" in which as many as fifteen thousand Parisians perished.[1]

Since then, Montmartre had been transformed from what was still a somewhat rustic site (it had been incorporated into Paris in 1860) into a unique, yet still peripheral, part of the capital. The journal *Illustration* provided a contemporary description of the butte, one far from that to which tourists rush today. Montmartre was a jumble of *banlieue* styles, many "offering the same ramshackled, sad appearance."[2] If it was less rural, it was no less poor.

At the crest of the butte, Victor gazed upon the Basilique du Sacré-Coeur de Montmartre, the construction of which began during the "Republic of the Moral Order" in the early 1870s to celebrate the Versailles victory over the Paris Commune. Victor described it as "sort of a fake Hindu style, monumentally bourgeois." From Sacré-Cœur, Victor could gaze down upon an "ocean of gray roofs, over which there arose at night only a few dim lights, and a great red glow from the tumultuous squares."[3]

The Montmartre Victor encountered was a site of contrasts. Victor remembered, "Our Montmartre had for neighbors, but without giving two cents about, cabarets of artists and bars haunted by women wearing feathered hats, who wore dresses reaching down to their heels." The windmill of the Moulin de la Galette announced the dance hall of the same name. The Chat Noir, the Moulin Rouge, and Les Quat'z'Arts around place Pigalle attracted tourists and wealthy Parisians—*le beau monde*—arriving in taxis in what was still something of a foreign land. The poet J. P. Contamine de Latour recalled, "Once you'd climbed [Montmartre's] rough steps, you felt as though you were hundreds of miles away from the capital. . . . Everything about it was rustic and peaceful. Streams down the middle of streets . . . and birds twittered in the luxuriant greenery that covered the old, ruined walls."[4]

The place Blanche with its brasseries, cheap cafés, and dance halls had come to rival place Pigalle. *Mondaines* came to see and be seen in what amounted to a subprefecture of pleasure, a capital of debauche, a privileged territory for prostitutes.[5]

Bohemian artists and writers had already colonized Montmartre when, in 1904, Pablo Picasso moved into an apartment in a tangle of poor dwellings at Bateau-Lavoir, off place Ravignan below Sacré Coeur. Like many Parisians, Picasso would sometime carry a Browning revolver for protection; Montmartre had a reputation for crime.[6] At least at the beginning, like most Parisians he had very little money. He drank at the modest Le Zut cabaret on rue Ravignan. It was in his tiny studio in Montmartre that Picasso launched Cubism in 1906–1907 when he painted *Les Demoiselles d'Avignon*. In 1909, his financial situation improved enough that he moved to a nicer apartment, but not far away, on boulevard de Clichy near Pigalle. He still liked and thrived in Montmartre. The young Italian artist Amedeo Modigliani also headed for the butte upon his arrival in Paris in 1906, finding a place to live in what was little more than a shack.[7]

In Montmartre, the avant-garde reacted against the cultural restraints of artistic tradition and convention, continuing the revolt against Romanticism. In this sense, their "violent dissent" had something in common with the anarchist revolt of Victor and many others against hierarchical bourgeois society and its state.[8]

Why did Montmartre become something of a "privileged terrain" for anarchist revolt, attracting newly arrived radicals like Victor? Did its narrow, steep streets, some of which were little more than stone staircases, and paths, back courtyards, *caves,* and attics provide an easy means of remaining hidden? Because some anarchists rejected festive meals and alcohol, did the rampant, public festivity—even debauchery—of Montmartre, which stood in stark contrast to the abject misery of many residents, encourage anarchism?[9]

And it was not just Montmartre. To the east lay La Chapelle, an essential part of the expanding sprawl of plebeian Paris in which anarchism thrived. La Chapelle was a chaos of small railway depots, workshops, factories, and warehouses, interspersed with vacant lots. Many female workers, including seamstresses, lived in this area. Their children took their apprenticeship on the tough streets of the La Chapelle neighborhoods. An increasing number of dilapidated houses stood along the roads, with flower pots in the windowsills and laundry hanging every which way, drying before again becoming soiled by soot carried from nearby chemical plants by the wind. The buildings, most of them constructed in great haste during the 1880s, were three or four stories high. Unlike houses of "standing" constructed during the same period along boulevards Rochechouart and Clichy, their facades consisted of just about any building material that could be found: planks of wood or pieces of metal, cardboard—anything except solid stone. The houses of La Chapelle offered—if that is the appropriate term—tiny apartments into which were crammed as many people as possible. The ceilings of many of them were already in a state of virtual collapse, as were doors weakened by use and suffering assaults by aggressive neighbors.[10]

The historian Daniel Halévy once said of La Chapelle that it was not "part of Paris," but rather "a passage, a current of air." Snow and rain entered at will. When a renter informed his landlord that rainwater from a storm was pouring into the apartment *comme vache qui pisse*, the owner retorted, "You only have to pick up an umbrella." The arrival of the Métro changed very little, except bringing the roar of the trains and probably prostitutes—and "bad boys," some of whom were pimps—from other quartiers. There, at least at night, they ruled. Thugs from La Chapelle carried their provocations to Montmartre. The tattooed thugs did not dance the tango.[11]

The so-called Belle Époque was not *belle* for very many Parisians, including Victor. Contemporaries used the expression "*fin de siècle*" or "1900." The very idea of a "Belle Époque" before World War I was a construction that first appeared during the late 1930s—and then, above all, with the lingering sense of the "world we have lost" during the time of Vichy France during World War II when Paris was occupied. Following the war, when France was no longer a great power and its colonial empire was disappearing, it was again easy to imagine that the years before *la Grande Guerre* were the halcyon days.[12] They were not.

Victor remembered: "One of the particular traits of Paris at this time was that it included . . . a vast world of people coming and going, of the disillusioned, the miserable, and even the seedy."[13] He would never forget:

> The opulent Paris of the Champs-Elysées, Passy, and even the great commercial boulevards were to us a foreign or enemy city. Our Paris had three centers: the vast working-class city which began somewhere in the lugubrious zone of canals, cemeteries, vacant lots and factories, toward Charonne, Pantin, the pont de Flandre, reaching the heights of Belleville and Ménilmontant, there becoming an intense plebeian capital, whose residents try to make ends meet in their anthill, having as its frontiers the city of railroad stations and of pleasure, surrounded under the iron bridges of the métro by sad quartiers.
>
> There were found small hotels, "merchants of sleep" where for twenty *sous* one could catch his breath in an attic without air, bistros haunted by pimps, swarms of girls with their hair up in buns and wearing polka-dot aprons on the sidewalks. . . . The rumbling wagons of the métro suddenly disappearing into their tunnel under the city.[14]

Victor encountered two cities of Paris. The overstated elegance and good times of the wealthy meant nothing to the vast majority of people living in Paris and its region. Not including its suburbs, the great city had a population of more than 2.8 million people—many times that of Victor's Brussels. The capital grew because of immigration from the provinces into the peripheral, poorer arrondissements. New residents formed urban villages within the burgeoning capital. Chain migration brought Auvergnats from central France to the eleventh and twelfth arrondissements. Poor Jews from Russia and Eastern Europe moved into the Marais in the fourth, between the rue des Francs-Bourgeois and the rue de Rivoli, particularly the *Pletzl* ("petite place") centered on rue des Écouffes. Limousins migrated to the fourth and fifth arrondissements, while Bretons headed for the fourteenth arrondissement and out north to Saint-Denis. There were some transplants of means, but not many. Generally prosperous

Swiss and Americans were a small part of the social geography of Paris, living around the Opéra and the Champs-Élysées, along with wealthier Parisians.[15]

The largely plebeian suburbs also continued to grow rapidly, housing those who could not afford to live in even the poorest parts of the city. The suburbs within the *département* of the Seine now included 1.3 million people with the industrialization of the periphery. Saint-Denis grew from 15,700 in the Second Empire to 71,800 in 1914, Boulogne-Billancourt from 7,000 residents to 57,000, and Ivry-sur-Seine from 7,056 to 38,307. By the turn of the century, 26 percent of the population of the Paris region lived in the suburbs, double that of 1861. A railway line circled Paris beyond the city walls, connecting the peripheral communes.[16]

The availability of space and a transient workforce; proximity to the Seine, canals, and railroads; and standing beyond the *octroi at the edge of the city*—the customs barrier where taxes were imposed on goods brought into the city, which accounted for half of the municipal budget— encouraged manufacturing beyond the walls of the city. Raw materials arrived via the Seine River and the Canal Saint-Martin. In 1914, 154 of the 307 manufactures that had more than one hundred workers were in the peripheral arrondissements of Paris. This included most of the "dirty" industries, expelled from the center of Paris, a process begun by Napoleon III and Baron Haussmann during the 1850s and 1860s. This had been largely achieved through chaotic expansion driven by market forces.[17] The chemical and textile industries, particularly clothing, had moved to the suburbs. Two-thirds of the *grandes enterprises* (fourteen firms) employing more than five hundred workers—producing automobiles and soon airplanes, electric motors, and gasoline, oils, and tires—were found beyond the walls of Paris, although some heavy industry remained in the twelfth, fifteenth, and nineteenth arrondissements. Beyond the city limits, the Renault and Dion-Bouton automobile manufacturers, in Boulogne-Billancourt and Puteaux, respectively, as well as the French Society of Munitions in Issy-les-Moulineux, employed more than two thousand people in 1914.[18]

This contributed to the gradual de-industrialization—at least in terms of the size of enterprises—of central Paris. In 1911, nine hundred seventy-eight thousand workers lived in the capital, although most worked in small firms (90 percent of employers had fewer than ten employees, and eighty thousand workers labored at home). Much of artisanal production remained in Paris itself, such as in the first arrondissement. The neighborhoods around rue Sentier in the second arrondissement remained the center of the garment industry, for instance, although much of the work was done by women sewing at home. The effect of this shift was to further separate the two Parises: one becoming increasingly fancified, catering primarily to the wealthy, and the other one becoming the site of factories of various sizes and poor workers.

Well into the middle decades of the nineteenth century, employers had remained present in factories, but now foremen, promoted from within the enterprise or brought in from the outside, enforced an increasing number of regulations. Workers commonly referred to factories as *bagnes*—prisons—because of the strictures of industrial discipline.[19]

Between 1902 and 1913, 37 percent of people who died left nothing to their descendants because they had nothing to leave. For some ordinary people, an improving economy brought a slight increase in the quality of life, even if for the majority of workers getting by remained extremely difficult. Anarchist newspapers ran articles lamenting the rising cost of food, particularly meat. Misery was everywhere to be seen in People's Paris.[20]

Transient workers came to Paris and its suburbs, while others departed in search of a job, somewhere. Work was largely uncertain, and when it could be found, workdays lasted twelve, fifteen, and even more hours a day. Barbers and hairdressers labored fourteen hours a day and sometimes even more, tramworkers ten to fourteen. The expansion of white-collar work was dramatic, rising from about one hundred twenty-six thousand in 1866 to three hundred fifty-two thousand in 1911. About five thousand women worked in department stores such as Bon Marché, Printemps, and Galeries Lafayette. These had come into existence during the 1850s and 1860s, strategically placed on Haussmann's *grands boulevards*. The harsh conditions confronting department store clerks are often forgotten. They, too, were subject to long workdays and sudden dismissals. Many women working in the *grands magasins* slept in chilly dormitories above the stores.[21]

French industrialists, the new *seigneurs*, ignored what minimal protection laws provided workers, laws that lagged far behind those available in monarchical Britain or autocratic Germany. Employers routinely ignored the 1906 law making a weekly day of rest obligatory. If workers protested, there was always someone to replace them. Of two thousand bakers in Paris, only two hundred allocated a day of rest. Wages could be cut for the slightest infraction or imperfection. Workers were vulnerable to accidents at work; in 1909 and 1911, almost four hundred thousand were reported—as required by an 1898 law that was often ignored.[22]

At least three hundred fifty thousand women worked in Paris. The proportion of female workers in the workforce had risen from about 15 percent in 1870 to around 33 percent in 1914. More than 40 percent of women working in Paris were domestic servants, some of them commuting often daunting distances on foot from the plebeian heights of Paris into the *beaux quartiers*. The majority, though, were lodged miserably in attics or under staircases in the fancy apartments where they worked.

Female workers, many of them producing the famous "*articles de Paris*"—purses, gloves, and other quality goods—earned little more than half what male workers brought home, sometimes for the same work (in Paris in 1906, an average of seven and a half francs a day for men and four and a quarter for women). Textile work provided the major occupations, however varied, and at least twenty-five thousand women produced artificial flowers and feathers. Female workers enjoyed virtually no state protection at all and many suffered sexual harassment from foremen and male workers. French women remained unequal before the law, which made it impossible for them to combat daily harassment or sudden dismissals. Households headed by single women faced devastating and usually inescapable poverty.[23] The level of education for women remained considerably behind their male counterparts. Untimely pregnancies remained a constant risk not only for unmarried or uncoupled women, but for married females as well.

Some working women turned to prostitution *pour faire sa fin du mois*—to pay the bills at the end of the month—some with the knowledge and indeed permission of their husbands. For women living alone, this "fifth quarter" was necessary to keep afloat.

Tens of thousands of Parisians made their living selling whatever they could wherever they could, pushing or pulling their carts through the streets of the capital, the sound of their bells and shouts announcing what they had to offer for sale or could repair. Women who sold fruits and vegetables (*marchandes aux quatre saisons*) set up their wagons along major arteries, and "market strong men" carried provisions on their shoulders, above all in and around the great market of Les Halles in central Paris.[24]

Working-class life in Paris remained fragile, precarious. Underemployment and unemployment were inevitable parts of the working-class experience. Older workers seeking to be hired faced daunting challenges. Furthermore, much industrial work—such as boilermaking and the clothing trades—remained seasonal, leaving many workers with long periods of generating no income. Sometimes, smaller enterprises simply closed their doors, leaving those who worked there with absolutely nothing. More than two-thirds of a family's income went to purchase food, and when things were tough, there was little more than a large loaf of bread on the table. In 1911, 82 percent of the population of Paris was classified as poor, and 72 percent of those were indigent.[25]

The vast majority of families had no savings at all because they needed to spend whatever income they had just to keep going. Between 1902 and 1913, 37 percent of people who died left nothing to their descendants because they had nothing to leave.[26] Rents rose rapidly after 1905, and more than two-thirds of working-class families rented their lodgings. For some people, an improving economy brought a slight increase in the quality of life.[27] But the rise in incomes for working people had stopped at the turn of the century, so "getting by" remained extremely difficult for the vast majority. Poor people purchased food in small quantities, not being able to afford more. The price of meat had risen dramatically, doubling since 1905. People bought second- or third-hand clothing or, when they could afford to, ready-made attire.

Most families, as had been the case for Victor's family in Belgium, could not survive without credit and pawnshops. Hard times easily became disastrous ones—expulsions from rooms, living without shelter, begging to get by. Arrests for vagabondage soared. A journalist looking closely at working-class quartiers reported that "the constant preoccupation of workers is to eat and drink."[28] In April 1911, an editorial in *Lectures pour tous* lamented:

> Misery is everywhere in Paris, and it seems that "progress," instead of bringing out its disappearance, has only kept it going and multiplied it. It is in the winter months that the problem of existence is the most anguishing for thousands and thousands of poor people.[29]

Winter was indeed the hardest. Heating of any kind could be rare, and illnesses like tuberculosis preyed on hungry, cold, and overworked people living in crowded, dirty homes. In Paris, thirty-two thousand residential buildings out of eighty thousand were considered unhealthy. In the first decade of the twentieth century, municipal authorities were listing "*îlots insalubres*"—sometimes entire blocks, many in central Paris, including the quartiers of Saint-Merri and Beaubourg in the Marais, around rue Mouffetard, neighborhoods in Belleville and Clignancourt, and many more—that were so unhealthy they were zones of tuberculosis. The disease killed seven of every one thousand residents in buildings housing the poor. In Saint-Denis, the percentage of unhealthy residences—veritable breeding places for disease—jumped to an appalling 58 percent and in Saint-Ouen to 62 percent. In 1911, 45 percent of housing was assessed at "overcrowded" or "insufficient" in terms of size. Despite the efforts of associations for reasonably priced dwellings (*habitations à bon marché*), Paris lacked at least fifty thousand apartments.

In 1903, only 10 percent of the houses in Paris were connected to sewers. About fifty thousand apartments in Paris consisted of only one room. Toilets, such as they were, stood in the courtyards on the ground floor or halfway up the communal staircase. A quarter of the buildings in Paris had no lavatories at all, and in the plebeian suburbs the percentage was far less than that. If baths were taken, they were in municipal establishments. Water from the Seine and the Marne was bad enough, but well water was even more dangerous, with cesspools inevitably nearby. Women did the family washing in public washhouses. When electricity was present, it often flickered.[30] Streets were badly paved, or not paved at all, little more than mud left by the incessant Parisian rain. The flea markets at porte de Clignancourt, porte d'Italie, and porte de Montreuil affirmed for Parisian elites the association of the periphery with gnawing, inescapable poverty. And so did the tanneries along the horribly polluted Bièvre River that slowly worked its way through the thirteenth and then fifth arrondissements, before emptying into the Seine near Notre Dame.[31]

Apollinaire's poem *Zone* reflected elite views of the suburbs of Paris. It presents a theme of the displacement of poverty, amid shanties "with their jumble of materials and perspectives." Likewise, Eugène Atget's *Zoniers* photo album, from 1912 to 1913, emphasized marginal types in the marginal zones, some showing only "a simple dwelling or work without the worker." Atget also highlighted the social exclusion of the poor from the center of the city into the Parisian periphery.[32]

In *quartiers populaires*, family disputes exploded in dank, tiny rooms. Many working women suffered violence at the hands of their men. Poor children had no more hope than their parents. Many very young children were passed, depending on the circumstances, to aunts, grandmothers, and other relatives.[33] Children started working as soon as possible—in principle, children were to remain in school until they were thirteen, but this law was routinely ignored.

Children's labor contributed about 20 percent to the income of the families of workers. When Léon Jouhaux, who would head the Confédération Générale du Travail and later win the Nobel Prize for Peace, went out on strike as a worker, his son had to leave school to go to work and earn thirty *sous* a day for his family.[34]

The daunting number of abandoned babies—4,232 in 1903—made it clear how desperately poor so many Parisians were. Of every five babies born, one did not live past three years of age. Until infant mortality began to decline in about 1906, a third of all married couples (and probably even more in *unions libres*) had lost at least one child to illness. This was particularly true in *quartiers populaires*.[35]

Alcoholism took a frightful toll as well.[36] Absinthe—"the green fairy," of which three hundred sixty thousand hectoliters was produced each year—ravaged and killed. Women found the drink attractive because it was somewhat sweet and could be mixed with water. Eau-de-vie such as Calvados, made from apples, and similar strong liquors from every imaginable fruit added to the prodigious consumption of alcohol. All this contributed to the French nationalists' fears that the stagnation of the population would prevent the army from having enough soldiers to one day take back Alsace-Lorraine, which included the *départements* lost by France in the Franco-Prussian war of 1870–1871.

The giant French wine lobby, in a country with 1.6 million *viticulteurs*, continued to insist that "wine is the healthiest and most hygienic of drinks" and that the French, unlike the gin-guzzling British and the bourbon-drinking Americans, did not have a problem of alcoholism. The number of places licensed to sell alcoholic drinks increased by a third between 1881 and 1911, reaching close to half a million in the latter year, even as the French population had really stopped growing (1891: 38.3 million; 1911: 39.6 million). In France, there was one store selling wine and other alcohols for every eighty-three inhabitants. By one estimate, in 1901 the average consumption of wine by a Parisian (counting infants and children, who presumably were not drinking) stood at 191 liters a year—and at 317 liters in the suburbs. In Belleville alone, in 1910 there were 448 merchants selling alcohol and doing brisk business.

Victor would have been very familiar with the kind of poverty he came upon after he arrived in Paris: he had seen it before in Brussels. And he now observed the great wealth of the elite in central Paris, which undoubtedly reminded him of the fancy quartiers of the Belgian capital. Anarchism drew followers who were appalled by the extreme poverty afflicting many in Paris, by workers confronting overbearing employers and foremen, by low wages, by suddenly being fired with no explanation, by rising rents, and by the ravages of tuberculosis and alcoholism.

Chapter 4

ANARCHISTS IN CONFLICT

Having arrived in Paris in late 1908, Victor needed a little money to keep afloat. He found work in nearby Belleville as a draughtsman in a small machine manufacturing company. He also gave French lessons to Russian immigrants—some of whom were exiled revolutionaries—and translated Russian novels and poems for a Russian journalist, who then published them. All this work brought in barely enough money to purchase onion soup for dinner at Les Halles. In his spare time, he immersed himself in French and other literatures: "Paris called to us, the Paris of . . . the Commune, of the CGT [Confédération Générale du Travail], of little journals printed with burning zeal, the Paris of our favourite authors, Anatole France and Jehan Rictus [Gabriel Randon]." Anatole France's anticlericalism and his activism in the campaign on behalf of Alfred Dreyfus would have attracted Victor. Rictus's poetry spoke to the poor in the language of the street, lamenting "the suffering of the penniless intellectual dragging out his nights on the benches of foreign boulevards, and no rhymes were richer than his."[1]

After work, Victor often took the Métro toward the Latin Quarter, "our third Paris, that which to tell the truth I prefer." He headed to the Bibliothèque Sainte-Geneviève near the Panthéon to read for the remaining hour and a half before it closed. He started up a short-lived reading and discussion group—"an eclectic group for social studies" called *La Libre Recherche*—with about twelve participants. They met in a sordid locale on rue Grégoire-de-Tours, near brothels whose red lanterns beckoned clients not there to read and discuss. Nearby, the rue de Buci offered louche bars. Victor had the impression of being in the Paris of Louis XVI among ancient doors and eighteenth-century figures announcing what goods or services could be purchased there. He remained briefly in Belleville but then found a room in the attic of a hotel on the place du Panthéon. He could cross boulevard Saint-Michel and go into the Jardin du Luxembourg to read near the place where the troops of Adolphe Thiers had gunned down Communards during Bloody Week in May 1871.

Victor met up close "a terrifying world, that of the ultimate indigence, of accepted degradation, of the fate of man under the stones of the great city," some of the poorest of the poor, drawn from *les bas-fonds*, the lowest and by reputation most dangerous Parisians. Some were on their last legs, begging and exhibiting to often horrified passersby real or imagined wounds and ulcers. Ragpickers waited for the gates of Paris to swing open early in the morning at porte d'Asnières, porte d'Italie, or porte Saint-Ouen, so that they could sell what they had collected beyond the walls or find what they could inside the city. No electric lights illuminated the huge piles of garbage through which they sifted.[2]

For Victor and Rirette, the offices on rue du Chevalier de la Barre in Montmartre of *L'Anarchie*, which the anarchist individualist Libertad had founded in 1905, quickly became a focus of their life together. Victor had gone there almost immediately after arriving in Paris from Brussels in late 1908. Unlike Rirette, Victor had never met Libertad, and the latter's anarchist individualism continued to loom large in the development of Victor's anarchism. Victor's first article in *L'Anarchie* was published on March 24, 1910, signed "Le Rétif," and his editorials subsequently appeared frequently.[3]

Born in Bordeaux in 1875, Libertad was abandoned by his parents and brought up in a charitable institution. His legs had atrophied from a childhood disease, and he could walk only with the help of crutches. This gave him overdeveloped shoulders, which bore his weight as he lurched along. After some schooling, he worked as an accountant in a small town in the Dordogne, before being fired for organizing what must have been a very small anarchist gathering. He then somehow managed to get to Paris in 1897 at age twenty-two, surviving by begging—"with such a formidable voice that one could hardly refuse." The anarchist journalist Sébastien Faure came across Libertad living on a bench on boulevard Rochechouart in People's Paris and took him in for a time. At Faure's house he sometimes slept on a pile of old newspapers, but it was better than being outside in the cold. One day, a comrade dropped by to see Faure and, seeing Libertad, muttered, "One has the impression of being right in *la cour des Miracles!*," the place in Ancien Régime Paris to which supposedly some beggars returned at the end of their day to remove what passed for horrible wounds.[4]

On September 5, 1897, Libertad went into the Basilica of Sacré-Coeur de Montmartre because bread was distributed in addition to Communion hosts. The catch was that to get something to eat one had to stay for the Mass. When *Père* Lenières said in his sermon, "It is unhealthy ideas that provoke scandals," Libertad hobbled forward from the rows of poor wretches and interrupted the priest's sermon, shouting with his southwestern accent, "It is you who are causing a scandal and who have unhealthy ideas. . . . I demand the floor! I demand the floor! . . . I am poor, and thus I am closer to your Christ than the Holy Father in Rome with diamonds in his hat. And you up there, the good pastor, you are an accomplice of the political schemers who exploit human misery!" He thundered on, addressing the faithful amid chaos: "And you there with your moronic heads! You come here on Sunday to have a clear conscience so that you can peacefully cheat those who work for you during the week. Heap of scoundrels! You bunch of cattle!" Libertad used his crutches to fend off those coming to silence him. Finally, a vicar went to the sacristy and brought back a bedsheet, dropped it from the priest's pulpit on the anarchist's head, and, with help, rolled him into it. The police arrested Libertad for vagabondage. When asked to respond as to his means of existence, he replied, "I am habitually without work and have no means of existence, nor a home." He was jailed for two months. At least there, Libertad was assured of something to eat.[5]

Destitute and dressed in the well-worn blue smock of a typographer, wearing sandals, and with his long hair blowing in the wind, Libertad harangued passersby with his booming voice, quickly attracting crowds on street corners or in front of café terraces, or in public meetings, where he was an almost inevitable presence, also often attracting the police who arrested him time and time again. Libertad spoke loudly and well. Invariably, as he attracted crowds, some laughed at him, but often he won people over to his side. He spoke in various rented rooms and halls. Sometimes the number of those attending, paying about forty centimes to participate (of which the owner of the place received twenty-five centimes), was insufficient to cover the fee for the hall. So in 1902 Libertad started up anarchist *causeries populaires* (lectures and public discussions) in Montmartre, and three years later the *causeries populaires* began at 22 rue du Chevalier de la Barre.[6]

Libertad began to write in *Le Libertaire*, and in 1902 he was one of the founders of the *Ligue antimilitariste*. No one was really sure of his real name—"My name? I don't care. They can call me whatever they want!" His theme was constant: "When the oppressors have been eliminated from the earth, it will be the coming of the anarchist society and men will be united by their love of life!" Yet "revolt was not his only mistress." He was known to have lived with two sisters and to have never declared the resulting babies to the authorities: "Public records? [*État civil*]," he spat out, "never have heard of them!"[7]

In April 1905, Libertad started *L'Anarchie*, helped by the take at *causeries*. The anarchist newspaper, which appeared on Thursdays usually in four but occasionally two pages, emerged as the center of anarchist individualism in the French capital. Two years later, Libertad managed to bring together enough equipment to print the newspaper in the building he rented on rue du Chevalier de la Barre. Down

The anarchist Libertad.

a steep incline from Sacré-Coeur, across from an old, high house with green shutters, stood—and still stands—the three-story building. Libertad published *L'Anarchie* in the basement. On the ground floor were the newspaper's offices, a room large enough for anarchist *causeries,* and other rooms to lodge up to ten visitors or comrades who didn't have a place to sleep. It was an article of faith that anarchists would welcome them and not ask what had brought them there.

Victor Kibaltchiche described the street: "[H]ouses from the previous century still standing, a small misshapen intersection stretches its cobblestones up to a crossing of two streets, one a steep hill and the other of completely gray stairs . . . the *'causeries' popu-laires* and the publication of *L'Anarchie* took up all of the low house, from which could be heard the roar of the printing presses, songs, and intense discussions." The police would later insist that the printing letters were stolen from print shops in which some *compagnons* worked. A police report referred caustically to Libertad as "the king of Montmartre."[8]

Libertad was nothing if not provocative. Under his editorship, *L'Anarchie* wondered aloud if it might not be a good thing if prostitutes knowingly passed along venereal disease to bourgeois as a means of exacting revenge. He outraged policemen on one of many occasions referring to them as "imbeciles who watch intelligent people go by," encouraging the hostility of the crowd that assembled to the uniformed agents.[9]

In August 1907, on rue du Chevalier de la Barre, Libertad pointed to two policemen and provoked, "Look at the murderers!" Three months later, he was again arrested, allegedly for threatening to kill a policeman. At his trial early the next year, he denied having said that workers should break their tools (owned by their bosses) and burn their factories, claiming he only said that they should "burn down the unsanitary factories, as well as unsanitary houses." He was acquitted.[10]

In April 1908, on boulevard Barbès, Libertad and several friends were singing "Down with war!" accompanied by several guitars and violins. When a policeman asked if they had permission to sing in the street, Libertad replied that they needed none. When the police insisted that all this had to stop, he announced, "Comrades, these policemen want to arrest me arbitrarily in order to beat me up. If they want to take me in, they will need a carriage!" Then he dropped to the ground. The police tried to arrest him, but the crowd prevented the police from doing so, as Libertad shouted "Death! Down with the cops, down with the cows [cops]!"[11]

Libertad loved the chaos and the people of the street, mocking all authority. He had particular contempt for socialists who participated in elections, thus in the mind of most anarchists propping up the bourgeois state. "The elector, there is the enemy!" he insisted, although he provocatively put forth his candidacy as the "abstentionist candidate" in elections for an arrondissement municipal council. He used the occasion to denounce universal manhood suffrage as a fraud serving to legitimize oppression. Libertad held that those promoting immediate revolution were "jokers" like the others. Don't wait for the Revolution! Make your own Revolution—be free and live freely, he insisted. Be yourselves. Libertad became the patron saint of individualism. He reminded his followers, "The most difficult enemy to defeat is in yourself, anchored in your brain. It is one, but wears different masks: it is the belief in God, the belief in the Patrie, the obsession with the family, the existence of property. It calls itself Authority, the holy Bastille of Authority, to which everyone is supposed to bow."[12]

In *L'Anarchie*, Victor's editorials focused attention to the challenges faced by the poor. Unhappiness abounded in Paris and other French cities: "No one dares accept the famous opinion of Professor Pangloss: all is for the best in the best of possible worlds."[13] In an editorial, the young anarchist Rirette Maîtrejean called attention to the obvious: "the high cost of rents and food, and the immense effort necessary even to have something to eat." The cause was "ever more atrocious exploitation."[14]

During the first decade of the twentieth century in Paris, on one side stood "those who have money and do not work . . . and those who work and have nothing."[15] Money talked and the poor walked. In a time of considerable hardship for ordinary people, many dreamed that France would one day have economic and social justice.

As workers faced unemployment, underemployment, and dead seasons, undercut by the increasing mechanization of factory production, three kinds of social movements seemed to offer hope for change. The first was Socialism. Reform Socialists believed that sweeping electoral victories would bring about a new state. Revolutionary Socialists counted on revolution to bring the downfall of capitalism and the existing French state. Jules Guesde led France's revolutionary Socialists. Greatly influenced by Karl Marx, and known as the "the red Jesuit" because he was rigid and doctrinaire as well as humorless, Guesde had organized the Federation of the Socialist Workers of France Party in 1879 and then, four years later, the French Workers' Party, the first modern political party in France. Guesde considered electoral campaigns a means of propagating Marxian socialism. In 1905, thanks to the leadership of the charismatic Jean Jaurès, a former philosophy professor, reformist and revolutionary Socialists were uncomfortably unified.

The second possibility for mobilized workers was Revolutionary Syndicalism (under the umbrella structure of the Confédération Générale du Travail, the CGT, which had been founded in 1895). The Chamber of Deputies had legalized unions in 1884, and by the early twentieth century French unions had more than a million members. "Syndicalists" saw strikes—and one day a general strike—as the means of bringing the state and capitalism to their knees. They viewed the shop floor as providing a natural way to organize workers, while providing something of a vision of what a society of equals would be after a revolution. Revolutionary Syndicalism, as proclaimed at the Congress of Amiens in 1906, carried the struggle of workers away from politics to a uniquely economic front.

Anarchism had emerged as a third option during the last decades of the nineteenth century. It was one response to the growth of powerful centralized states and their increasing capacity to extract resources, command allegiance, and conscript bodies for war. These centralized states and the large-scale industrialization that accompanied them were transforming European society. Nationalism was fully part of state-making. States worked with determination to increase the number of speakers of the dominant language—a push that anarchists firmly resisted. Spain provides a good example of the adage "A language is a dialect with a powerful army." Thus it is not surprising that anarchism found followers in non-Castilian parts of Spain and in southern Italy, where tax collectors, government officials, and soldiers, speaking a different language, stood as the face of the state. Victor remembered workers being "pulled in opposite directions by two antagonistic movements, the revolutionary syndicalism of the CGT, which, with a fresh and powerful idealism, was winning the real proletariat to the struggle for positive demands, and the shapeless activity of the anarchist groups." Indeed, many anarchists and other workers were attracted to the structure and organized demands of the CGT.[16]

Anarchists dreamed of abolishing the state, and thus the privileges so cherished by the wealthy. The poet Camille Mauclair recalled, "It wasn't so much that we wanted the miserable to be happy . . . as that we wanted the happy to be miserable . . . the label ["anarchist"] covered all the grounds of our discontent. . . . I hated indiscriminately deputies, policemen, judges, officers, all the supporters of the social order, as much as I hated philistines, and I believed mystically in catastrophic revolution and the red dawn."[17]

Anarchists believed that once states had been destroyed, people could live in harmony in natural groupings. They believed fervently that people were basically good, but that their lives were blighted by the existence of states and the props of capitalism, organized religion, and professional armies. A stateless society would bring about the disappearance of social disharmony, making possible the full development of the individual in a world free of conflict. As Victor put it, "Anarchism rises above class interests. It appeals to all men who energetically hold onto the will to live free." He went on: "Anarchism swept us away completely because it both demanded everything of us and offered us everything. There was no remotest corner of life that it failed to illuminate; at least so it seemed to us."[18]

Many anarchists were influenced by Mikhail Bakunin, the Russian revolutionary who memorably asserted that "destruction is a creative passion" and who looked to the Russian peasantry for the expected revolution. Another Russian anarchist, the geographer-prince Peter Kropotkin, was a man of peace. Yet he is sometimes credited with coming up with the scary term "propaganda by the deed," the belief that an assassination of a tsar, general, or police chief could be the spark that would inspire ordinary people to throw off the chains of the state. In 1892, Ravachol (the Dutch-born François Koenigstein) tried to kill magistrates with bombs he planted in elegant Parisian residences. He had already killed before and would have continued to do so had he not been captured and guillotined. During the era of "propaganda by the deed," anarchists killed six heads of state, including French president Marie François Sadi Carnot and US president William McKinley, who was assassinated in Buffalo, New York, by a man whose fare to that city in upstate New York had been paid by an Italian anarchist group in New Jersey.

Émile Henry's bomb attack in Paris in February 1894 on the Café Terminus, near Gare Saint-Lazare, initiated the era of modern terror. Henry, twenty-one years of age and the son of a man who had been condemned to death in absentia after the Paris Commune, went out to kill not officials representing the state but just ordinary people listening to music and having a beer before bedtime. He was also an intellectual, which at the time made him unusual among anarchist terrorists. Before his execution in April of that year, Henry assured judge and jury that the state could not destroy anarchism, insisting that "its roots are too deep." Most anarchists, in the wake of these high-profile attacks and assassinations, rejected "propaganda by the deed" and moved in more positive directions, including propaganda by the word, cooperatives, and seeking influence in trade unions. The vast majority of anarchists were not violent, but it was the small number of violent anarchists who preoccupied public attention.

As anarchism gained ground with workers during the last years of the nineteenth century, anarchist committees started up and their public meetings became more frequent. The anarchist press again came to life, and newspapers advertised lectures, debates, and *causeries populaires*. A police report correctly assessed that these anarchist gatherings, which were informal lecture series, served as something of an organized center for Parisian anarchists. Their searing editorials played a major part in the way that competing anarchist tendencies defined and promoted their positions. This became even more important with the new century, as differences in outlook between different anarchist groups became even deeper and increasingly bitter.

Most anarchists, a majority of whom were workers, rejected the hierarchical organization that characterized socialism. Other anarchists drifted toward producer and consumer cooperative movements, although this evolution generated considerable hostility from comrades who saw such a trend as moving toward socialism. Recent interest in neo-Malthusianism (whose adherents sought to limit population growth because of fears that existing resources were inadequate to sustain more people) also divided anarchists. Yet most anarchists were favorable to neo-Malthusianism, believing it was part of the transformation of society, and many saw it as part of control over their own sexuality. Some believed in a woman's right to abortion; others did not.

In the first years of the twentieth century, some anarchists moved toward Revolutionary Syndicalism, or "Anarcho-Syndicalism" as it was sometimes called, particularly in Spain. Trade union membership in France grew from about two hundred thousand in 1906 to seven hundred thousand in 1912. To syndicalists, *bourses du travail* (labor exchanges)—which many French cities had—offered something of a vision of a future transformation of society once the state and capitalism had been destroyed. French elites feared exactly such an occurrence.[19]

When Victor arrived at rue du Chevalier de la Barre and began attending *causeries* that sometimes took place twice a week, he walked right into contentious debates among communist anarchists, anarchist individualists, and, increasingly, illegalists. He had it right when he assessed that anarchism was "built upon contradictions, torn apart by tendencies and sub-tendencies."[20]

Victor, like Libertad, had embraced anarchist individualism: "Let's not wait for a problematic revolution. We live in a society . . . in the state of permanent revolution [and] we have faith in ourselves, in the ability of the individual to transform himself and to struggle non stop for the transformation of society." In any case, "every anarchist is by definition revolutionary." He put it this way: "[t]he evolution of minds that foresees the great social upheavals has hardly begun. We deduce that the revolution is still far away." Victor's advice: "make your own revolution by being free men and living in comradeship."[21]

It took courage to live "*en-dehors*" (on the outside):

> To be an anarchist is to leave the beaten paths on which for hundreds of years generations of sheep have walked without reflection, break with routines, reject commonly held believes, be contemptuous of public opinion, have disdain for rejecting smiles and treacherous laughs, insults, and calomnies.[22]

Victor would take the route that pleased him, working hard "to be 'me,' a free man among the slaves, strong among the weak, brave among the cowards."[23]

The Revolution, anarchists believed, had to begin within the individual. "Individualists," influenced by the philosopher Max Stirner, encouraged ordinary people to "sculpt their 'me'" in order to achieve "the revolution in oneself."[24] Like all anarchists, they rejected military service and organized religion. They also denounced sexual repression and, for some, marriage as compromising the individual.

Victor insisted that the anarchist had to "resist and take action continually." The masses were blocked by "the habit of believing, the habit of obeying, the habit of being guided." Laws were powerless to transform society. The "parliamentary illusion" simply deluded ordinary people. From the individualist perspective, "Bestial violence, hatred, the sheep-like mentality of [political] leaders, the gullibility of the masses—here is what must be annihilated in order to transform society. . . . Without the renovation of mankind, there is no salvation!" The bases of anarchist morality could be found "in our very lives. Because it is life that inspires our insubordination."[25]

Some "libertarian individualists," espousing "conscious egotism," lived in small groups on the margins of society. This took some of them to the suburbs. Anarchist communities there were intended to transform the self as a first step in the conversion of many in society to the ultimate possibility of revolution.

Individualist anarchists scorned leaders who called for immediate social and political mobilization. Victor remained scathing about the political and union demonstrations he had observed in Belgium: "Look at them about seven in the evening as they file down the streets, glum or marked by alcohol, broken by abhorrent tasks, not even giving the vigorous impression of beasts of burden. Watch them, the days of *fêtes*, going about in raucous bands among the hiccups of a drunken binge, [singing] the sorry and obscene songs of the people."[26]

Individualist anarchism thus defiantly broke with "communist anarchism," whose adherents believed that revolution was near and who were proponents of collective action and willing to undertake alliances with socialists and syndicalists. To Victor and other individualists, "Marxism and Syndicalism are incurable forms." The concept of organization itself flew in the face of anarchist spontaneity. *L'Anarchie* editorialized: "When anarchists want to undertake something together, they do not need something in writing—their free consent always suffices." Individualists encouraged "acts of individual revolt in order to diffuse libertarian ideas," which would ultimately bring about individual and then collective emancipation. They insisted they were building toward a revolutionary future and the transformation of society. Between October 1910 and June 25, 1911, 2,908 attacks occurred on railway lines—above all, the cutting of telephone and telegraph lines. The police invariably suspected anarchists, and in many cases they got it right. They would count thirty-nine "individualist" groups in Paris and its suburbs, scattered throughout the plebeian neighborhoods.[27]

Some individualists became "illegalists." Illegalism had first developed in France during the late 1890s, as well as in Italy and Belgium. Illegalists contended that any acts against society were justified. They argued that since property was theft, such heists or counterfeiting were simply taking back that which belonged to everybody. It was *"la reprise individuelle"* (the individual taking back). One could hold up a wealthy person at gunpoint or break into a wealthy person's safe, because the money or objects being taken were not stolen but simply taken back from someone who benefited from the protection of the state, thus stealing from the poor. Work brought scanty remuneration, while labor further enriched people of means. Illegalists were not only on the margins of society but also in defiance of all of its codes and laws. Believing that no immediate escape from the capitalist state was possible, they would no longer be exploited. Illegalists insisted that such acts were part of a "permanent revolt against the established order." Thefts became revolutionary acts. Illegalists represented a new, younger generation of anarchists, most of whom were workers. Traditional anarchists like Sébastien Faure and Jean Grave (a follower of Peter Kropotkin and the author of *La société mourante et l'anarchie* [*Moribund Society and Anarchy*]) rejected them, although the latter opened up his newspaper columns to illegalist views. And so, later, would Victor Kibaltchiche.[28]

Marius Jacob became the most eminent "illegalist." Born in Marseille in 1879 to a working-class family and beginning his career as a typographer, Jacob traveled to Australia as an apprentice sailor. He deserted the ship, commenting bitterly, "I have seen the world and it is not beautiful." He returned to France and became a burglar. Jacob's band of thieves sent out scouts to gather information about possible targets for operations. They divided France into "zones of activity," and in principle they stole from only those whom the burglars designated as "parasites." In the desire to separate "*reprise individuelle*" from "theft," Jacob asked members of his band to contribute at least ten percent of the take to anarchist propaganda. After hundreds of burglaries, he was arrested in 1903; three years later, he was sent to the Hell of Cayenne, a notorious French penal colony in French Guiana, where he remained, despite almost twenty escape attempts, until 1927.[29]

The number of illegalists in Paris slowly increased during the early years of the twentieth century. A police report noted in July 1907 that young unemployed men "who frequent the milieu of anarchists and anti-militarists, [were] living from plunder and theft." They stole bread and milk, among other things, following the passage of suppliers. Some raced by to take things very early in the morning as grocers and other merchants started to put their goods out on the street. The report assessed that "this way of living at the expense of society is now strongly recommended in private conversation in all the libertarian groups of Paris."[30]

Most illegalists stole very little and did so in order to have something to eat. One day, in a fairly poor neighborhood on rue Clignancourt, a poet friend of Rirette's was walking with an illegalist who had had nothing to eat the day before. But he had an idea. His dog was trailing behind the pair. As they approached a poultry store, the merchant was putting out his finest chickens for customers. At his master's command, the dog leapt up and grabbed a chicken and ran down the street. While the merchant ran after the dog, the illegalist grabbed a second chicken and thrust a third in the hands of his astonished friend. "Let's get out of here!" the illegalist shouted. But then he stopped: "Wait, I forgot the watercress!" He returned to take two bunches of it. When they returned to the illegalist's apartment, the dog and presumably the chicken were waiting. "Never had such a good meal," the poet related to Rirette.[31]

Although the anarchist press helped differentiate the two major anarchist groups—on the one hand "communists" in the anarchist sense working for revolution that they believed they would see in their lifetimes, and on the other hand individualists and illegalists—the separation between them could easily be exaggerated. Go-betweens often left one group for the other, or participated in both. And although anarchist groups may have had increasingly different views of the possibility of revolution, they were often in contact, at times coordinating activities. They even raised funds together to allow for the publication of newspapers and brochures. Moreover, as anarchists came and went, not all of them were fully aware of the ideological and strategic differences between the two groups. The editors of L'Anarchie, for their part, insisted that all anarchists were illegalists because they were outside the law.[32]

Some individualists had become obsessed with "scientific theories," wanting to introduce "rationality in all aspects of daily life." In order to live "scientifically," they lived in small groups on the edge of Paris in a "free association of egos."[33] They took up vegetarianism and other ascetic régimes, refusing, among other things, meat, salt, pepper, coffee, vinegar, and any alcohol, including wine. They considered alcohol to be responsible at least in part for brutalizing the mass of workers, keeping them from understanding their real interests and developing as individuals. These anarchists ate a lot of macaroni, garden vegetables, and cheese. And only some of them believed that tea was acceptable.[34]

Victor's philosophy was neither that of the illegalists nor that of the dominant individualists. In Paris, Victor quickly turned against illegalism as a dominant current of individualism, and thus turned from the influence of Libertad. Most illegalists who knew him believed, for their part, that Victor was too close to socialism and too much of an intellectual who preferred contemplation, writing, and persuasion to burglaries and violence. By virtue of his articles, he was already known to those frequenting anarchist *soirées* and debates. On March 21, 1908, before he moved to Paris, Victor first signed an article in *L'Anarchie* with the *nom de plume* "Le Rétif"—"the stubborn one" who refuses to compromise [with the state and bourgeois society].[35]

Although he still felt himself "lost in space," Victor began to sign editorials on the first page of *L'Anarchie*, which was growing quickly and soon had a print run of six thousand five hundred copies. Among the individualist anarchists he met in 1909 on rue du Chevalier de la Barre was a short, slim young woman "with a Gothic profile"—Rirette Maîtrejean.[36]

Chapter 5

RIRETTE MAÎTREJEAN

By the time Victor first encountered Rirette Maîtrejean, she had become an increasingly visible presence in Parisian anarchism. She was born Anna Estorges in the village of Saint-Mexant, Corrèze, on August 14, 1887, the daughter of a poor farmer. But with prices plunging for farm goods, Anna's father Martin moved the family to Tulle, five miles away, finding work as a mason. Even as a young child, Rirette had a passion for study, with the goal of becoming a teacher. She wanted to prepare at the regional teaching school for possible admission to the École Normale and eventually a good teaching post. Rirette's father agreed with this choice, but he soon fell ill with enteritis and died in 1903 at the age of forty-four. With absolutely no money—one grandfather had already passed away and the other, reduced to ragpicking, died soon thereafter—and not yet of an age to secure a teaching position, Rirette's only option was to find work as a domestic or begin some sort of apprenticeship. Neither path interested her. Her mother insisted that she marry, not necessarily someone of her choice. After all, marriage remained for many an economic arrangement where love was not necessarily a factor.[1]

Defying her mother, in the winter of 1904 Rirette took the train to Paris, where she lodged with an aunt in the eleventh arrondissement. This was a traditional and obvious trajectory for a poor girl

Rirette Maîtrejean.

from the Limousin, except that domestic service or some other similar work was not what she wanted. She arrived in the capital at age sixteen with "a proud idea of my independence." Yet she needed money in order to survive. Work in the garment industry by sewing at home was a possibility, but she quickly discovered that thousands of young women became virtual slaves working almost around the clock in order to pay the rent on the sewing machines they got from merchant-capitalists, thus gaining little or nothing from their work.

Rirette saw the exploitation of workers up close. Yet she would remember that despite the misery all around her, "a breath of liberty passed through our souls . . . a reaction against the social suffocation that then ruled." That liberty took the form of anarchism, which "spontaneously developed in our minds." It was "a sort of springtime, the springtime of [the new] century. There were bells ringing in the air, appeals made by intellectuals to the people, a great revolt against slavery."[2]

Rirette gradually joined the world of speeches, discussions, and debates about how to bring social justice to France. With two young men, she attended her first *causerie*, where she heard Libertad speak. As always, he wore the blue smock of a printer as he shouted, "Me,

I am an anarchist!" People were not born free, he argued. Freedom had to be conquered and anarchism was the way: "To free yourselves, you must fight!"[3] Rirette agreed.

Plunging into the world of Parisian anarchism, Rirette followed the *cours d'études sociales* at the Sorbonne and attended lectures followed by debates given at the "*universités populaires*" that had sprung up in many French cities—notably, the first one, the "Cooperative of Ideas" in faubourg Saint-Antoine (which had been a center of militancy in the Revolutions of 1789 and 1792, the June Days of 1848, and the Paris Commune). For a small sum, she and other young workers and intellectuals, including some women, attended lectures and debates, borrowed books to read, and took courses in foreign languages.[4]

The gatherings in faubourg Saint-Antoine and those at the Cité Angoulême in the eleventh arrondissement were held in cramped, rented halls. A few times a week, Rirette would walk to the end of a "dark courtyard whose leprous stones oozing misery opened into an uncertain wall giving way to sort of a shop into which air could only enter via a single small window. Furnishings consisted of a huge wooden table and several worm-eaten benches. A large lamp exuding smoke provided light." She was surprised to find the hall walls adorned by several "decors of modern art," lending a bit of beauty to otherwise desolate rooms.[5]

On Wednesdays, speakers, some obscure, some well known, would choose "the most important subjects" upon which to speak. Outsiders turned up from time to time, some seemingly astonished that they had not come upon anarchist orgies. Usually these were serious affairs, but occasionally they brought comic relief. Once, a group of anarchists impatiently awaited a speaker who was very late. Eventually sounds of chaos could be heard outside. The speaker had been approaching the Cité Angoulême wearing only a pair of shorts. Several policemen surrounded and arrested him, and when they interrogated him on his attire, he explained that he dressed "following his ideas." The pores of his skin had to be completely open to the air so that "the noxious substance developed by sudoriferous glands" could be free in order for him to think. Three doctors who examined him found him completely sane.[6]

There was a communal spirit to many of these gatherings, even if the debates became heated at times. Anarchists shared what they had. Rirette knew one who regularly gave almost every *sou* he had to the cause of publishing anarchist propaganda. She was aware that his family provided a certain sum for him each week, but he kept precious little for himself, sleeping on the floor in the hallway of a building when the outside temperature was in the twenties, exposed to the *courants d'air* (drafts) that obsess the French. He once purchased a dozen spoiled herrings because they were cheap and enough to feed him for a week. Anarchist groups willingly accepted comrades they did not know to their dinner tables, although those regularly there enjoyed certain rights—perhaps the first spoonfuls—and such meals invariably went on with mutual respect.[7]

Rirette decided to become an individualist. She had heard Libertad speak and had taken his words to heart, especially when he had thundered, "It is not a hundred years from now that one must live as an anarchist. It is now." She was also impressed that women appeared to have a more important role among individualists than they had among revolutionary anarchist-communists. Several female activists became her friends. For the moment, she believed that the advantages of individualism outweighed the disadvantages, though she remained wary of the fact that many "individualists" had become "illegalists."[8]

On weekends, a small number of "individualists" began to go to the Gare Saint-Lazare or the Gare d'Orsay—paying the fare if they had any money, sneaking onto trains if they did not—and then out into the countryside. *L'Anarchie* announced these outings. The revelers carried musical instruments and something to eat. In the forests of Saint-Germain-en-Laye, Sénart, or Rambouillet, they picnicked; listened to anarchist lectures; or simply discussed, debated, and sang anarchist songs, which themselves offered an essential form of propaganda. A picnic in Saint-Germain in 1907 included *déjeuner sur l'herbe* at noon; "a great public meeting on propaganda" at four, including a lecture on "the social war"; songs by the poet-singer Charles d'Avray; and an early *diner sur l'herbe* at six o'clock, followed by a lengthy "concert among comrades," beginning an hour later. Unlike anarchist songs twenty years earlier, these songs no longer saluted "heroic" anarchist attacks, but rather denounced societal inequalities and the plight of ordinary people.[9]

A typical poem went like this:

As the earth belong to everyone as communal property,
He who, first of all, acquires a fortune,
First of all commits a theft, as you know by heart,
That everything is really for everybody, and nothing is to be unfairly
    exploited.

Rirette, who was part of a group of anarchists espousing free love, soon discovered that she was pregnant by someone she had recently met. Her mother came up to Paris to help her daughter and found work as a domestic servant in the eleventh arrondissement. One rainy afternoon, at the corner of rue des Envierges and rue Piat, Rirette dashed into a café to get out of the rain. Sitting at a table, two men— probably pimps—began to bother Rirette, mocking her obvious distress. Just then, a tall young man jumped to her defense, intimidating the two aggressors and scaring them off. Her rescuer was Louis Maîtrejean, a young saddlemaker from a village in the Haute-Saône in eastern France with a forceful mustache and prominent cheekbones, who had seen Rirette at *causeries*.[10] Rirette and Maîtrejean shared what they had to eat that evening and for several evenings after that. In the summer of 1905, they took up residence together.

Rirette gave birth to Henriette, known as Maud, in January 1906, and the following September Louis and Rirette undertook a civil marriage, although many if not most anarchists repudiated the institution linked to recognition by state and church. Rirette was nineteen. Louis's name was entered on the birth register as Henriette's father. In 1906 their child Sarah—nicknamed Chinette—was born, just ten months after the birth of her sister. Maîtrejean and Rirette continued attending anarchist *soirées* and debates on the rue du Chevalier de la Barre and at Cité Angoulême. Whenever they went out, Rirette's mother, who was living nearby, took care of the babies.

Rirette and Maîtrejean lived with their two children in plebeian Belleville in the twentieth arrondissement, where the saddlemaker could find work, changing addresses three times in ten months. This was the way of life for the working poor. Life was tough in one of the most impoverished, dilapidated, and crowded parts of Paris; the quickly erected facades of buildings began to crumble, and broken windows let in torrents of Parisian wind and rain.

The neighborhoods in which Rirette and Maîtrejean lived were typical of Belleville, a place of hundreds of shops of artisans and craftsmen. Belleville was less properly "proletarian" than other parts of the Parisian periphery. There were really two Bellevilles. In upper Belleville, *rentiers* and other bourgeois could be found, lending a more conservative appearance that stood out next to working-class lower Belleville, which had drawn workers from *quartiers populaires* of the tenth and eleventh arrondissements. Forty years earlier, the Commune reinforced the negative image of lower Belleville in particular in the minds of many elite Parisians, who identified the neighborhoods with radical politics, alcoholism, syphilis, crime, and delinquency.[11]

There was not always work to be found for Maîtrejean, whose generosity and anarchist ways frequently brought an unanticipated mouth to feed, in the person of a comrade passing through with nowhere to sleep or eat. Rirette spent her days taking care of the babies, doing laundry, trying to find food they could afford at the market, and preparing meals.[12]

The young couple began to drift apart—gradually, but definitively—even though Maîtrejean was a good worker and father who brought home his pay every Saturday without stopping at a bar along the way. And he remained loyal to the struggle of the unions and the illusion that revolution was not far away. Yet the conditions of life, seen in the abject deprivation of young children in the neighborhood, drove Rirette to despair as she worried about her own babies. She felt this especially keenly after she and her friends visited an experimental anarchist school in Saint-Germain-en-Laye, founded in 1904. Here, children's education seemed very successful, in harmony with the rustic environment and based on respect for the pupils and rejecting the authoritarian structures of ordinary schools. Rirette's return to Belleville after the outing made the contrast seem enormous—indeed, disturbing. How could she find a suitable environment in Paris in which to raise her daughters?[13]

To make matters worse, Rirette had little opportunity to go beyond the radius of a few blocks. There was increasingly little for the couple to discuss. Rirette continued to attend *causeries*, and she thrived on the exchanges she had there; Maîtrejean, meanwhile, was innately suspicious of intellectuals. Rirette put it this way: "Intellectually, we had nothing in common. Any idea a bit elevated made him dizzy. As for me, I was only happy with lofty ideas."

In 1907, Rirette met and fell in love with Mauricius, a well-known anarchist orator. Born Maurice Vandamme, in 1886, the well-read Mauricius grew up on place du Tertre in Montmartre, the son of a bankrupt jeweler and a mother who sold paints and other materials to artists. He contributed articles on medicine and human biology to *L'Anarchie*, and, like Rirette, he actively espoused neo-Malthusianism. Yet Mauricius had developed the reputation as a "talker" and not a man of courage—a theoretician, nothing more. His rather bourgeois appearance somewhat irritated Rirette, but on several occasions it allowed him to avoid arrest during police roundups. And, at any rate, his countenance was very different from her husband's. She wrote Mauricius a letter, telling him, "I am completely yours," and assuring him that her husband no longer meant anything to her, except as a friend she admired. Louis Maîtrejean, who still loved Rirette passionately, hesitated to show his jealousy—anarchist couples were not supposed to do that. As Mauricius put it, "The stability and permanence of a couple were viewed as retrograde, monogamy as a [bourgeois] appropriation." Louis understood that Rirette would no longer be in his life, and he suffered in silence. Early in 1908, Rirette left their small apartment and moved in with Mauricius, taking her little daughters with her. In the spring, Rirette, Mauricius, and the two girls moved to a small house on the Seine in Champrosay in the commune of Draveil, twelve miles southeast of Paris.[14]

By then, Maîtrejean had abandoned saddlemaking for counterfeiting—"cash in chocolate," a common illegalist tactic—although it brought him only thirty francs a week instead of the sixty francs he had earned making saddles. Rirette suggested that this might have been because Maîtrejean had been devastated by her leaving him and that perhaps he wanted to show her "he was also a perfect illegalist." He justified counterfeiting by asserting that such a practice would ultimately destroy the French franc. In June 1910, Maîtrejean was sentenced to four years in prison for counterfeiting.[15]

In April 1908, Rirette went to rue du Chevalier de la Barre to see Libertad. He had been her idol, and now she found him alone, crying like a child. Libertad believed himself to be a victim of a cabal of "scientific" anarchists who had worked to undermine his influence while he was in jail for a short time. Moreover, the sharp division continued between individualists like Libertad and "communist" anarchists who believed in organizing for revolution. Libertad's rivals, and even enemies, within the anarchist movement were at work.[16]

Things turned worse for Libertad. For all the lovers he took, a woman named Jeanne Morand seemed always to be at his side, "silent and sad." But Libertad announced that this woman was not his "girl-friend," and in late May, Libertad told Rirette that Jeanne Morand had left him. Yet if Libertad had been abandoned by "his immediate entourage," he still retained some degree of influence, as French workers reacted to increasingly hard times by going out on strike.[17]

Despite the reliance of police, gendarmes, and soldiers on increasingly brutal tactics in dealing with demonstrations, anarchists seemed unable to increase their influence among ordinary people, many of whom shared their critiques of Georges Clemenceau's government. When Libertad spoke early in 1908 on the rue du Chevalier de la Barre, he admitted that "anarchism is in a state of rest and even of lassitude." Furthermore, Libertad's influence among individualists was being challenged by a group led by Georges Paraf-Javal, a leading "scientific" anarchist who had co-founded the Ligue antimilitarist in 1902 along with Émile Armand, an illegalist, and Libertad himself. Paraf-Javal printed two brochures directly attacking Libertad. In turn, Libertad accused Paraf-Javal and his followers of being "more scientific than anarchist."

Libertad and his followers felt increasingly isolated, particularly as many anarchists moved toward the union movement and the *bourses du travail*. Police observers worried that this would put an end to ideological factions within anarchism and lead to "one single unified revolutionary wave." This was not to be. Yet *causeries* continued, and a policeman reported that "the anarchists danced and behaved like fools." Even depressed, Libertad believed such events would continue to provide attractive propaganda for anarchism that even Clemenceau could not stop.[18]

Clemenceau, who at the time was prime minister and minister of the interior, was despised by anarchists. He was a leader of the Radical Party, whose proponents were anticlerical but socially moderate. Clemenceau was a bully and a renowned dueler who detested socialists, unions, and the Catholic Church almost as much as he detested his American ex-wife, whom he had had followed by a detective, jailed, and deported. He made his allegiances clear during the bitterly contentious years before Victor's arrival in France. On March 10, 1906, an explosion deep in the Courrières mines in Pas-de-Calais killed more than one thousand one hundred miners. Just before the massive demonstrations on May Day, a tradition that had begun in 1890 in France, Clemenceau, who relished his identity as "France's first cop," ordered the arrest of leading union leaders and brought an addition thousand troops to the capital.[19]

Over the course of the year, more than two hundred thousand workers in the building, textiles, metallurgical, chemical, and transport industries went out on strike. They demanded that wages not be lowered; they also demanded a shorter work day and the implementation of the law obliging employers to grant one day of rest per week. The affirmation of Revolutionary Syndicalism at the Amiens gathering of the CGT that year frightened employers amid talk of a possible general strike. Clemenceau remained determined to turn police and troops loose during demonstrations and strikes. He ordered twenty-six thousand soldiers to Paris to complement the standing garrison of fifty thousand in the capital. He was quite willing to turn to state violence to confront what he considered working-class rampage.[20]

Police repression of demonstrations and strikes had noticeably increased in intensity when Clemenceau had become prime minister and president of the Conseil in 1906. When he "received" a delegation from the CGT a few days before the planned demonstrations of May 1, he told them, memorably, "You are behind a barricade, while I am in front of it. Disorder is your means of action. My duty is to impose order!"[21]

The French state made such coordinated repression possible, and the upper classes called for it. Armed troops, gendarmes, and police could be sent against demonstrators and strikers without the slightest hesitation. On behalf of the French Republic, Clemenceau used violent tactics of repression with ease and virtual impunity. This left no doubt in the minds of anarchists of all varieties—and of socialists and syndicalists as well—that their criticisms of the centralized and powerful state were justified.

The strikes generally failed to secure the demands of the workers. To anarchists, such defeats demonstrated not only the sheer evil of the state but also the impossibility of carrying out a revolution through unions and, for that matter, socialist political organization. Libertad denounced unions as "the ultimate imbecility." Yet many anarchists—the "communists"—still had faith in unions as the way to prepare future revolution.[22]

For their part, the upper classes were reassured by Clemenceau's repressive tactics. A Parisian lawyer had intoned, "Contempt is the voluptuousness of the moment. . . . Never has authority managed better without respect."[23] The popular novels of Paul Bourget, celebrating the French bourgeoisie, identified workers and socialists as the enemy. Clemenceau's determined repression of strikes would inspire Bourget's *La Barricade* (1910). If entrepreneurs exploited workers, so much the better. An infusion of muscular Catholicism would help counter what Bourget considered the ongoing "social war."[24]

During subsequent strikes in Draveil, twelve miles south of Paris, in May and June 1908, it became clear that in response to the violence of the "forces of order," some strikers and demonstrators were willing to reply in kind.[25] Most union members favored a general strike but did not believe that they would see a victorious insurrection in their lifetimes. The internal forces of the French state had grown more powerful since the Paris Commune. However, this did not mean that all workers rejected the use of violence in the conflict against employers, strikebreakers, and police.[26]

Events in the grim southeastern suburbs in the spring of 1908 only reaffirmed Rirette's anarchist militancy. Early in May, a bitter strike broke out in the desolate suburbs of Draveil, Villeneuve-Saint-Georges, and Villeneuve-le-Roi. Thousands of workers labored for thirty bosses, extracting sand in quarries over a thirty-kilometer stretch along the Seine. Building the new Métro and train tunnels and canals required an enormous amount of sand. These workers, many of whom were Breton, Auvergnat, or Italian in origin, were a hardy, tested lot. Injuries were commonplace, and for many workers three liters of wine each day was the only thing that could keep them going.

After a short-lived strike in November 1907 that brought a return to the paltry pay level of fifty centimes an hour, on May 2, 1908, about eight hundred workers who extracted five hundred to six hundred tons of sand a day went out on strike. They demanded seventy centimes an hour, plus twenty-five more for work in water, thirty for night work, and eighty centimes for additional work beyond their daunting workdays. The twenty-six bosses signed a pact of solidarity, vowing to defeat the strike, and brought in strike breakers. The strike was marked by fighting, sabotage, and even arson, with many acts carried out by anarchists. Some workers armed themselves with pistols. Anarchist speakers went out from Paris to address the strikers. Libertad was among them. In a fiery speech he told the workers, "When the earth has been freed from its oppressors, this will be the coming of an anarchist society when mankind will be united by their love for life."

On May 23, two hundred of the strikers tried to prevent scabs from working and were attacked by police and soldiers. Next, workers pushed four scabs into a restaurant and held them there until the subprefect managed to obtain their release. On May 28, gendarmes tried to enter a meeting of strikers being held in the Restaurant Ranque. Forced back, they began to fire into the restaurant, killing two people: Émile Giobellina, who was only seventeen years of age, and Pierre Le Foll, a carpenter.

Rirette went out to Draveil-Vigneux every day to participate in what she called a "festival of common misery." On June 2, as she arrived at the site of the strike carrying food she had gathered on farms along the way, Rirette learned of the restaurant shootings. Rirette went to see Giobellina's body, having discovered that the boy had no family. Someone, she insisted, should be there. Others had the same idea, and Rirette joined about ten thousand people in a solemn procession toward the cemetery where the young man was to be buried. Cavalrymen blocked their entrance.

Georges Clemenceau sent in more troops to back up the police and gendarmes. Two days later, ten to fifteen thousand people followed the casket of Pierre Le Foll to the cemetery of Villeneuve-le-Roi, amid shouts of "Down with the capitalists!" Violent confrontations between workers and soldiers occurred along the route.

A quickly organized investigation into the shootings concluded that the gendarmes had no orders to go into the restaurant and that, worse, they could not demonstrate any aspect of "legitimate defense." But that was the end of it; no one would be prosecuted for the deaths.

On July 30, a huge mobilization of union members, socialists, and anarchists took place, as building workers and others arrived by train from Paris in support of the strikers and to protest the harsh repression. They marched toward the cemetery where Émile Giobellina had been buried. Cavalrymen cut through the demonstration with their swords, killing four demonstrators and wounding a hundred more, including a thirteen-year-old. The clash left sixty-nine soldiers, gendarmes, and police wounded as well. Indeed, some of the demonstrators had brought pistols. The police arrested more than a score of union leaders, among them Victor Griffuelhes, the general secretary of the CGT, who spent two months in jail. A deputy mayor of Draveil was among the injured—his arm would be amputated while he was in prison.

Both Rirette and Libertad were there that day. Rirette's leg was broken by a huge rock thrown at her by a soldier during the confrontations on July 30. She escaped arrest only when a doctor convinced the police that she needed to be taken in an ambulance to medical care because she risked paralysis. Libertad avoided arrest only by throwing himself into the Seine, surviving despite being handicapped and not knowing how to swim.[27]

Gradually, negotiations started, and in the end the strikers received a tiny raise of five centimes, the workday limited to ten hours, the guarantee of one day of rest per week, a little more pay for night work, and the closure of exploitative bars run by foremen. Sixteen people who had been arrested were freed without being charged. It became clear that *provocateurs* and informers had been at work within the ranks of the strikers. Yet again, Clemenceau's strategy had been bloodshed.[28]

For Jean Jaurès's *L'Humanité* and other newspapers on the left, Clemenceau's responsibility for the tragic events seemed clear. The

Commission Administrative de la Bourse du Travail noted, "Yet again Clemenceau wants to show that he is the master of France. Laws mean nothing to his bloodthirsty existence." The commission denounced the "government of murderers." The conservative *Le Temps* had a very different view, describing the CGT as "a purely insurrectionary committee" and declaring, "We will deal with it as such."[29]

Rirette would never forget what she had seen during those weeks in Draveil. In five years in Paris, she was much changed. And for Libertad, the strikes would be his last stand. He died four months later, in November 1908, at age thirty-three—eight days after being kicked in the stomach during a brawl following an anarchist talk on rue du Chevalier de la Barre. He hobbled on crutches to Lariboisière Hospital near the Gare du Nord. Before Libertad died of peritonitis (although rumor has long since had him being poisoned), his only visitor was Mauricius. No one came to claim his body.[30]

Chapter 6

A LOVE STORY

Rirette had first caught sight of Victor Kibaltchiche in the spring of 1909 at an anarchist meeting in Lille that she attended with Mauricius. She was not impressed. Victor had "worried" dark eyes, his mouth was small and contemptuous," and his hands were "very meticulous," not those of a worker. Reflecting his family's origin, Victor wore a Russian shirt of white flannel, embroidered with light silk, covering his "frail" chest. He spoke softly, reassuringly, carefully choosing his words, with "precious" gestures. "He displeased me enormously. What pretension!" she remembered. Victor's impression of her was not much better. He asked Mauricius, "Who is this little goose who is accompanying you?"[1]

In July 1909, after leaving her girls with militants she knew, Rirette and Mauricius made a brief trip to Italy and planned to go on to North Africa. But in Rome Rirette fell ill with meningitis and had to return to Paris. Rirette's relationship with Mauricius had become stormy by that point, and the abbreviated trip did not help things. Yet she returned to France with characteristic optimism about anarchism, although she and Mauricius went their separate own ways.

Again Rirette ran into Victor Kibaltchiche, at an anarchist *causerie* on the rue du Chevalier de la Barre. Victor annoyed Rirette, as well as other comrades, even more—"he exuded being an intellectual"— when he rose to speak during these debates. On several occasions

Rirette countered his arguments, and Victor always responded politely. A comrade made fun of the tension between them: "If you talk together for only an hour, you will find agreement," he assured her. When they met again at the *Université populaire* on rue de Faubourg Saint-Antoine, Rirette began to have a different impression. Soon Rirette again bumped into Victor, this time in the Jardin du Luxembourg. He seemed alone, a bit disconcerted, and sad. They chatted, and Victor opened up to her, describing his young life in Brussels and what he had left behind there.[2]

After that, Victor and Rirette began to meet every day in the Jardin du Luxembourg. On occasion, they walked into the distant woods on the edge of Paris during the day. Some evenings, they strolled along the quays of the Seine, discussing poetry, music, and life. When the weather was good and they had a few *sous*, they would take a *bâteau-mouche* to Saint-Cloud. Rirette, now in love, found Victor "beautiful as a god . . . with a very pure oval face with his delicate and sensitive mouth and a somewhat distant smile, giving the impression of considerable nonchalance."[3]

With virtually no money, Victor and Rirette moved into an attic room offered them by a philosopher friend in the fifth arrondissement, not too far from place de la Contrescarpe, paralleling rue Mouffetard. Their apartment was close to the setting for Honoré de Balzac's *Père Goriot,* near where the novelist had once lived. For a time, because of their friend, they gave lessons to a seventeen-year-old baron whom the former had taught, until he ran into some trouble and his parents refused him further education. But no matter. No money, no problem.[4]

When the baron-student's parents stopped paying, Victor and Rirette found themselves "lacking only money, although they had enough to purchase tea." And they had Rirette's two girls, who were a joy, as well as *causeries* to attend and their friends who came to visit.

Victor's friends became Rirette's friends. He introduced her to René Valet, a shy anarchist locksmith he had met in a bar in the Latin Quarter. "One has to extract his words" from René, but little by little, "he came to life," emerging as a "lively restless spirit." Influenced by Victor, Valet could recite passages from Anatole France and from the anarchist Rictus. They discussed literature and poetry in the cafés around Sainte-Geneviève or the boulevard Saint-Michel, or in Victor and Rirette's apartment. With no funds to purchase kerosene, they read by the dim light of a candle. In such moments, the long face of Valet—who became known to his friends as "Carrot Hair"—took on "an expression of extraordinary suffering," relating things "sad, so sad . . . his appearance is both painful and brutal." He dressed in wide corduroy pants with a blue flannel belt. Valet spoke slowly, softly, and sometimes with great bitterness, particularly when it came to his bourgeois family, who lived nearby.[5]

René Valet was born in 1890 in Verdun, and his family lived on boulevard Port-Royal. He was an intelligent young man, and he, like Victor, took advantage of his proximity to the Bibliothèque Sainte-Geneviève. Valet's family was "well considered" in their neighborhood. His father was an entrepreneur in public works projects. René had been a student in the nearby École Lavoisier. He had

René Valet.

79

grown up with two older sisters and an elder brother; when his brother passed away four years earlier, a change had come over René.

In 1910, Valet briefly served as secretary of Jeunesse Révolutionnaire de la Seine, an antimilitary group that included anarchists and syndicalists. He was arrested and condemned to a suspended sentence of fifteen days in jail that year for "outrages" against police. An industrial electric company in Suresnes (beyond Bulogne-Billancourt), where he had worked, accused him of thefts in September 1911. But what had been removed from the company was found outside, along with an official order for Valet to report for military service. He left for Belgium, with funds provided by his father who apparently was fed up with him, and he managed to avoid being conscripted. Returning to France thanks to a porous frontier, Valet worked briefly in Brest and on the construction of tracks between Pontoise and Dieppe and distributed antimilitary propaganda. He spent a couple of weeks in prison for assault during a strike.[6]

For all of their seeming incompatibility when they first met, Victor and Rirette had several interests in common that brought them together, in addition to anarchism and the lectures and debates in the causeries. Victor recalled: "Anarchism swept us away completely because it both demanded everything of us and offered us everything." Intellectuals, they shared a passion for poetry, literature, and music. They enjoyed strolling through the Jardin du Luxembourg, discussing what they had read and ideas in general. Rirette recalled that their love began with daily meetings there. Both also loved on occasion watching dawn arise and walking along the quays of the Seine in the evening. Victor and Rirette also took short trips together into the countryside beyond Paris. Moreover, both had survived extremely challenging times when they were children and adolescents. They both were used to making the best of the little they had. For his part, Victor quickly adapted to life as a couple shared with Rirette's two daughters.[7]

Victor remained preoccupied by the challenge of mobilizing anarchists against the French state. Could not the expansion of the ravages brought by international capitalism and state power be countered by massive demonstrations in Paris and other cities, which could increase the appeal of anarchism? Three giant Parisian demonstrations had offered Victor hope. He joined massive protests following the execution in Barcelona in October 1909 of Francisco Ferrer, an educator falsely accused of conspiracy in the bloody attempted assassination of Alphonse XIII by Mateu Morral Roca three years earlier. Before being shot in a moat of the fortress of Montjuïc in Barcelona, he yelled to the execution squad, "I forgive you, my children. Aim well!" On October 13, an angry crowd of twenty thousand poured into the streets of Paris. Demonstrators marched from place Clichy to place Villiers, to boulevard Batignolles and then through the fancy neighborhoods of Malescherbes-Courcelles, where they showered the elegant bourgeois apartments with rocks. The protesters then swarmed toward the Spanish embassy, before being driven away by police firing pistols into the air, intent on protecting, above all, the major boulevards, accurately described by Victor as "bordered by banks and aristocratic residences." Marchers destroyed kiosks, gas pipes, and several omnibuses and attacked monuments, some shouting "Death to the inquisitors!" At one point, a man stepped out and fired a Browning at Louis Lépine, the prefect of police of Paris, shouting "Assassin! I am going to take care of you!" Lépine was lightly wounded, but not badly enough to prevent him from ordering a second charge against the crowd, which had constructed several barricades using café tables and chairs. Pitched battles left wounded on both sides. Aggressive shouts echoed: "Death to the cops!" "Death to the cows! Death to the gendarmes!" and "Death to the bourgeois!" The repeated use of violence by police and soldiers and the killing of several demonstrators raised the stakes and intensity of conflict.[8]

On June 26, 1910, another confrontation between demonstrators and police brought violence. The occasion was the funeral of Henri Cler, an anarchist and syndicalist cabinetmaker, born and living in the faubourg Saint-Antoine, who had been killed by a blow to the head with the butt of a policeman's rifle. Victor and Rirette were among the tens of thousands who marched from the faubourg Saint-Antoine to the cemetery of Pantin. Marchers shouted against the "social order" that had killed their comrade and attacked policemen, and the cavalry charged, again wielding swords and slashing about a hundred people.[9] Marchers vandalized some shops and a factory on boulevard Belleville that had remained open, as they yelled "Close up! Close up!" When a master smelter fired at demonstrators, a marcher drew a Browning and wounded him with a shot. More confrontations occurred near the cemetery.

The third *cause célèbre* of opponents of the French state was the execution of Jean-Jacques Liabeuf a couple of days later. One evening the twenty-year-old worker had struck up a conversation with a streetwalker, earnestly trying to convince her to leave her established *métier*. Seeing the two walking together, two policemen arrested Liabeuf as a pimp. He was convicted and sentenced to prison. Feeling stained forever by the verdict, upon his release Liabeuf got a pistol and went out for vengeance. He shot and killed one of the policemen who had arrested him, and he wounded another. Victor remembered that Police Prefect Lépine, "whose goatee presided every year over the bludgeoning of the May Day demonstrators, demanded his execution." Liabeuf was convicted of murder and condemned to death by guillotine. On the night of June 30–July 1, throngs of people moved toward the imposing La Santé prison on boulevard Arago, "always ghastly by day and sinister by night," to protest his execution. Among the demonstrators, someone shot and wounded two police agents. The cavalry charged, slashing away. Victor wondered aloud how the bourgeois occupants of the elegant apartments, with their curtains "tightly closed on the principle of everyone for himself—and God for everyone" near the prison could appear to not have any idea what was going on, or to care. To Victor, "Our place is in the turbulent crowd during these angry days. . . . Along with education through words and writing, there is education to be done through action. . . . To retaliate against authority is a necessity that anarchists should not ignore." In Paris, the movement of protest seemed spontaneous: "The faubourgs poured toward the center, by hundreds of thousands, workers and ordinary people moved by overwhelming indignation." Victor noted with pleasure that "revolutionary groups follow rather than guide the masses." He saw in the violence another sign of bourgeois panic: "In order to guillotine Liabeuf, they had to fill up an entire *quartier* with soldiers. Our masters have a master: fear."[10]

Thus, as he remembered, the massive demonstrations gave Victor, in particular, and Rirette hope. They also contributed moving Victor away from anarchist individualism and toward a sense that collective action could ultimately achieve great goals. Confronted by popular protest, the French state seemed panicked. Increasingly secure in their relationship, Victor and Rirette now looked more optimistically to the future.

Chapter 7

A BITTER SPLIT

―――――――

For Victor and Rirette, 1910 and 1911 were busy years. Victor was writing more and more for *L'Anarchie*, and the pair spent their time meeting old and new anarchist friends at *causeries*, debates, café conversations, and the newspaper office on rue du Chevalier de la Barre. Before long, increasingly stark differences in anarchist circles began to cause rifts between Victor and Rirette and Victor's old and their new friends.

An old friend of Victor's soon reentered their lives. Victor had related to Rirette his friendship in Brussels with Raymond Callemin, the "dreamer" who had been seemingly inconsolable when the young Russian student, Macha, whom he had met in the Royal Library in Brussels, had returned to her native country. Raymond had remained impulsive, with his omnipresent sarcastic smile. "Poor kid," assessed Victor.[1]

The adolescent friendship of Victor and Raymond Callemin was already in the past. For one thing, Victor now renounced illegalism. His old friend was not only proud to be an illegalist who committed burglaries, but Raymond was a "scientific anarchist," convinced that a strict diet—essentially vegetarian—was essential to individualistic anarchism. Callemin scoffed at his old friend's esteem for the Russian revolutionary tradition. On the wall of his room in Brussels, Victor had placed portraits of Russian revolutionaries who had been executed. For her part, Rirette considered Victor's old friend "a dreamer," and, ultimately, perhaps a dangerous one.[2]

Callemin had gone back and forth between Paris and Belgium between 1909 and 1911, meeting up with the anarchist team of *L'Anarchie* and turning up at various *causeries*. He never stayed in one place very long. Seeing uniformed troops and tricolor flags flapping in the breeze in Paris had confirmed for Callemin the idiocy of the very idea of "*la Patrie*." Raymond's "*Patrie*" was "the entire earth, without any borders."[3]

After a long bicycle trip to Central France and stops in Lausanne and Marseille, Callemin was forced to return to Paris after confrontation with the police. The trip took all his money, and in Paris Callemin had to depend on the largesse of *camarades* to get by. He went to the offices of *L'Anarchie*, where he ran into his old friend Victor Kibaltchiche.[4]

Callemin was just one of many anarchists from Victor's years in Belgium who found their way to Paris. Most were illegalists, and the group grew in number in the French capital. Édouard Carouy, a thick-faced Belgian Walloon metal turner, whom Victor had met in Brussels, carried his strong Belgian accent to Paris in 1910. "Built of herculean strength, his face thick, extremely muscular, illuminated by small, tentative, and crafty eyes," Carouy was not particularly intelligent, lacked education, and did not speak well in French or in Flemish, which he had learned while working in Flanders.[5]

Born in 1883, Carouy was the son of a couple of Belgian farmers in Montignies-lez-Lens who died when he was three years of age. Carouy—sometimes known as "Raoul"—had grown up in the care of neighbors, who placed him at age fourteen into an apprenticeship with a metal turner in Brussels. He spent twenty days in jail for putting up antimilitary posters in 1908. Upon his release, he went to the Belgian anarchist newspaper *Le Révolté*, briefly serving as its manager.

Carouy worked in Malines and on the barges of the Meuse River before moving to Paris, where he took a room for two months in a

Édouard Carouy.

shabby hotel beyond the Butte Montmartre; Jean de Boe, Victor and Raymond's friend from Brussels, was also staying there. Both men were booted out of the hotel because they were constantly inviting people to stay with them.

Using an assumed name, Carouy worked briefly in an automobile factory as an ironworker, but his boss would later remember that he did little work and that he stole. When he moved on, the theft of expensive tools stopped. After he left, fellow workers who had doubts about his identity opened a drawer and found official documents for other people and military papers, as well as a Browning pistol.[6]

One day Carouy showed up at the offices of *L'Anarchie* with a friend. For a moment, Victor was afraid. The Belgian had a violent temper and had once reproached him for a minor disagreement over a few *sous* in Belgium. He was also notoriously tight-fisted, despite being an illegalist. Victor kept his cool this time, and Carouy simply asked Victor what he should read. "Élysée Reclus," the anarchist geographer, was the answer.

Not all their interactions were so easy. One evening, Victor, Rirette, and Carouy were walking along boulevard Saint-Michel. Victor and Rirette's total fortune amounted to three francs and a few centimes; Carouy knew this. Upon a nod from Victor, Rirette began distributing all the money the couple had to little children they encountered along the way. Carouy was beside himself. "We haven't become suckers like that, have we?" he snarled, repeating his displeasure again and again. The next day, he related the story to every anarchist he saw, insisting that Victor and Rirette were worthy of dying of hunger for being so stupid. Yet when he had a little money Carouy purchased birds in a cage, and then released them. He fell in love with Jeanne Bélardi, the wife of an anarchist counterfeiter known as Brutus, whose fake coins Jeanne delivered in the suburbs on her bicycle. Brutus was none too happy about Carouy's interest in Jeanne; the two men battled over it with knives on rue Ramey, leaving the Belgian slightly wounded.[7]

The French and Belgian authorities began to take notice of this strong connection between Paris and Belgium in the illegalist world. In September 1911, an officer in the Belgian gendarmerie sent the French police authorities a list of "our anarchists who are now in Paris and who go back and forth frequently between that city and Brussels." Édouard Carouy led the list, described as dangerous and "always armed with a Browning revolver." Callemin and de Boe were also on the list. And so was "Kabaltchiche" [sic], reported as having left for Paris with his "concubine" Georgette Estorges [sic, Rirette], then identified as "Estogues, Anne Henriette, Madame Maîtrejean, born in 1877 [sic]."[8]

One illegalist became a particularly close friend to Victor and Rirette. Victor first met André Soudy in a public meeting in the Latin Quarter.[9] Rirette had already met the pale, gray-eyed young man, nicknamed "Pas-de-Chance," in a bar frequented by anarchists. Born in 1892, he was the son of hôteliers—"À la Maille d'Or"—who had gone broke in Beaugency on the Loire River west of Orléans. Soudy had refused the ceremony of the first communion because he

André *"Pas-de-Chance"*
("No Luck") Soudy.

had argued with the priest in charge. Soudy, Victor noted, "grew up in the streets," and his young life perfectly reflected "a childhood without possibilities, of impasses." Soudy's father had placed him as an apprentice grocer, and André had gone to Paris, working from six in the morning until nine at night at various small stores. He had acquired the argot and accent of the faubourgs. Soudy complained to his parents about the high cost of living in Paris. He lived alone, moving from place to place, barely getting by. Fired several times, including for alerting customers to the fact that they were being cheated by the weight and quality of the products they were purchasing, Soudy took several of his employers to the Conseil de Prud'hommes, a court-like institution that adjudicated labor disputes, after being let go. Between 1909 and 1911, he was in court several times for theft, selling stolen goods, making seditious statements, committing "outrages" against police authority (earning a short jail term in La Petite Roquette prison in December 1910), and vagabondage. In one case, Soudy was fired by a grocer on rue Léon in the rough quartier of la Goutte d'or for insolence "and especially for having made anarchist statements." Soudy spent several months in another prison for distributing anarchist propaganda during a strike. He lived for a time with a female cousin. She left him to get married, leaving the young man heartbroken. Soudy now managed to survive by selling postcards to tourists on the Pont Alexandre III, stealing cans of sardines from grocery stores, committing burglary, and pickpocketing on the bridge.

The story of Soudy was that of thousands of young men arriving in Paris at the time. He worked where he could, moving from one small room to another in the Marais and then on the impoverished rue du Bièvre in the thirteenth arrondissement, and one in the more prosperous seventh arrondissement. He found roommates where he could, sharing one rent of five francs a week on the impasse Guépine and rue Jouy in the Marais with Édouard Coupeau, who was twenty years old and "without any known profession or occupation." They only stayed a month, leaving their landlady Madame Journet with "the most sad memory of them" as well as "a quantity of anarchist brochures."

During his second stint in prison—or perhaps earlier—Soudy contracted tuberculosis. He noted sadly, "I am a *pas de chance* (no luck) nothing to be done about it." He said, over and over, "I'm jinxed . . . everything gets me." In 1910, he spent several months in a tuberculosis sanatorium in Angicourt (Oise). In late January 1911, he had treatment in the Hôpital Saint-Louis. He also had picked up syphilis, probably from his cousin. Victor would visit him in the hospital, bringing him oranges to cheer him up.[10]

True to his nickname, Soudy's luck kept running out. As he was about to go into a hospital in January 1911, Soudy loaned his room to an anarchist illegalist, who stole a mailman's bicycle. When Soudy's friend was arrested, he gave the police Soudy's address, where police found burglary tools. Soudy was in prison from mid-February until late August of that year, where his tuberculosis no doubt worsened.[11]

Upon his release, Soudy kept afloat through small thefts. On weekends, he joyfully took Rirette's two little girls for walks at Buttes-Chaumont, buying them little cakes. They adored him.

Soudy was a sentimental man, and the syrupy songs of café singers could move him to tears. He wanted to fall in love, but he "did not know how to meet a woman without appearing ridiculous." When someone called him "comrade," he seemed reborn, firmly believing that one should "become a new person" and that anarchism pointed the way. In the meantime, "the most stinging jokes helped him to live," as he was convinced that his life would not be very long, "given the price of medications." He remained unfailingly loyal to friends, and proud to be an illegalist.[12]

Soudy regularly attended *causeries*, where he was usually in good spirits and enjoyed rousing debates with fellow anarchists. One evening, when a professorial type was at the podium, Soudy shouted from the first row of the balcony, "*Vous êtes une bille!*" ("You are an imbecile!"). The hall exploded in laughter. The speaker, visibly shaken, continued. When a second speaker began, Soudy thundered again, "*Vous êtes une deuxième bille!*" The shaken speaker finished with difficulty. A third speaker was greeted by "*Vous êtes une troisième bille!*" Chaos. And then virtually the entire audience began to shout in unison: "*Bille! Vous êtes une bille!*" The evening ended.[13]

Victor's intellectualism and critiques of illegalism were well known among this new group of illegalists. Georges-André Roulot, known as "Lorulot" (born in Paris in 1885), had become editor of *L'Anarchie* in 1909 after Libertad's death and had infused the newspaper with individualism and illegalism. He defined illegalism as "the permanent and reasonable response of the individual to everything that surrounds him—it is the affirmation by each person of his own existence and his desire for complete development."[14]

Although Lorulot and Victor tended to disagree about illegalism, they still appeared together in *causeries* announced in *L'Anarchie*. They shared a common enemy and were "Against all Bastilles"— thus, all kinds of authority, whether erected in the name of republicans, royalists, or socialists.[15]

But when in July 1910 Lorulot rented two buildings at 16 rue de Bagnolet (now rue de la République) in Romainville to create an ideal anarchist community, it wasn't quite clear how Victor and Rirette would fit in. Such a way of life would include adherence to a strict vegetarian diet and the practice of regular exercise. A rigorous life would, in Lorulot's mind, along with *L'Anarchie,* provide propaganda for anarchism. Such a free setting (*milieu libre*) seemed a logical place for anarchist individualists, *"les en-dehors."*

Romainville had been incorporated in 1867 into the commune of Les Lilas; by 1911, it had a population of about five thousand six hundred. Like almost all of the suburbs north of Paris, Romainville had become a working-class town. A site of gypsum mines (gypsum was used as a fertilizer and in plaster), some of the commune was not built up and represented an extension of the "zone" beyond the old fortifications of Paris. The capital itself could be reached from Romainville via a tramway whose route ended at Charles Garnier's opera house.[16]

The property on rue de Bagnolet, which was set off from the street by an imposing wall, included a large garden with trees and lilacs and offered a rural image that pleased its anarchist occupants. There was also space for illegalists to practice firing their Brownings. Upon entering the property, visitors came upon a building of two floors with *caves* below. There were several bedrooms, in one of which slept Jean-Joseph Huc, a former counterfeiter and convict known to his friends as "Ripolin," who gardened, and his girlfriend, Marie Bader—known as "Ripoline." Another room provided space for anarchist travelers who had nowhere to stay. A second building included a large room for a sizable printing machine, a storage room for stacks of newspapers that had not been sold, and a large shower room. There were smaller gardens in the courtyard, where fruits and vegetables were grown; the poultry occupants of the courtyard offered eggs.[17]

Rirette and Victor arrived in Romainville as summer was approaching in 1911. There they met the illegalist Octave Garnier. He had joined those who were going on the offensive against Victor and Rirette's intellectual approach to anarchism. Garnier, whom Victor described as stout and rather squat, with light brown hair, was "a dark, handsome boy, silent, with astonishingly dark and intense eyes." He had been born in Fontainbleau, where his father was a road worker. Garnier wanted to make his mother proud of him. He told her, "You'll see, Mama, how you will be happy. You know that I am not afraid of work."[18]

After leaving school at age thirteen, Garnier worked for a baker. However, several arrests for theft put an end to that. He then survived as a *terrassier* (a road worker or ditch digger; he was sometimes known as Octave *le Terrassier*), and continued to steal. Garnier was convicted of several political offenses—and was once badly beaten because of his role during a strike. He spent two weeks in jail for assault during a construction workers' strike. Just after his release, he avoided conscription in 1909 by fleeing to Belgium, leaving his worried mother in tears. In Charleroi he met Raymond Callemin, Édouard Carouy, and Jean de Boe. He and Callemin became "inseparable" companions, and Victor noticed that Garnier clearly exercised great influence over Callemin and Édouard Carouy. Garnier returned to Paris because the Belgian police were looking for him.[19]

Marie-Félice Vuillemin, known as "Marie *la Belge*," was Garnier's "Rubensesque" girlfriend. Twenty-two years old, she had been born

Octave Garnier.

Marie-Félice Vuillemin,
known as "Marie *la Belge*,"
Octave Garnier's girlfriend.

in Mons, where her mother worked in a mine. In April 1909, Marie, who had been condemned to three months in jail for theft, left for Paris. There, she married Auguste Schoofs, a thirty-two-year-old housepainter. The couple stayed together only about a month in the tenth arrondissement in Paris. Marie worked in a small manufacture on rue Béranger, not far away. The couple quarreled constantly, and during the summer of 1911 Schoofs hit Marie hard enough to send her to the hospital. After being bandaged in Hôpital Saint-Louis, she returned to Belgium, to Charleroi, living with her mother and working cleaning houses.[20]

In Charleroi, Marie met Garnier, who had just been released after several days in jail for what she described as "anarchist deeds." For two months, they lived together in a furnished room, with Marie going by the name "Madame Garnier." Marie then accompanied Garnier to Schaerbeck, a suburb of Brussels, where Garnier worked constructing a tunnel and Marie did more cleaning. Back in Charleroi, a *cafetier* for whom Marie had briefly worked was robbed—presumably by Garnier, Édouard Carouy, Marius Metge (another anarchist sometimes known as "Mistral" because he came from the Valley of the Rhône), and two others, although only the latter fell into police custody. In March 1911, Garnier and Marie left for Paris.[21]

Garnier left an impression—rarely a positive one—on those he met. A friend Marie had made while living with Schoofs had not seen her for ten months. One day Marie showed up with her new lover, Garnier, whom she never formally introduced to her friend. The couple stayed for two hours. Garnier said he was a road worker, finding employment where he could. Marie added that he was a deserter who had found refuge in Belgium. Before leaving, Marie asked her friend to loan her one and a half francs, explaining that they had nothing for dinner and had to walk all the way back to Romainville, where they now lived. Marie's friend was "a little frightened" by the new man, whom she described as having "a piercing and angry look." She asked Marie that the next time she came for a visit, she come alone, adding "above all."[22]

Victor described Garnier, who slept in a room on the first floor, as a "rootless force . . . searching for some impossible new dignity about which he seemed unsure." Garnier rejected all discussion with intellectuals. "Phrases! Phrases!" he would mumble softly as he went out arm in arm "with Marie and set about preparing some dangerous nighttime crime."[23] Victor said of him, "No other man that I have met in my whole life has ever so convinced me of the impotence and even the futility of the intellect when confronted with tough primitive creatures like this, rudely aroused to a form of intelligence that fits them purely technically for the life struggle." On one occasion,

Garnier had showed one of his neighbors a long, loaded revolver, adding that "with this, one does not fear anything."[24]

Victor and Rirette's first meal in Romainville was a total disaster. Lorulot asked Rirette to prepare dinner, but when the individualist anarchists realized that she had put some vinegar into a dish, all hell broke loose. Callemin shouted, "She put vinegar in there!" Garnier snarled, "What audacity!" "It's come to this!" added Carouy. Lorulot, Callemin, Garnier, Carouy, and Valet considered vinegar an "antiscientific" ingredient, capable of compromising their individualist idea of a perfect anarchist life. Individualists believed that oil was the nectar of existence and should be consumed in great quantities, which Lorulot did every day—thus, "oil anarchy." Salt and pepper were unacceptable, along with coffee, alcohol, and chervil (which Garnier considered to be an aphrodisiac). Lorulot's advice for workers who demanded higher wages so that they could have enough to eat was that they should eliminate such expensive items as meat and fish from their diets. This sort of individualist denounced those who rejected such rules as the "unintelligent" who had not evolved with the times. The list of acceptable foods included mashed corn, milk purée, vegetables, macaroni with cheese, tea, and sugar. Bananas were a natural food, "chemically the complete, natural element."[25]

Rirette was hurt by all this, while Victor was largely unconcerned. However, this was the end of everyone eating at the same table. Rirette seemed relieved when, in a setting clearly identified with "water drinkers," a friend dropped off six bottles of Médoc wine. She drank one bottle, and then on another day she drank a second bottle. When she came back to open the third, she found that the remaining bottles were empty. She sensed that some of the self-proclaimed "water drinkers" had come by and had given in. Anarchists came and went from the house, seeking "a momentary refuge." Some occasionally left a little money for pamphlets taken or meals consumed. Others simply ate, discussed, and slept, before moving on.[26]

Rirette was torn; she was somewhat tempted to opt for such a life in a rural setting, but by now she was also committed to life in the city, far from her village in Corrèze. She also knew that in such idealized communities, face-to-face relations were not always ideal. Lorulot had the reputation of being a shirker, more interested in sunbathing than assisting in work around the farm. When there was work to be done, Lorulot simply disappeared. On one occasion, when others went to look for him, they found him sitting on a fallen branch, reading poetry, quite nude. When his colleagues complained, he replied, "You are the laborers, you work! I am the brains and I think."[27]

In the meantime, life went on, accompanied uncomfortably for Victor and Rirette by the *"régime lorulotique"*—that is, without salt, pepper, coffee, and wine.[28] Huc gardened. Callemin counted. Valet set the print for editions of *L'Anarchie*, and Carouy and Garnier carried out the printing, along with Victor's friend Jean de Boe. De Boe had followed the others to Romainville, living nearby with Marius "Mistral" Metge.

Élie Monier was also part of the group. A tall, thin anarchist florist, he was born in Estagel in the Pyrénées-Orientales in 1889, the son of struggling farmers. He had been placed as an apprentice flower gardener with a wealthy family living in a chateau. A later assessment held that these contacts with "well-off people" embittered him, "and seem to have made him independent, undisciplined, and, later, an enemy of society." He left for Paris at the end of 1909 to avoid military conscription. There he met anarchists involved with *L'Anarchie*, beginning with Lorulot, with whom he went on the road in the Midi and in the small industrial town of Boucau, which had forges along the Adour River in the Pyrénées-Atlantiques. When Monier left for Belgium to avoid arrest, he traveled with the papers of a Turkish anarchist named Simentoff. He sold whatever he could find in markets and fairs. For several months, Monier went back and forth between Belgium and France. He also managed to get to Carcassonne, where he burglarized a tax office in September 1911.[29]

In the midst of all this, there was also some fun to be had. The group took frequent excursions into the countryside. On one occasion, Rirette joined Carouy, Soudy, Callemin, Octave Garnier, and his Belgian girlfriend, Marie Vuillemin, for a trek on bicycles to Nogent-sur-Marne to rent canoes. When Marie's tire went flat, Callemin proved anything less than gallant, casting some doubt on Rirette's belief that anarchists treated women better than nonanarchists. Yet overall the afternoon and its picnic went very well, amid singing, a deep appreciation of nature, and good humor.[30]

The police were well aware of the anarchist presence on rue Bagnolet. A police inspector watching the headquarters of *L'Anarchie* reported on June 20 that he had not seen Mistral (Marius Metge), Édouard Carouy, or Octave Garnier. There were usually about a dozen men at the house and four or five men in the two buildings, "but these people have the specialty of never revealing their names nor their nicknames in the vicinity of where they live." Only a raid would determine if the three men were actually there. When an agent asked any questions, the reply from residents of the house was usually something along the lines of, "Our home is not a branch of the prefecture of police!"[31]

During the summer, a highly placed police official from Paris and three police agents went out to Romainville with Louis-François Jouin, deputy director of Security since 1909. Jouin was an energetic, reliable, and generally respected policeman of modest means who had worked his way up the ladder in the police hierarchy after beginning as an inspector of rooming houses in the Search Brigades. He had only a certificate of primary schooling, and his first job for the municipality was monitoring the sewers of Paris. He then entered the army as a volunteer in 1891, serving as a sergeant in North Africa. When he was not out tracking down anarchists, he lived a quiet life with his wife and sixteen-year-old daughter.[32]

There were suspicions that the anarchist community in Romainville was committing burglaries. Jouin and the policemen had gone out to investigate. They knocked on the door. When no one answered, they went in, coming upon a man teaching a number of boys and girls. There were posters on the wall and newspapers here and there. Jouin predictably and aggressively warned, "Hands up! Empty your pockets!" The police began to open the drawers of armoires, searching for fake military documents used by those dodging the draft. They asked Raymond Callemin what he and the others were doing in Romainville. Callemin replied, "We live according to our ideas." Who is your leader? The reply: "We do not have a leader." Do you often work? "When there is work." Are you anarchists? To this, Callemin replied, "If to be an anarchist is to not recognize the right of someone to impose his will on us, then we are. Science tells us that a man should be able to live as he wants." They would continue their revolt "as long as you will still have prisons." Callemin asked exactly what the visitors had against them, when those living in the community drank water but not liquor, never smoked, and were vegetarians: "Is this why we are tracked as criminals?" There was no evidence of any illegal activities, so the police had no choice but to leave, carrying away some unimportant papers.[33]

Had Jouin known where to look, he might have found evidence of thefts. The burglaries of Garnier, Carouy, and Callemin—of which Victor and Rirette disapproved, but looked the other way—brought the anarchist community some resources.

In the community, everyone shared everything, with the right to be lodged and fed and have one's clothes cleaned. Victor earned a little on the side doing French and Russian translations. One day, Victor asked Carouy for some money. The latter snapped, "I risked my skin, my old friend, to bring in some money. If you want us to share it, then you only have to do the same!" For his part, Victor strongly believed that the risks inherent in such thefts—as in the case of counterfeiting—were too great and that the illegalists' self-professed independence would inevitably lead to prison, where it was indeed difficult to be free. He also believed that such crimes and the obsession with money that characterized illegalists were incompatible with the true development of the individual and the anarchist way of life. For her part, Rirette questioned whether the theft of a can of sardines would ultimately change society. It was war between "the sentimental" and "the scientifics." Such "fanatic popularizers!"—in Victor's description—reduced science to that of "an algebra which becomes the catechism of the individualist revolt: me against everyone."[34]

And there were more troubling disputes. On one occasion, Garnier became absolutely furious when the others refused an article he had written with the title "Salt Is Poison." Garnier drew his Browning revolver before things calmed down.[35] On another occasion, Rirette believed that Carouy had come to the apartment she shared with Victor with the intention of killing him.[36]

There were fights, too, about the direction L'Anarchie was going in. In June 1911, Lorulot left Romainville for Paris. He had argued violently with Garnier, Callemin, and Carouy, but it was only the latest blowup. Once, as L'Anarchie was about to be printed, Rirette eliminated from it a provocative phrase of Lorulot's that had denounced "smokers, opium addicts, morphine addicts and Baudelarians" as "idiots." She had quickly asked Lorulot if he had ever read Baudelaire, and he had replied, "Never!" When the edition appeared, Rirette discovered that the sentence had miraculously reappeared. How? Callemin had reinserted the sentence, it turned out, because this was also his view. Another time, Lorulot attacked the illegalists in an editorial in L'Anarchie, which Victor could not really refuse to publish since Lorulot had edited the newspaper. That Victor inserted the piece accentuated tensions with the illegalists. In Paris, Lorulot started up a new individualist anarchist newspaper, L'Idée Libre.[37]

L'Anarchie still had a following, but it was not prospering under the unsteady hand of Lorulot. Lorulot had begun to pressure Victor and Rirette to take over the newspaper. Rirette was against the idea, warning Victor that "we will be surrounded by illegalists!" who continued to denounce them, led by the abusive Garnier. Yet Victor repeated, over and over, "There is something to be done, there is something to be done." In the end, Rirette went along with it. Victor would be the editor of L'Anarchie, and Rirette would serve as the newspaper's manager, as long as they would have no financial obligation to the newspaper. Raymond Callemin would be the treasurer as well as the principal printer. Thus, the two quarreling factions would remain with the anarchist newspaper in Romainville—Victor and Rirette on one side, and the "scientific individualists" and "illegalists" led by Raymond Callemin on the other.[38]

One evening in July, Victor rose to speak in a *causerie*; he noted that the prisons were full of anarchists and that it was better not to transform "certain means of action" into a goal or an ideal. Thus, the rupture was consummated. Victor was denounced as "having sold out," and he barely missed getting punched out. For his part, Callemin, who took himself for the real theoretician of illegalism, insisted that his old friend from his days in Brussels was an intellectual dreamer who should not be taken seriously.[39]

More disputes inevitably followed. Three weeks later, the illegalists began to leave Romainville. Huc left when police suspected him, with reason, of counterfeiting. Carouy, who lived in absolute terror of jail, departed when he became a police suspect in a burglary in Maisons-Alfort. Carouy moved to Saint-Thibault-des-Vignes, not far from Romainville, dyed his hair black, and sold odds and ends (including fake jewelry and items he and others had taken in burglaries) at markets in the Paris region. Victor and Rirette had tried to reason with him, to get him to stop, but they got nowhere. At times, as he sat in a café on rue de Seine, Carouy dreamed aloud about living in the countryside and having a small garden.[40]

Garnier and Valet also left, in part because of increased police surveillance of their residence in Romainville. Monier, who had taken the name Simentoff, also departed. He began delivering wine for Pierre Cardi, a Corsican anarchist who had come to Paris in 1906. Cardi's store on the rue Ordener was across the street from a branch of Société Générale.[41]

Raymond Callemin departed with his sarcastic, caustic smile, leaving behind his perfectly clear and balanced accounting of the financial situation of *L'Anarchie*. In July 1911, some of his friends were arrested. Raymond vowed "to take vengeance against this criminal society." He moved to Vincennes. With other illegalists, he began to discuss the means "to make felt even more strongly the shouts of our revolt."[42]

And so, after three months in Romainville, the team of *L'Anarchie* moved back to Paris. Fewer resources were coming from bookstore sales of brochures and other publications, as well as of the newspaper itself. The annual rent of one thousand francs could not be met. Perhaps a move back into the City of Light might improve the fortunes of *L'Anarchie* and propaganda for the anarchist cause. In the middle of an October night, the remaining anarchists moved "*á la cloche du bois*"—that is, with the help of comrades and without paying the rent they still owed.

The bitter split between Victor and Rirette and the illegalists had contributed to the departures from Romainville. Yet for a time the two sides continued to coexist. After all, they had a common enemy: the state. Victor and Rirette continued their friendship with René Valet, and to a lesser extent with Callemin. However, Valet was clearly under the influence of Garnier and Carouy, who seemed to have pressured him to leave Romainville.[43]

Once Victor and Rirette were back in Paris, Rirette rented an apartment on rue Fessart in the nineteenth arrondissement in Belleville. The apartment offered considerably less space than the property in Romainville. It included a living room transformed into an office, the inevitable room reserved for newly arrived anarchists without a place to stay, and the room in which Victor, Rirette, and the girls slept. Behind the building was a series of small gardens, typical of Belleville, and at the back a hangar larger enough for the printing press. Rirette took care of all the newspaper's correspondence. The apartment stood on the second floor, halfway between the place des Fêtes and Buttes-Chaumont, thus convenient for outings to the park for Rirette and her two little girls. André Soudy was the only illegalist who came around to visit often. Rirette treated Soudy like a lost little brother, and he took the girls to play in Buttes-Chaumont. And, as in Romainville, policemen—in uniform or not—were frequently stationed outside the building, observing the comings and goings of anarchist visitors.[44]

Having burned his bridges with the illegalists, Victor now undertook in *L'Anarchie* a vigorous campaign against them. He had his work cut out for him. Criminal acts were becoming the face of the public's perception of anarchism. Kibaltchiche dreamed of an anarchism based on love and feeling, in which illegalism and the "scientism," which seemed so eccentric—even stupid—and counterproductive, would have no place. His old friend Callemin's obsession with the so-called scientism of extreme individualism had now led to his being routinely, and sometimes mockingly, called Raymond *"la Science."*[45]

Victor, as editor of *L'Anarchie* (although Rirette held that title on paper), worked to take the newspaper in a new direction "in the sense of a return from individualism to social action. . . . I wanted to affirm the doctrine of 'solidarity and revolt' in the present." Three years earlier, he had written in the *Le Communiste* that, "To be in solidarity with economic rebels does not mean to advocate theft or to elevate it to that of a tactic."[46]

Victor didn't have much luck convincing the illegalists he knew. Marius Metge, who came to Victor and Rirette's home occasionally, had his own ideas about illegalist tactics. Metge was originally from the small Rhône railroad town of Le Teil in Ardèche, raised by his grandmother. Metge had begun as an apprentice cook in Nîmes and then worked in that métier in England. He thus had the obvious nicknames of *"Le Cuisinier,"* *"Le Pâtissier,"* and *"La Cuistance"* or *"Le Cuistancier."* Like Soudy and other anarchists, he had gone to Belgium to avoid military conscription—where he had met Carouy, Garnier, and Valet—and returned to Paris in 1910.

Marius Metge had fallen in love with an illiterate Breton servant, Barbe Le Clerch, who had come to Paris from the small town of Le Faouët in Morbihan. The number of Breton immigrants to Paris had increased dramatically beginning in the 1880s, particularly to the vicinity of the Gare Montparnasse, their point of arrival in the capital.[47] Barbe was one of more than twelve thousand domestics from Brittany working in Paris. The mayor of Le Faouët could find nothing for which to reproach the young woman: "This young person before she left Le Faouët was of good morality, reflecting her upbringing by her mother, who, given her state of indigence, was obliged to place her daughter" in domestic service in town, near her village. Now in Paris, Barbe Le Clerch worked here and there as a domestic. She wrote—through the auspices of a Breton public writer—to her mother several times, but her mother had absolutely no idea about her life.

Barbe Le Clerch had lived with Metge in Romainville, not far from the offices of *L'Anarchie*. The sister of the owner of the building recognized her from a police photo as one of the women of the anarchists who lived in the building between December 1910 and April 1911. For a time, she worked as a domestic in Les Pavillons-sous-Bois. That residence was subsequently burgled, and it appeared that Le Clerch provided information to Metge. The couple moved to Suresnes and then to the grim northern suburb of Garches.[48]

Two men broke into the post office in Romainville on the night of October 17, 1910, after the illegalists had moved away from that suburb, stealing more than eight thousand francs' worth of stamps, as well as sixteen hundred francs in cash. They climbed over a wall and shattered a window. Police suspected Metge, whom they believed to be a friend of Carouy and another suspicious anarchist, Louis Rimbault.[49]

The illegalists in Romainville had burgled in order to survive. Yet such small crimes brought only small amounts of loot. Following their departure from that suburb, their exploits in August brought in three hundred and then four hundred francs, followed by seven hundred francs for the burglary of a post office and four thousand francs for the burglary of a villa in Nantes. In September, a burglary at the post office in Chelles (Seine-et-Marne), fifteen miles east of Paris, yielded four thousand francs and that of a tax office in Compiègne, fifty miles northwest, in early November netted three thousand five hundred francs. But other nighttime action brought in very little, despite the risks of being caught.[50]

While Victor and Rirette were moving in a different direction, their old Romainville comrades were doubling down on their old ways. Octave Garnier began to dream of a bigger robbery that would be worth the risk. Raymond Callemin, "obsessed with revolt," was also intent on pulling off "an audacious coup." Garnier's attention turned toward the use of an automobile for such an exploit. Such a modern contraption could be stolen with relative ease, a new weapon to be turned against the bourgeois state. He had learned how to drive, but he was not very good at it. Garnier needed a comrade who knew how to drive well. So for the moment he hesitated to steal the kind of large and powerful automobile that would be required "to carry out a coup that would keep them from need for a certain time."[51]

Callemin also had learned how to drive, but also not well. He mentioned to Garnier and one or two other illegalists that he had met someone with lots of experience at the wheel.

PART TWO

Chapter 8

JULES BONNOT

Octave Garnier and his friends found someone who could drive: Jules Bonnot. "A small, sturdy man with a thin moustache wearing a worker's Sunday-best clothes that were too tight," Bonnot had arrived from Lyon. He needed money. He was looking for men capable of and willing to, in his words, "play for keeps, willing to succeed or to die." On December 12, 1911, Garnier, Valet, Callemin, and Carouy had returned from various small "coups" in the suburbs. They met with Bonnot, probably in the apartment of Bernard Gorodsky, an anarchist printer who lived in Montmartre. Callemin remembered, "We discussed the project and in the end we fell into agreement." Bonnot was wanted for murder. He had nothing to lose.[1]

Jules Bonnot embodied the frightening turn of anarchist violence. He was born in 1876 in Pont-de-Roide (Doubs), twelve miles south of Montbéliard and nine miles from the Swiss border. The small town in eastern France had a population of about twenty-six hundred and several mills sawing lumber from the rich forests of Franche-Comté. Bonnot's father was an illiterate smelter, beaten down by impossibly hard work, low wages, and the constant fear of being let go. Bonnot's mother passed away when he was four years old, and he resented the siblings from his father's second marriage. His uncle Charles, a policeman in Paris, became

completely unstable, before returning to Franche-Comté and passing away. The children were raised by Jules's grandmother.

After a difficult, unsuccessful, and brief stint in school, where his
teachers described him as "lazy, undisciplined, insolent," at age fourteen Jules began an apprenticeship as a mechanic. A year later, he
got a job in the Peugeot factory in Sochaux. His elder brother Justin
also worked there, until, after an unhappy love affair, he committed
suicide by throwing himself into a river. Jules had constant disputes
with his employers, whose authority he simply rejected and who
probably with reason suspected him of theft. His first brush with
the law was an arrest for using explosives instead of a rod and reel
for fishing; his second arrest, at age seventeen, got him ten days in
jail for a brawl at a dance in Besançon. Other arrests followed for
miscellaneous brawls. Bonnot fulfilled his military service, beginning in November of 1897. He did well enough, reaching the rank of
corporal in the 133e infantry regiment. Jules was noted for excellent
marksmanship, and he also received a certificate of good conduct.[2]

After he left the military, Bonnot began hanging out with anarchists, which made it difficult for him to find regular work. In August
1901, he married Sophie Burdet, a young seamstress, the daughter of
a farm couple in the village of Vouvray in the Ain with whom he had
been lodged while in the army. For a time Jules worked in Lyon, then
in Ambérieux, followed by Bellegarde near the Swiss border. At this
last place Jules lost his job, seemingly because of his espousal of anarchism. Unable to find regular work, he and his wife left for Geneva,
where Sophie's mother had gone to live. There Bonnot found some
employment. Sophie gave birth to a baby girl, named Émilie, but
the infant died several days later, perhaps because the couple had no
money to pay for urgently needed medical treatment. A son, Justin-
Louis, was born in February 1904.

By now, Bonnot began to spread anarchist propaganda, and Swiss
authorities expelled him. A brief stint followed in Neuves-Maisons
near Nancy, and then Bonnot and Sophie returned to Geneva, before
the police expelled Jules again from Switzerland. Returning to Lyon,

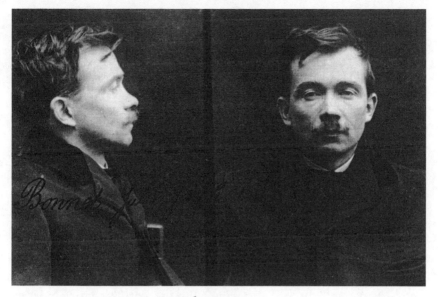

Jules Bonnot.

he found work in the Berliet automobile factory in Montplaisir. He and Sophie lived in the home of a Berliet factory foreman called Besson, a union secretary.[3]

Bonnot lost his job at the Berliet factory after participating in a strike. Now the police identified him as an anarchist. Long periods of unemployment and underemployment took him from place to place looking for a job. He worked as a mechanic in Saint-Étienne between October 1905 and April 1906. There a police report assessed him as "very violent and above all nasty." While Jules was working in Saint-Étienne, Sophie left him for Besson, their lodger. The new couple ran off to Geneva with Justin-Louis. Jules wrote to his wife, noting that he was not "under the influence of anger" but that he had decided to "return to his most absolute rights," in other words, to take her back. He signed the note "Your husband who has not forgotten you, Jules Bonnot."[4]

The letter did not have the desired effect, so in August 1906 Bonnot again wrote to Sophie in response to a letter she had written apparently denouncing him. He asked if she really believed all that she had written to him: "I really tried to forget you but I couldn't because it always came back to me that I cannot understand how you had the courage to leave me at the moment when I most needed you. Think of the future of your son. You tell me you think of him. I don't want a divorce nor your money. It's you I want." Besson had accomplished "the most cowardly of crimes because it is not punishable." He had stolen Bonnot's wife. Bonnot went on, "You know that I have spent money trying to get you back, at the risk of dying of hunger as I was ill. You know that I am suffering greatly. Do not prolong my suffering. I finish my letter by kissing you." Bonnot would never see Sophie or his son again.[5]

With his formidable skills as a mechanic, Bonnot managed to find some steady work driving automobiles. He received his driver's license on September 17, 1907. The next year he and Albert Petit-Demange, who had also worked in the Berliet factory, opened an automobile repair shop, and then a second one. The shops became ideal places to store bicycles that the two men or others had stolen. At night, Bonnot and his friend burgled houses. "Business" went well enough that Bonnot rented several other places to store what they had stolen.

In 1908 Bonnot took a room in a house occupied by Jean-Baptiste Thollon, an alcoholic cemetery guard, thirty-five years of age, in plebeian La Guillotière in Lyon on the road to Vienne. Bonnot fell in love with Thollon's wife, Judith. The two went on romantic excursions in the adjacent cemetery, while her clueless husband drank and went about his work.[6]

Needing another person to help out in his enterprise, Bonnot hired an Italian anarchist and former baker, Joseph Platano (born in Poneragno in 1883; he also went by "Sorrentino," his family name, "Mandino," or "Mandolino," depending on the circumstances), to help him out in a city where Cesario, another Italian anarchist, had assassinated French president Sadi Carnot in June 1894. When the police were on to them, Jules Bonnot left briefly for Geneva and busied himself with more safecracking there. In 1910, he went to

London for several months, probably to see about selling stolen cars. Needing some money to tide him over in the British capital, he seems even to have worked for a time as a chauffeur for Arthur Conan Doyle. The English writer, who was bringing Sherlock Holmes to the world's attention, undoubtedly had no idea that he was being driven skillfully around London by a real-life criminal.

Back in Lyon later that same year, Jules Bonnot continued to steal. On the night of March 31–April 1, he took six motocyclettes and three bikes from a certain Monsieur Weber in Lyon. Bonnot decided to accelerate, as it were, his one-man crime spree through the use of automobiles—stolen, of course. In the first adventure, Bonnot used a car simply to reach a new and tempting target. He and his sidekick Platano drove to Vienne in April 1911, twenty miles to the south along the Rhône. Dressed in their Sunday best and stepping out of a gleaming luxury (stolen) automobile, they explained to notary Monsieur Girard some sort of project that would bring easy money to all three participants. Bonnot and Platano's next trip to Vienne took place in the middle of the night on April 19–20, 1911. Undetected, with the help of a welding blowtorch, they cracked Girard's well-stocked safe and left with thirty-seven thousand francs in gold and bank notes, which had been deposited the day before by a wealthy merchant from Lyon. Platano headed to Italy with some of the loot, while Bonnot calmly returned to Lyon.

Sometime earlier, Jules Bonnot had stolen a car in Lyon and driven it up to Paris. He took the automobile to a garage owner named Joseph Dubois, who lived in Choisy-le-Roi just southeast of Paris. Dubois was French, but he had been born in Odessa and was a veteran of the Foreign Legion. He was also an anarchist who had served time in jail for burglarizing a church. Dubois sold the stolen automobile, and for some time Bonnot stayed with the *garagiste*. Together they stole a car in Blois, before Bonnot returned to Lyon.[7]

In October 1911, an informer tipped off the police about what was really going on at Bonnot's automobile repair business. When Bonnot and Petit-Demange were away, police searched the Route de Vienne shop and found stolen motorbikes, bicycles, burglary tools, and various accessories that had been taken from stolen cars, including some from a luxurious automobile stolen in Vienne in January. The motorbikes and bicycles could be identified as having been stolen from Monsieur Weber. The police arrested Petit-Demange, but Bonnot got away when a neighbor told him that the police had come looking for him. He thanked the good neighbor, said he could not imagine why the police were after him, and announced that he was off to buy a newspaper. Jules Bonnot was a wanted man. It was time to get out.[8]

Early on the morning of November 26, 1911, Bonnot crammed some clothes in a bag, along with five Browning pistols—thus the illegalist argot, to *bouziller*, or "lodge a Browning bullet in the body of someone"—and one hundred bullets. He dressed up a bit so as not to raise suspicions as he and his friend Platano, who had returned from Italy, drove a stolen—naturally—olive-green Buire luxury car on the long road to Paris. As they reached the region of Brie, Bonnot drove over a chicken and a dog. Platano laughed, "Who are you going to kill now?"[9]

Platano never made it to Paris. About 10:30 in the morning a rural guard in the village of Pamfou in Seine-et-Marne, on the road from Melun to Montereau, heard a shot. Thinking he might nab a poacher, he hurried in that direction, and then a second shot sounded. He came upon the critically wounded man lying in the light snow in Le Châtelet-en-Brie. He turned and saw a man dressed in black leather run to a beige Rochet-Schneider automobile, jump in, and drive away. The guard rode his bike to get help, and the bleeding man was taken to the farm of the village mayor. A summoned doctor could do nothing for him. Platano died without revealing anything. He was ultimately identified by the name "Mandino"—one of his aliases—found on a tag in his coat, in which he had 450 francs, a considerable sum. A tailor confirmed by telephone—another accoutrement of the *fin de siécle*—that he had sold the clothing to a man called Mandino. Mandino had asked that the clothing be delivered to a shabby Parisian hotel. The word "Saulieu" written on a small piece of paper led police to a hotel in that town where Platano and his companion had stayed, and to a restaurant there where the two had dined without exchanging even a word.

Bonnot did not get far before the automobile broke down in Moissy near Melun. Someone saw him trying to restart the motor several times, without success. Exasperated, he went into a small restaurant and ordered two eggs and half a bottle of wine for lunch. He stood out because his fine boots were covered with mud. And he seemed preoccupied, leaving quickly after discarding his driving clothes. He took the next train for the hour trip into Paris.

Police soon discovered through the engine number that the Buire automobile, eighteen horsepower, had been stolen at about four in the morning on January 18 in Vienne. Platano had briefly worked as a chauffeur for the owner of the stolen vehicle. Accessories from the car had been found in Bonnot's shop in Lyon.

Witnesses, including some who had seen him catch the 2:31 p.m. train to Paris, described a man about thirty years of age. That description was sent to police stations: a man about thirty years of age with a little brown mustache, "1.60 to 1.63 [meters tall], stocky, oval face, dark complexion, rather gray looking, not very engaging, well-kempt, wearing a large dark raincoat, black melon-shaped hat, and dirty boots." In Saulieu, Le Châtelet-en-Brie, and Moissy, those who had seen him identified Jules Bonnot from police photos. The *juge d'instruction* in Melun soon put out a warrant for Bonnot's arrest for murder. *L'Excelsior* named him as the suspect in its edition of November 30.[10]

So why did Bonnot kill his sidekick Platano? The police concluded that the two men had been waiting for an accomplice on the train to toss them the loot from a big theft and that Bonnot had eliminated Platano to avoid having to split the money. Or had Bonnot suspected that Platano was ready to betray him? Or had—as Bonnot later claimed to anarchists in Paris—Platano accidentally shot himself while checking out a Browning revolver with which he was not familiar, and the second shot the rural guard heard was the *coup de grâce* that Bonnot fired to spare Platano further suffering. If Bonnot's account was indeed true, illegalists in Paris debated whether this was the correct thing to do. Victor Kibaltchiche and Rirette Maîtrejean had not yet met Bonnot, but "from the grapevine we gathered than an individualist from Lyon, Bonnot by name (I did not know the man) . . . had killed Platano." Victor did not believe Bonnot's story about Platano's demise, and he rejected the idea that an anarchist could end a colleague's life in such a way. Rirette also had her doubts. Their opinion was an unpopular one. When Victor made this point at an anarchist meeting, he received a visit from his old friend Raymond Callemin, who apparently even threatened to "*bouziller*" him. "If you don't want to disappear," Raymond warned, "be careful about condemning us. . . . Do whatever you like! If you get in my way I'll eliminate you!"[11]

On December 2, police in Lyon, having learned that Bonnot had stayed there, searched the residence of the cemetery guard Jean-Baptiste Thollon and his wife Judith. The police found burglary tools, including eight welding torches capable of piercing steel plate, and moulds to produce counterfeit money. Both Thollons claimed they did not know the tools had been left by Bonnot. The police also found letters from Bonnot that left no doubt about his relationship with Madame Thollon. And the police discovered twenty-five thousand francs in bank notes wrapped in paper, which Judith insisted she knew nothing about because her lover had sometimes left her similarly wrapped anarchist propaganda. Yet it seems that Bonnot had placed that sum in an envelope and sent it to Judith, addressed to "*J. T. Poste restante, la Guillotière, Lyon*," with the note "Put this where you want. It is only a beginning. I am at the moment in Paris. Burn this letter when you receive it."

The police also found receipts for rent in the name of Jules Renaud—in reality, Jules Bonnot. This led them to the five places he had rented to store stolen goods and to divide up the take. A search of one of Bonnot's rented places turned up more burglary tools, car tires, various items of clothing, and two stolen motocyclettes, including another taken from Weber. A second search of the Thollon residence revealed some of Bonnot's clothes; he had taken care to appear as a well-heeled gentleman, as when he had gone to Vienne to check out the notary whose office he had later robbed in the middle of the night.

The Thollons were taken under arrest to the Palais de Justice in Lyon. Both continued to proclaim their innocence. The cemetery guard's boss expressed confidence in Thollon, as did the other renters in their residence. Yet there had been worries about people coming and going, and it turned out that Bonnot's accomplice Petit-Demange had stayed there, too. Platano had also come around. Perhaps Thollon knew more than he let on. The police suggested that he might well have hidden suspicious items among the tombs in the cemetery. Certainly he was "under the influence" of Jules Bonnot—as, obviously, was his spouse.

The police of Lyon moved forward with an investigation of two other accomplices of Bonnot, hoping, perhaps, that someone would lead them to the man himself. David Bélonie, born in Gignac in the Lot to a mother whose boyfriend quickly abandoned her after the birth, could speak some of seven languages. He became an anarchist counterfeiter and an occasional pharmacy employee. The other accomplice was a swindler who had worked for Le Comptoir Français, which produced small gambling machines for bars. Bélonie sent him gambling machines from Lyon, presumably to sell for profit. On January 3, 1911, Bélonie took one of the motocyclettes that Bonnot had stolen from Weber in Lyon and transported it to London.[12]

In a headline on December 5, *Le Progrès de Lyon* loudly proclaimed, "We now know who killed Platano. It is Bonnot. It remains only to arrest him." The front page flashed a police photo of Jules Bonnot, taken in Lyon when he had been arrested on November 11, 1909, for assault and battery. The Parisian newspaper *L'Excelsior* on December 5 was the first to refer to "the Bonnot gang," but only in the context of the murder of Platano and the thefts and burglaries carried out with others in and around Lyon.[13]

For now, though, Bonnot remained at large in Paris. Where in the City of Light could Jules Bonnot—anarchist, thief, and probably murderer—find a place to stay? David Bélonie, Bonnot's old friend and accomplice from his Lyon days, pointed Bonnot toward a rooming house on rue Nollet in the seventeenth arrondissement. Bonnot, in turn, recommended the establishment to Eugène Dieudonné, a twenty-eight-year-old anarchist cabinetmaker from Nancy.[14]

Bonnot's self-proclaimed anarchism found him a welcome home in Paris. His first stop was the offices of *L'Anarchie*. No one there recalled seeing Bonnot before, but his reputation as an uncompromising tough guy had preceded him.[15]

Jules Bonnot increasingly presented himself as less convinced by theories of anarchism than as a rebel who aggressively refused to submit to the rules and laws of organized society. Older than those who were becoming his associates in crime, he seemed a bad guy (*"mauvais esprit"*) capable of violence, particularly as he contemplated more lucrative crimes. Bonnot was cold, aloof, suspicious, and secretive, hardened by an impoverished childhood and tumultuous adolescence. But his was not unusual behavior for people on the margins in a France in which undercover policemen and police spies and other informers were everywhere and no one could be easily trusted. Informers were surprisingly successful in infiltrating the anarchist milieu.

As soon as Bonnot reached the circle of anarchists linked to *L'Anarchie*, he opened up attacks from the illegalist perspective on Victor Kibaltchiche and Rirette Maîtrejean. Rirette first saw Jules Bonnot with a little mustache and "giving the impression of being old" in a meeting on rue de Bretagne in the third arrondissement. She instantly did not like him.[16]

Upon his arrival in Paris, Jules Bonnot turned almost immediately to planning crimes. He soon found the trio of illegalists that had been looking for someone exactly like him. On December 7, he went to the shop in Montmartre where *L'Idée Libre*, "a monthly review of social education," could be purchased. This was Lorulot's "scientific" newspaper. There Bonnot met Raymond Callemin, recognizing him thanks to Dieudonné's description, and Monier. They had found their driver.

Chapter 9

THE BONNOT GANG STRIKES

On the night of December 13–14, Jules Bonnot, Raymond Callemin, and Édouard Carouy waited in the shadows for Monsieur Normand and his spouse to return from the Opéra de Paris to their luxurious residence in Boulogne-Billancourt, a western suburb. When the couple had returned, turned off the lights, and gone to bed, the three men climbed over a garden wall into the garage and stole the Normands' black and dark green Delaunay-Belleville, twelve horsepower with a value of fifteen thousand francs. It was exactly the car they had in mind—fast, powerful, and large enough to hold the welding torch that Garnier needed to cut through large safes.[1]

Normand woke the next morning to find his prized automobile gone, and he offered a reward of five hundred francs for its recovery. A newspaper that reported on the theft suggested that perhaps a nearby quartier "of very bad reputation because the Italians who stay in furnished rooms are for the most part unsavory," played a role. For many French of means, Italians were an unwanted other. It was enough of a distraction to keep the press and the police off the trail of Bonnot and give the three men time to plot their next move.[2]

Bonnot and his new friends were ready for action, armed with 9mm Brownings, semiautomatic, light, and accurate. If they ran into trouble, they knew that Parisian policemen were unarmed. In the middle of the night of December 20, Bonnot, Garnier, Callemin,

Carouy, and perhaps Valet met in La Villette, amid butchers from the nearby slaughterhouse. The plan, at first, was to rob a villa in Romainville, but when they got close to the house they spotted the owner and abandoned that idea.[3]

Finally, at around three in the morning, the men made a decision. The elegant automobile moved toward a second target, one that had been suggested by Pierre Cardi, a Corsican anarchist. For a while Cardi had run a wine shop on rue Ordener on the other side of Montmarte in the eighteenth arrondissement; across the street from the shop was a branch of the Société Générale bank, and each morning, a courier carrying cash and securities arrived on a tram, unarmed. Now, well before dawn, Garnier practiced driving—in case something happened to Bonnot—by going down and then up the Champs-Élysées. Bonnot then took the wheel and they drove to rue Ordener in the eighteenth arrondissement, checking out the street and those that adjoined it. The *quartier* was decidedly *populaire*. Thus, with even taxis few and far between, the Delaunay-Belleville automobile immediately attracted attention. At five in the morning, as Paris slowly awakened, a few ragpickers could be seen going through garbage at the same time that workers hustled off to workshops and small factories. Garnier sat in the seat next to Bonnot, and Callemin sat in a back seat next to a fourth man. They waited.[4]

At 8:45 in the morning, one of the men in the car stepped out and gunned down Ernest Caby, the courier carrying funds and securities to the branch of Société Générale, shooting him three times. Two *gardiens de la paix* tried to stop the car, but the bandits sped away, with Jules Bonnot at the wheel.

By 9:30 a.m., the audacious robbers were driving through Saint-Denis just north of Paris. In the car, the men vowed to defend themselves until death. They were certainly well prepared: Callemin was himself carrying six revolvers, one of which could fire eight hundred meters, and his partners each had three pistols and four hundred bullets.[5]

On rue Ordener, Henri Mosier had heard sounds like tires popping. He yelled to the driver and his companions, "Hey, guys, your tires have blown!" He heard someone in the car say to the man at the wheel, "Move forward, forward, forward!" Next to the driver was a man standing up with a revolver in his hand, looking back and firing in the direction of the curious who were following behind the car. When Mosier started to run after the car, which had picked up speed, the man shot at him twice. When the car turned left, he lost sight of it. He described the driver as about twenty-five years old, with a dark "Italian" complexion and a small black mustache, wearing an old, dark-colored raincoat with a black jockey's cap. The man who fired at him was thin and pale, with a chestnut-colored mustache, a long black pardessus, and a black bowler hat.[6]

In the confusion, witnesses offered contradictory accounts as to the color of the big car—black or white—and even the number of occupants of the automobile—four or five—although most everyone agreed that there were at least four bandits. The man seen shooting Caby appeared to be twenty-five to thirty years of age, with a long and rather dark face, wearing a long gray raincoat and a gray cap pulled down over his ears. Someone noted the license plate as being 660-X-8. One of the men had remained in the automobile the entire time.

The robbers stopped in Pontoise, fifteen miles northwest of Paris, to discover that the take was considerably smaller than anticipated. Moreover, they knew that the securities would be extremely difficult to sell. They had missed an envelope in Caby's pocket stuffed with twenty thousand francs.[7]

The bandits sped north through the *octroi* in Beauvais. Upon arriving in Rouen, Bonnot and his friends realized they had missed the turn for Le Havre and ended up in Dieppe. That evening on a beach in that Norman town, residents gathering seaweed watched in astonishment as a number of men tried in vain to dig out and start up a luxury automobile, as the wind carried away the hat of one of them. The men then quickly abandoned the car.[8]

In the abandoned automobile, police later found the clothes of a mechanic and the card of a car repair shop in Levallois, just to the west of Paris. The owner of the shop knew many drivers, including the chauffeur who worked for Monsieur Normand. The pieces came together. Apparently the robbers had removed the car's license plate. A child came across it in the gardens of a casino.[9]

At 1:30 in the morning of December 22, Bonnot, Garnier, Callemin, and a fourth man arrived in Paris by train. A police report on passengers purchasing tickets for Paris from Dieppe indicated the presence on a train in third class of a man twenty-five to thirty years of age, very pale, with a small black mustache, wearing a raincoat and a bowler hat.

Yet one police report already had the robbers on the ferry carrying passengers from Dieppe to Newhaven, England. Indeed, the director of the Office of Security sent a telegram to British authorities asking them to monitor the arrival of travelers on ferries from France in that English port. Leaving the car on the coast near a ferry port would encourage this interpretation. Another had the bandits sitting in a café near the Gare du Midi in Brussels, dividing up the take. In reality, upon their return to Paris, the bandits went—for the moment—their separate ways.[10]

The night of December 23–24, several men broke into a gun store at 70 rue Lafayette, taking more than one hundred handguns. At the time, there was no reason to link the robbery with the raid on the Société Générale bank. During the night of January 9–10, a similar robbery occurred at Smith and Wesson on boulevard Haussmann. Thirty-four guns were taken, including revolvers but also a number of rifles, and more than fifteen hundred francs in cash.[11]

The Société Générale offered a reward of twelve thousand five hundred francs for information leading to the arrest of the bandits. There had been a spate of holdups of bank couriers of late, but not like this. Headlines announced, "A Crime of Unprecedented Audacity!" and "Stupifying Act." Newspaper hawkers yelled out, "Ask for the Crime of rue Ordener! A Courier Shot in Broad Daylight! The Murderers Fire on the Crowd!" *Le Petit Journal* included on its front page a drawing of the gunning down of Caby, "based on the testimony of witnesses."

How could such a robbery take place with seeming impunity on a crowded street in Paris, with its legions of police? After the holdup on rue Ordener, news about the revolutions in China and Paraguay, a short war between Italy and Turkey fought over Libya in the fall of 1911, and the aftermath of the Second Moroccan Affair that same year slipped to the back pages. A French force had violated the terms of the Algeciras Conference five years earlier by going into the town of Fez. Germany sent a gunboat to Agadir, bringing rising tensions between France and Germany. On Sunday, December 24, *Le Petit Journal*, which advertised itself as having the greatest circulation of any newspaper in the world, sported a photo of the automobile found in Dieppe.[12]

On December 27, *Le Petit Parisien* advised readers that the police were closely watching "louche individuals" in Montmartre, including anarchists and tire thieves. In illegalist circles, Garnier's name was the first to be widely mentioned as a participant. The Spanish Cubist painter Juan Gris was arrested when he was mistaken for Garnier; he was released when the Fauvist André Derain came to the station to confirm his identity. *La Lanterne* informed eager readers that the security police were sure that the crime had been the work of a band of anarchists. In the meantime, Alfred Peemans, the official in the Société Générale who had been at the scene, used a sizable collection of police photos and was able to identify Carouy as one of the bandits.[13]

Parisian police had a reputation for being mediocre but also violent and playing a political role despite the pretense of neutrality. Louis Lépine, prefect of police, wanted to change that image. Born in Lyon in 1846 into a family of modest origin, he had quickly given up law for administration, serving in Saint-Étienne as prefect of the Loire. Like his predecessors, Lépine did not come out of the police force itself. Lépine was a professional administrator who built a reputation for insisting on efficiency as the absolute goal of maintaining public order in the Third Republic, to which he was devoted as a republican conservative. Overseeing the daunting responsibilities of the post, Lépine's goal was to be a model functionary respected for his good work. He was patriotic and proud of the army, on several occasions affirming that "a Frenchman is born a soldier." Lépine made no secret that he detested socialism and anarchism, which to him represented a lack of discipline as well as disorder and irreligiosity. The police should become masters of the streets. Socialist, syndicalist, and anarchist demonstrations and activities got in the way. Irritated by what he considered frequent and unfair hostility to the police in the mass press, Prefect of Police Lépine wanted Parisians to love their police.[14]

However, the Bonnot Gang, terrorizing Paris and its region, presented a daunting challenge for the police. In his capacity as prime minister and minister of the interior, Georges Clemenceau in 1907 had created mobile units that became known as "the brigades of the Tiger," adding to their number in 1911. The number of police agents in Paris had been increased to seventy-five hundred following the anarchist attacks that had begun in 1892. But unlike those attacks, which were bombings carried out by individuals against specific targets, Bonnot, Garnier, and their colleagues were committing crimes in and beyond the capital, escaping to rob and kill again. The number of nonuniformed policemen now stood at an imposing one thousand. The Security police numbered close to 350 men, headed by Octave Hamard (appointed December 30, 1911) from his office at 36 quai des Orfèvres on Île de la Cité.

However, the inability of any of the police authorities to put an end to the bandits terrorizing Paris and its region laid bare tensions and the lack of effective centralization, coordination, or even basic communication among the security, or "judicial" police, the gendarmerie, and the municipal police. For that matter, the gendarmerie, with Paris having its own legion, had been virtually ignored by the judicial police. While the municipal police were, in principle, under the authority of the mayors of the arrondissements of Paris, paid by the municipality, and their day-to-day organization in arrondissement police offices (*commissariats*) focused on the surveillance of neighborhoods, the ministry of the interior and thus the officers of Security remained superior authorities.[15]

The investigating magistrate (*juge d'instruction*) in the Bonnot case was to be Maurice Gilbert, a lawyer forty-one years of age. Deputy Director of Security Jouin and his staff—including a veritable army of informers in the pay of the police—were put at Gilbert's disposition. The holdup on rue Ordener put Hamard under pressure: under his watch the *Mona Lisa* had been stolen from the Louvre in August 1911 (it was recovered two years later).[16]

Victor guessed that his old friend Callemin, along with Garnier and Bonnot, had committed the holdup because Bonnot—"now hunted and trapped"—needed money. Victor understood that the term "without possible escape" now also applied for different reasons directly to Bonnot, Callemin, and Garnier. There were now five illegalists on the loose, "wandering in the city without escape, ready to be killed somewhere, anywhere, in a tram or a café, content to feel utterly cornered, expendable, alone in defiance of a horrible world."[17]

A reward of one hundred thousand francs had been offered for information leading to their capture. Moreover, the bandits would need a steady supply of money as they moved from place to place. Several illegalists appeared to have joined them out of solidarity, including René Valet and André Soudy.[18]

On Christmas night, Victor and Rirette heard a quiet knock on their door. It was Callemin and Garnier, exhausted, their clothes battered and their shoes covered with dirt. They had been afraid to find lodging with anarchist comrades for fear of compromising them with their presence. "It's nice in here," commented Garnier. Victor told him to be quiet, as the two little girls were sleeping. Rirette asked them in. Victor broke the silence with, "So! Here you are back from Dieppe!" Callemin offered a faint smile, and he and Garnier nodded. Callemin spoke while looking at his old friend Victor disapprovingly. They had thought that Bonnot's idea—to figure out the

itinerary of a bank courier carrying lots of money and rob him—
would be a relatively easy and lucrative project. Then afterward, they
had no idea where to hide, relating simply that, "We went around in
Paris." Garnier added that he had been the one who had shot Caby.
Garnier, a man of few words, was "the killer of the team." (Rirette
remembered: "Callemin thought for him. And Callemin thought
very badly.")

Raymond Callemin added that the worst of it was "the crowd . . .
of imbeciles, of ferocious guys." They had been forced to fire at them
as they drove away. Victor inevitably asked them why they had done
what they had done. "What's the use of making little speeches?"
Callemin replied aggressively. "We didn't get anywhere just discussing in public meetings. They are so beautiful, theories!"

Rirette waited for Victor to provide the *coup de grâce* and ask, "And
now, have you somewhat progressed?" He wisely resisted, offering
cigarettes instead. Garnier mumbled, "We have to start up again."
Callemin asked for some tea and Garnier a coffee—their insistence
in Romainville on the evil of such drinks seemed far in the past.
Victor could not resist saying, "You are drinking tea and coffee. I
fear that you will make even further concessions!" Victor speculated
that Callemin had come to see him "to recapture the memories of
his adolescence when, sentimental and melancholic, he went around
with me in the streets of Brussels."

When nearby church bells struck twelve times, the two left, very
quietly. Victor and Rirette had not told them that the police had
rented a room in the adjacent building to keep the anarchist newspaper offices under surveillance.[19]

A break in the search for the perpetrators of the audacious holdup
and getaway came, now almost predictably, through the mass press.
Monsieur Chaperon, who worked as an employee in the town hall
of Bobigny and was a "correspondant" of the best-selling *Le Petit
Parisien*, told the paper—but not the police—that he had seen the
Delaunay-Belleville automobile in his suburb in a recently opened
garage, that of Jean-Georges Dettweiller.

Dettweiller, born in Paris in 1875, had begun his working life as a locksmith on rue de Flandres, until he left for a two-year term of military service beginning in 1894, after which he returned to his job until 1905. He had earned seven to eight francs a day and had the reputation of being a very good employee. Dettweiller moved to Bobigny near the route de Bondy, close to the communal limit with Drancy. Dettweiller still occasionally worked in a factory on rue du Faubourg Saint-Denis. The garage amounted to a hangar still under construction. The property was surrounded by a red brick wall and a wooden barrier. The family occupied only one part of the house with two floors, the rest lodging two other couples[20]

Dettweiller's father had been a *quarante-huitard* (an [eighteen] forty-eighter), a democratic-socialist deported from France following Louis Napoleon Bonaparte's coup d'état of December 2, 1851. The younger Dettweiller, who had briefly been a wine merchant in Paris, had attended some anarchist individualist *causeries populaires*.

The police acted quickly. Fearing that an article with this information that had appeared in the *Le Petit Parisien* would tip off the bandits, they raced to the garage that same day. They found Dettweiller, his spouse, their three boys (aged ten, eight, and five), and a four-year-old girl, the child of Jeanne Bélardi, who sold odds and ends in various markets. Sometimes the Dettweillers also provided lodging to Jeanne Bélardi's lover, "Raoul Leblanc."

Dettweiller readily admitted that he had stored the automobile for several days. He explained that "Leblanc" had brought it to the garage with several men Dettweiller did not know. When a search uncovered the burglary tools, Dettweiller and his wife were taken to a central police station. Dettweiller was already known to the police because of his anarchist leanings. Now the police were even more convinced of anarchist involvement in the holdup on rue Ordener.[21]

The police continued to stake out the garage. When Jeanne Bélardi, the mother of the little girl who was staying with the Dettweillers, arrived, the police took her in for questioning. The Lyon-born woman's husband, Brutus Bélardi, was in prison in Melun for counterfeiting. Jeanne sold fake jewelry in markets—"You know how difficult life is for a woman alone . . . battling as best I can in the struggle for life," with a child four years of age. Under questioning, it became clear that Jeanne Bélardi's lover Leblanc was really Édouard Carouy. She had met him a month earlier at an anarchist *causerie*. At first, their relations were simply cordial, and then they became more than that. But Carouy had left her. Jeanne was determined to see him again. Indeed, she and Carouy had stayed together in the Dettweiller's lodging for several days, before she moved on to a very cheap hotel, and then stayed briefly in the headquarters of *L'Anarchie* on rue Fessart. Her daughter had remained with the Dettweilers at the garage.[22] Dettweiller claimed that when four men had brought the fancy car to his garage on December 14 at about two in the morning, he had been asleep. The man who spoke said his name was Charles Delorme, who returned on the night of December 20. Dettweiller's accounting book had noted "the fourteenth, received from M. Charles Delorme one car in the garage, with the crank handle to be repaired," along with an address in Melun. Police found some belongings of the "Leblanc" couple, and a police indictment from 1909 for Jeanne Bélardi's husband and a letter of the latter from prison in Melun from September 1911.

When the four men returned for the automobile on December 21, Dettweiller continued, he asked for fifteen francs pay for the work he had done. They gave him twenty-five francs. Leblanc was not staying there that night, and he returned only on Christmas Eve. Dettweiller insisted that Leblanc had never told him that his friends were going to bring a car in for repair. He claimed that he never made a connection with the events on rue Ordener.[23]

Interrogated by the police, Madame Dettweiller related that her husband had told her "they came to bring the automobile of which Monsieur Leblanc had spoken" for some repairs. One day "he seemed to be repairing the crank handle." Eight days later, someone knocked on the door; when Dettweiller asked who was there, he heard a voice say, "We are here to get the automobile." Madame Dettweiller saw a light go on and heard the motor, thinking it was odd as it was the middle of the night, but the men had said they were going to a theater to pick someone up. She looked out and saw Dettweiller and three other men. The men drove the car away. They left behind five empty containers of fuel, which were then hidden under a wooden table.

Threatened with jail and having her children put into a facility for the poor, Dettweiller's wife now admitted that Leblanc—now clearly Carouy—knew the men who had brought the car to her husband's garage. Dettweiller continued to deny this and remained in jail. A neighbor told the police that her children had climbed into the car to play and that Madame Dettweiller became particularly angry, chasing them away and covering the automobile with a canvas tarp. The neighbor told police she thought this was suspicious, as if someone was trying to hide the car.[24]

Meanwhile, Jeanne Bélardi claimed that she did not know anything about Carouy's role in bringing the automobile, refused to provide any information about her lover, and was placed in temporary incarceration. She asked Rirette Maîtrejean to find a place for her daughter to live while she was in custody. However, the police soon released Bélardi, believing that watching her would bring leads.[25]

Louis Jouin, the deputy director of security, was now even more convinced that Carouy had been one of the men in the automobile on rue Ordener. Moreover, from police photos witnesses formally identified Carouy as having been involved in the Société Générale heist. His description was sent to police offices throughout the Paris region: "Very strong, muscular man. Height, 1 meter 66. Face high in color. Dangerous individual, his capture will be difficult, always carries a revolver." Carouy's photo was diffused in the mass press on January 1. Now knowing that he had frequented the team of *L'Anarchie* in Romainville, police closely monitored comings and goings at the newspaper's office. One difficulty confronting Lépine was that anarchists were obsessed with not providing any information that would compromise a comrade. With the increasing police presence and arrests, some anarchists began to head for the provinces to avoid interrogation.[26]

In the meantime, in Bobigny, Jean-Baptiste Chaperon, who had told the police about the car in Dettweiller's garage, received a letter written in red ink: "My good fellow. Don't think for a minute that you have escaped us. There is nothing you can do. We will find you no matter where. . . . You will get it (*tu sautera*)." It was signed "The avenger of the automobile." Four crosses had been drawn at the bottom of the page.[27]

Very early on the morning of January 3, 1912, in Thiais, five miles southeast of Paris, a ninety-one-year-old *rentier* named François Moreau was brutally stabbed to death—thirteen knife wounds— in his house on the rue de l'Église. His seventy-one-year-old maid, the widow Arfeux, was also dead, killed with crushing blows from a hammer and suffocated. A neighbor had become alarmed in the morning when the house remained tightly closed and unlighted. She had gone to find the maid's son who lived nearby. When no one responded to his knocking on the door, Louis Arfeux had gone to find the *commissaire de police* in the adjacent town of Choisy-le-Roi. Upon entering the house, the policeman had come across a horrible scene amid overturned chairs and open, rifled dresser drawers. The police surmised that one of the murderers had climbed the wall of the property and opened the door into the courtyard. The men then forced the lock of the front door of the house into the vestibule. On the second floor, they found the battered body of Moreau, his chest bloodied and his head showing the damage of repeated blows to what remained of its right side. In the next room lay the body of Madame Arfeux, "her head buried under pillows," her hands and feet tied. Securities and twenty thousand francs in gold pieces had been taken.

A witness related to the police that on the afternoon of January 2 two men in Choisy-le-Roi had asked if she knew Monsieur Moreau and if she could tell them the way to Thiais. The rumor in the village was that Moreau had a considerable sum of francs in his house. She heard one of the men say as they walked away, "Too bad it's broad daylight because we could take care of her and have what she is carrying." Seeing police photos, she identified Édouard Carouy and Marius Metge, who was known to the police as a suspect in burglaries in Romainville.

Alphonse Bertillon was assigned to the case. The controversial police criminologist became an expert in using physical factors such as hair color, presence or absence of a beard, shape of the nose, scars, and birthmarks to identify criminals. During the anarchist attacks in Paris in the early 1890s, Bertillon's physical descriptions of the bomber Ravachol had become widely known. Bertillon later came up with the idea of taking photos of suspects, one taken from the front showing the face and the other from the side. Above all, Bertillon became a specialist in the use of fingerprints (a process that had been used in Bengal in 1858 to establish identity, although fingerprints were used as identifiers in China as early as the fifth century). Yet the police criminologist remained marked—and for some even suspect—because of failures in the case of Alfred Dreyfus, when Bertillon had misidentified the Jewish captain as responsible for the infamous *bordereau* (detailed memorandum).[28] Bertillon's influence was such that his system came to be called "*le bertillonnage*" or "the Bertillon System."

Footprints on the scene indicated to Bertillon that at least two men had been involved in the terrible crime. In Thiais, after taking the print of a left thumb from a chest of drawers, Bertillon became absolutely convinced that Édouard Carouy was indeed one of the perpetrators. A left palm print seemed to indicate that Metge had also been there. Moreover, several local people recognized Carouy from photos as having been snooping around Thiais before the murder. Two days later, police identified Carouy and Metge as suspects in the atrocious killings.[29]

Chapter 10

THE BONNOT GANG AT BAY

———

For the moment, the police had no reason to suspect that the bank heist and shooting on rue Ordener were related to the violent, atrocious murders in Thiais. A first break in the bank robbery had come almost immediately. On December 23, police reported suspicious comings and goings at the residence of Louis Rimbault in Pavillons-sous-Bois. Rimbault, thirty-two years of age, had served on the municipal council in Livry-sur-Seine in the Seine-et-Marne for several years. After his hardware store failed, he moved with his Belgian wife and two children to Pavillons-sous-Bois, closer to Paris. He became a suspect in several burglaries and for dealing in stolen goods. On January 8, police searched Rimbault's residence and uncovered some stamps—believed to have been stolen from the post office in Romainville on the night of October 17—along with some anarchist propaganda and a number of revolvers, which Rimbault later claimed he had been asked to repair. Moreover, he had lodged three anarchists, including those with the first names of Raoul and Raymond. He told the police that the men had "even hit his wife in front of her husband when she seemed to take interest in what they were up to or seemed unhappy that they were staying with them." The police believed that Rimbault may have supplied anarchist burglars with weapons. Rimbault's father-in-law had bailed him out financially on several occasions but now stood ready to denounce him. Rimbault's residence had become a rendezvous for criminals. Perhaps he had been present at the attack on rue Ordener?[1]

Police searched Metge's room in Garches on January 10, and four days later they arrested him. Barbe Le Clerch disappeared the day of her boyfriend's arrest. Metge had lodged Carouy, and now was himself a suspect in the Thiais murders, although he denied any involvement. A search of the room turned up items taken in burglaries in Pavillons-sous-Bois, including a birth certificate and a military record booklet and stamps that had been stolen from the post office in Romainville the previous October. Fingerprints taken there corresponded to those of Metge, whom the resident in Pavillons-sous-Bois had suspected from the beginning. On January 20, the police arrested Louis Rimbault in the same place.[2]

In the meantime, several witnesses agreed that the man who shot Caby had been left-handed and was wearing a long raincoat and a melon-shaped hat that came down over his ears. Another participant was described as short with a dark complexion—"southern-looking," as people from northern France liked to say—with a trim mustache, and another man was described as a larger man, rather ruddy, and also sporting a mustache, this one more visible than that of his companion.[3]

On January 13, Raymond Poincaré, a conservative nationalist politician, became president of the Council of Ministers and formed a government, serving as minister of the interior. He made clear that reinforcing internal security against what he called an anarchist crime wave stood at the top of his list. Octave Hamard retired that month as head of Security. His successor would be Xavier Guichard, a professional policeman, who was the son of a Parisian doctor. When Guichard's career in the police began in 1892, he was a simple inspector whose passion was prehistory. In his métier, the hard-working and disciplined Guichard remained convinced that the wildly popular novels of Arthur Conan Doyle were "amusing" but "had nothing to do with the reality" of policing. His job was to put an end to the bandits who were terrorizing Paris.[4]

In the meantime, Jouin and his colleagues began to consider illegalists as possible suspects in the crimes of rue Ordener and the massacre in Thiais, and they began to explore the possibility that the two events were linked.

A Belgian trail opened up. The past September, Belgian authorities had charted the comings and goings of French and Belgian anarchists who had fled the draft in one or the other of the countries.[5] They were suspected of committing burglaries in Belgium and of then finding refuge in Paris. The Belgians were Raymond Callemin, Édouard Carouy, Jean de Boe, and Victor Kibaltchiche. All four were by then known to have lived in Romainville, when *L'Anarchie* was being published there. Soon the police believed that in the world of anarchist nicknames, "Gros Édouard" and "Raoul" might well be Édouard Carouy and Octave Garnier. On December 24, the former was seen in Bobigny, and police attention began to focus on that poor northern suburb. Garnier's photo and description appeared in Parisian newspapers.

Before his departure as head of Security, Octave Hamard had gathered photos and information on about twenty people thought to be Carouy's friends. Among them were two that corresponded to some of the descriptions of the men in the fancy automobile who had held up the courier of Société Générale on rue Ordener: Jules Bonnot, wanted for apparently having killed the Italian named Platano on a road in the Seine-et-Marne, and Octave Garnier, wanted for burglary in Charleroi in March 1911. Moreover, information provided by informers inside or on the margins of anarchist groups also identified Bonnot and Garnier as possible suspects. Police spies reported that a certain "Raymond" had been involved. One challenge for the police would be to find the location of these men, as they moved from place to place, sometimes *à la cloche du bois*. Jouin at first believed that Garnier and this certain Raymond were the same man, as nicknames were common.[6]

Every week at Jouin's office, hundreds of letters arrived that provided information about the suspects. Not many could be trusted. But a particularly detailed one came on January 18, claiming to be based on "rumors circulating among the anarchists." It stated that the shooter on the rue Ordener was "a certain Eugène Dieudonné, originally from Nancy, where he has doubtless returned to his parents. The others are three Belgians," with names that seemed to be Octave, Remend, and Deboit. The letter added "there's also Bonnot (from Lyon)." A subsequent anonymous letter mailed on February 3 claimed Dieudonné was the "principal aggressor" on the rue Ordener incident, noting that his wife Louise was now the girlfriend of Lorulot. This suggests the source's close knowledge of anarchist moves, indicating that some denunciations and information were coming from within anarchist circles.[7]

The police continued their search for Garnier. They discovered that Garnier and Marie *la Belge* had been living in Vincennes. They were no longer there when the police showed up at their former apartment on January 22. The concierge affirmed from police photos that it had been Garnier and Marie who had been staying there. Police found various burglary tools and train schedules to Pavillons-sous-Bois. They also found a package of stickers that included "Our enemy is our master!" and "Bourgeois luxury is paid for by the blood of the poor." Octave had signed the lease for the two-room apartment in June under the name Émile Rémond. After purchasing some furniture, Octave told Marie that a *compagnon* would arrive to stay with them, a thin young blond man about eighteen to twenty years of age. The concierge related this and recognized Callemin from a police photo as a visitor. The couple had told the concierge that he was Marie's cousin, and Octave called him "Julien." They generally left together at nine in the morning and returned twelve hours later, saying that they had been selling letters for printing shops. Octave provided funds for daily needs. During three nights each in July and August they did not return at all; they said that they had been involved in business projects in the suburbs.

On December 31, the pair had suddenly announced that they were going to the countryside "for the holidays," packing up two trunks.

Octave sent Marie to place de la Nation to get a wagon and a driver to cart the trunks. A very young *compagnon*, about ten years old, helped them move. But then Octave told Marie, "I have to leave to take care of some business," giving her two hundred francs, adding, "You figure it out, but you can't stay here." Julien followed him. Marie left the apartment two days later to return to Charleroi.[8]

On January 19, Marie went to visit a friend in the tenth arrondissement, finding her at an outside public laundry, a center point of working-class female sociability. They then went to a bar on the quai de Valmy. Marie paid for the drinks and returned the small amount of money she had borrowed the last time they had met. Her friend could not help but notice that Marie had several pieces of gold in her coin purse; this seemed strange as Marie never had more than a few cents. She explained that she had "inherited" the money. Then she left quickly, "because he is waiting for me to go to dinner." She promised to return for lunch the next Sunday.[9]

However, the next day, police arrested and interrogated Marie. First claiming another name, she finally admitted that she was the *femme* Schoofs. She claimed to be *sans domicile fixe* (homeless) but then said that she had stayed two nights in a store run by a Swiss anarchist who sold Lorulot's *L'Idée Libre* in Montmartre. How could she explain the seventy-one francs she had on her? She claimed that a mechanic named Jules Cambon had given them to her in Brussels. She had stayed with him in a cheap hotel in the Belgian capital, and they had taken the train together to Paris, and then separated at the Gare du Nord, when he had given her two hundred francs. She had lived on that, staying much of the time with Madame Lescure in the fifteenth arrondissement. Madame Lescure was Octave Garnier's mother.

Neighbors there recognized Marie from a police photo, as she was often seen in a first floor window. Marie insisted that she had no idea where Garnier could be found. When police searched the apartment of Garnier's mother, they found a trunk filled with burglary tools. Marie was released from jail on March 15 in the hope that she might lead authorities to Garnier. Then she disappeared.[10]

Police, by now, were fairly certain that Garnier was guilty. The final piece of the puzzle fell into place on January 22, when Ernest Caby, the Société Générale courier who had recovered from his wounds after the robbery on rue Ordener, identified Garnier as the man who shot him. He indicated that the man who shot him was left-handed. Parisian newspapers on January 24 carried photos of Garnier. *Le Matin*'s giant headline screamed, "The Man Who Shot Me—That's Him!" beneath a police photo of Garnier.[11]

Chapter 11

HOW TO UNLOAD STOLEN SECURITIES

With the police closing in, the bandits were confronted with the challenge of selling the securities stolen from the Société Générale. Some of them were high-risk speculations, including some from Spanish railroad companies. Such securities were traceable. Callemin knew that it was dangerous to sell them, because of all the publicity surrounding the heist on rue Ordener. About one hundred twenty-seven thousand francs worth could not be sold and probably ended up in the Seine. That left more than one hundred ninety thousand francs in securities in bearer form (*valeurs au porteur*).[1]

On January 20, Callemin and Bonnot left for Ghent, Belgium, where they met up with Garnier and tried without success to sell some of the stolen securities. They managed to steal a fancy automobile, a Minerva '11, from a surgeon, holding on to his case of surgeon's tools for an eventual sale or even use. In Ghent they learned that Callemin was a wanted man in France and that his photo had appeared in the newspapers. The bandits turned the securities over to Jean de Boe, who had worked with a trafficker of such stolen items, Van den Berg, who lived in Amsterdam, but he could not unload the stolen securities. De Boe had no success in Belgium either, and he reported that the securities could not be sold.[2]

Callemin, Garnier, and Bonnot then drove to Amsterdam, staying with an acquaintance of de Boe's, to whom they gave one hundred seventy-five thousand francs worth of the stolen securities in the hope that he could sell them there. They were able to unload enough that, as Callemin put it, "this improved our morale a little." They apparently burned securities that could never be sold. Bonnot and the others then sold the stolen car for eight thousand francs.[3]

Callemin, Garnier, and Bonnot returned to Ghent, where they came upon the garage of an industrialist named Heye. There were two cars inside, one a limousine. A small adjoining room with a bed was empty. Heye's guard was away, so the plan was to steal both cars before his return. As they got one started up, they heard the key opening a door. The thieves quickly turned off the lights in the garage. When the surprised guard entered, they pulled their revolvers, one of them barking out, "Not a word or you're dead!" When they told him to start the second car, the guard appeared not to understand the danger of the situation and just stood there, not reacting. The man, who was German, claimed that he did not understand French, which was not true. But one of the bandits spoke a little German and understood when the guard said he was not a chauffeur and did not know anything about automobiles. At that point, "the discussion started to heat up." Bonnot and Callemin worked on the car, without success. Then Callemin picked up a huge piece of wood and hit the guard on the back of the head, knocking him out. Callemin then hit him with an enormous car jack, and the man stopped moving. Suddenly a voice called out, "What are you doing there?" A man holding a lantern was trying to open a door into the garage, but the body of the chauffeur prevented him from doing so and he quickly disappeared. The bandits grabbed tools and ran outside. They ran into a night watchman, who asked in Flemish about the case that Garnier was toting. Callemin replied, "Things for our trip," and then shot the man several times, gravely wounding him. They walked along the road to Brussels, reaching the train station in Wetteren, where they took a train to Anvers and then Amsterdam. There they left Van Den Berg a package with more of the stolen securities.

In The Hague, the bandits found another automobile, this one belonging to a banker. With a full tank of gas, they started south with the goal of returning to France. Driving over bad roads and along canals in the mist, Bonnot decided upon a detour of forty kilometers. He jerked the car to the left, and the automobile slid down the bank of a canal, hitting a tree and thudding to a stop. Peasants, who thought the relatively well-dressed men were English, tried to help them pull the car out of the mud, using horses and ropes. Bonnot and his friends gave them some money, and when the peasants had given up and left, they pushed the automobile into the water. At 3:30 a.m. they left on foot for the nearest train station, twenty-five kilometers away. There they purchased tickets for Anvers, from which they could take a train to Paris.[4]

During the trip to Paris, Callemin left the compartment to go to the bathroom. He carried his pistol with him, loaded as always. In the tiny bathroom, he accidentally dropped his revolver. The gun fired, but luckily the sound was not heard because of the roar of the locomotive. The bullet lodged in Raymond's right arm. In great pain and holding the wound to somewhat reduce bleeding, he returned to the train compartment where Bonnot and Garner were waiting. The surgeon's case stolen in Ghent now proved fortuitous. Bonnot tightly wrapped the wound, reducing the flow of blood. There was much for them to fear—especially the sudden arrival of a train conductor before Bonnot had been able to care for the wound as best he could. Garnier stood watch in the corridor, his own pistol ready. As Callemin leaned back and Bonnot sat down, a conductor arrived to check tickets. With clenched teeth, Callemin managed to function through the pain, and the conductor noticed nothing. When the conductor moved on, Raymond fainted. Garnier had readied his pistol behind the back of the conductor had he seen anything suspicious. Upon their return to Paris and completely undeterred, the gang readied for their next coups, these being planned by Monier in the southeast around Alès, more than four hundred miles away from Paris.[5]

The Parisian press was covering the gang's every known move, and the police were hunting them down. Newspapers orchestrated the veritable psychosis of fascination and fear in the capital. But how would the anarchist press react to the violent crimes, allegedly the work of illegalists? *Le Libertaire*, the principal organ of anarchist communism, did not mention what had transpired. Jean Grave's *Le Temps Nouveaux*, which had always opposed illegalism, insisted that such crimes were becoming the public face of anarchism, insisting that "at the moment they commit such acts, they cease to be anarchists." Such acts had nothing to do with anarchism and were, for that matter, "purely and simply bourgeois," reflecting the "principles of egotistical individualism."[6]

Despite the fact that Victor Kibaltchiche had been a constant critic of illegalism and violence, his provocative editorial in *L'Anarchie* on January 4 nonetheless gave the impression that he defended illegalist violence. He assessed the role of the courier Caby, "who consented, this poor guy with his miserable salary, to transport fortunes." He therefore stood with "the miserable cowards who could never imagine audacity nor the will to really live, and now denounce the rebels (*les hors-la-loi*); and with the dogs who are the police, the journalists-police spies, the grocers sweating fear, and the rich who are more ferocious in their hatred of those who resist." He saluted those who had "firmly decided to not squander the precious hours of their life in servitude." Confronted by the realities of contemporary society, their choice had been between "servitude and crime. Vigorous and brave, they chose battle—crime." A week later, responding to an article in *La Dépêche de Toulouse* that had compared the bandits to wolves, he affirmed, "I am with the wolves, the wolves who are hunted, being starved out, and tracked, but who can bite back!" The causes of the violent acts of the bandits, he argued, would only disappear when the social order was transformed.[7]

On or around January 23, someone came to tell Rirette that Callemin and Garnier wanted to see her. They would await her on a corner of rue du Temple in the Marais. Rirette went as instructed and the three talked, standing on the sidewalk early in the evening as stores closed and metal screens slammed down. A policeman asked them to move away to facilitate pedestrians passing by, and they complied.

Garnier invited Rirette and Callemin to dinner, and they went into a cheap restaurant, sitting at the only available table, right in the middle of the room. Rirette would take their seeming indifference to being seen in a public place as reflecting a sort of fatalism that had engulfed the two. Next to them, diners were reading evening newspapers, which related that a reward of one hundred francs had been offered for the capture of the two men—who just happened to be sitting at a table next to them. A woman discussed this tidy sum with her companion. At their nearby table, Garnier easily recognized her Belgian accent and brazenly piped up that he, too, would love having such a windfall, but that certainly he would never have the good fortune. He then laughed out loud, while Rirette had difficulty swallowing her food. Garnier and Callemin had apparently given up trying to hide. Yet Garnier said in a lower tone of voice, "They don't dare arrest us, and this could go on a long time." Callemin replied only, "This can go on as long as we do."[8]

Chapter 12

THE POLICE IN ACTION

On the night of January 30, André Soudy slept in Victor and Rirette's apartment. Fearing the police, he left at four in the morning. A couple of hours later there came a much-louder knock on the door. It was Louis-François Jouin, as ever wearing a tie to signify his status as deputy director of Security, accompanied by several policemen. His long, sad face belied a pleasant and, for his position, not very aggressive personality. Jouin had come to ask some questions and to oversee a search of the apartment. In their search, the officers found two Browning pistols that had been stolen from the armament store on rue Lafayette. This burglary was almost certainly the work of Bonnot, Callemin, and Garnier. Victor and Rirette denied the theft, insisting that they had bought the revolvers from a "comrade" whose name they did not know.[1]

That afternoon, Victor was summoned to Jouin's office to sign the list of what the police had carted off with them. The policeman told Victor that he was very sorry to cause him any problems—and that he admired the anarchist writing of Sébastien Faure and realized that Victor was an intellectual, unlike many of his *compagnons*. He deplored the damage being done to the anarchist ideal by the illegalists acting outside of the law. But he advised Victor that the world "will not change very quickly." He suggested if he was taken into "preventative custody," his stay in jail could be long, but suggested that this could be avoided. He wanted information, promising that no one would ever know about their conversation and warning that "If you keep silent, you will get six months of preventative prison." Victor had nothing to tell the policeman. Jouin's threat was not idle. A tiny cell in the prison of La Santé awaited Victor. He found himself imprisoned alongside convicts who were awaiting the death sentence.[2]

Victor was arrested by virtue of the "Scoundrel Laws" (*les lois scélérates*) as they had become known. This meant that anyone could be arrested at any time for having the slightest relationship with known anarchists, violent or not. The laws facilitated a repressive onslaught against anarchists.

On December 9, 1893, Auguste Vaillant, a destitute man unable to afford to feed his family, had thrown a harmless small explosive device into the Chamber of Deputies to call attention to the plight of the poor (he became the first person executed in France during the nineteenth century who had not been convicted of murder). On December 12 and July 28, 1894, the French National Assembly passed in great haste laws that made it possible to prosecute virtually any anarchist, or anyone who had in any way helped an anarchist who was linked to some "deed" or "planned deed," even if they were in no way involved, or if they simply espoused anarchism.

With anarchism itself considered a *"secte abominable,"* the laws identified terrorism with anarchism. Jurists and politicians now felt free to refer to anarchists in terms that had previously been applied to "marginal social elements." Elite attitudes toward anarchists fit into the obsession with degeneracy and the concern with statistical increases in the number of people classified as criminals, alcoholics, or insane. The upper classes considered anarchists to be particularly dangerous because of their unrelenting opposition to social hierarchy, which they intended to destroy. The Scoundrel Laws defined anarchist crimes as offenses against common law, and therefore they could be punishable by death.[3]

The Scoundrel Laws offered courts a wide-ranging definition of what constituted "provocation," direct or indirect, and authorized harsh penalties for "apologies" for criminal acts. The assumption behind the laws was that a close solidarity existed between terrorists and anarchist intellectuals such as Victor and Rirette. The laws were directed at anyone who could be accused of "preparing an attack," a definition that included "the training of minds by propaganda." The notion of "propaganda by the deed" was extended to cover all sorts of basically harmless propaganda. It proposed a brand new crime: "an agreement established in the goal of preparing or committing crimes against persons or property." What constituted an "*entente*" was left purposefully vague. To take one well-known example: A "*malfaiteur*" (evildoer) commits a crime. He is then lodged by a comrade, and that evening he borrows a pen from his host to write a note to someone who is involved in or aware of the crime. Both the anarchist and the person who provided him a place to sleep and loaned him a pen could be convicted of the same crime. The law of December 18, 1893, also targeted "*associations de malfaiteurs*" (associations of evildoers), considered an *entente* for crime. The law of July 28 made "anarchist views a potential (*virtuel*) crime against common law (*droit commun*)"—and thus not considered a political offense and therefore subject to harsh penalties.[4] So armed, the police routinely trampled public liberties. Authorities banned an international workers' revolutionary congress that was to meet in Paris in 1900, the year of the World's Fair. Searches without cause became routine. And so did police beatings.

Judges inflicted harsh sentences on anarchists. The anarchist burglar Marius Jacob, whose band stole from people of professions he considered parasitical—such as bankers or *rentiers*—faced life in prison because some of the take from his nighttime burglaries went to anarchist propaganda. Such laws were not used against other "opponents" of the regime, such as *Action Française*, which worked for a restoration of the monarchy. The effect, at first, had been that many anarchists went underground and others left France. The anarchist press retreated. Moreover, some anarchist militants, particularly those who had been in the struggle for some time, withdrew from the fray. By the time Victor and Rirette had taken over *L'Anarchie*, anarchism had been revived. The police crackdown was amplified as well.[5]

After Victor's arrest, thirteen more "suspects" were rounded up. When the police burst into an accordion dance in Belleville, a brawl followed, with shots fired here and there. No anarchist suspects were present. Rirette wrote an article calling attention to the anarchists—"our prisoners"—who had been arrested, including Victor, and were being held in a cell in the prison of La Santé.[6]

In the meantime, Rirette remained free—undoubtedly because Jouin hoped she would lead them to the others. But she was interrogated three times, denying any link to the holdup on rue Ordener. Her daughter Chinette got to know Jouin well. The policeman told her not to be afraid of him, and Chinette said she recognized him—that he was the person who had taken away "Papa Louis," then "Papa André," and then "Papa Victor." "*Pauvre gosse*" (poor kid), commented Jouin sadly. Rirette was still legally the manager of *L'Anarchie*, which the authorities claimed served as a "gathering place for criminals." Rirette insisted from the beginning that she did not share the same ideas as the illegalists, but that she had remained in Romainville throughout the summer of 1911. Even so, Rirette was hardly in the clear.[7]

Early on the morning of January 31, two anarchist burglars were surprised at work in the small train station of Fleury-les-Aubrais just north of Orléans. They shot dead the stationmaster and hopped on the next train for Paris. When news outran the train, they jumped off into the night. Cornered by two gendarmes, they killed one before being captured. One of them yelled, "Long live Anarchy!" and put a bullet into his own head. The other, Joseph Renard, a friend of Louis Rimbault, was arrested. This bloody incident had nothing necessarily to do with the events in the Paris region, but it appeared to confirm the interpretation that anarchism and criminal violence were linked.[8]

The minister of the interior asked all of the prefects of France to provide information on how many anarchists in their *départements* owned automobiles or drove them as chauffeurs. Their movements were to be closely observed. After all, recent events had demonstrated that anarchist bandits "will not hesitate to employ the perfected means of locomotion to carry out their evil deeds (thefts, acts of sabotage, and more)."[9]

Parisians joined the police in looking closely at what they believed to be unlikely or suspicious automobile activity. Again, most of the tips led nowhere. For example, a well-off gentleman driving his "workers" to the post office near the place de la République at about 6:30 one evening watched as a young woman stepped out of a "superb limousine with a patent-leather interior." He heard her say to the driver "Do you think?" using the familiar "*tu*" and with an accent from the faubourgs. Then she went into a nearby building. The man contended that women owning automobiles did not usually *tu-toi*, particularly ordinary employees. The "good citizen" moved his car closer so he could discreetly have a better look at the car's driver. The well-heeled gentleman, immediately suspicious of an "accent from the faubourgs," carefully described the two men in the car, as if he had been asked to draw up a police description. All this made him think that what he had observed "appeared to me far from the customs of people of means." The small woman returned, getting back in the car with a tall man. The gentleman concluded that the men he had seen strongly resembled men believed to have held up the Société Générale on rue Ordener. But he refused to provide his name, "having no desire to become a target for the band of murdering robbers." Authorities could contact him with a notice in *Le Journal* and *Le Matin*. But he would soon be leaving on a business trip. Police spent hours if not days checking out such "tips." In this case, the people the "witness" had seen turned out to be "honorable." The owner of the car worked for the Bank of France. The driver was his regular chauffeur, and another man in the car was his son. The woman was his mistress, and the third man was one of her friends. Nothing could be simpler.[10]

The search for the bandits was not limited to land, as flying had emerged as a nascent sport. Prefects and police turned their attention toward aviation, listing "known aviation schools," of which there were now twenty-four, only one of which was in the *département* of the Seine. The minister of the interior worried that he had received information, from "a very serious source," that anarchists or other revolutionaries were trying to be admitted to "aviation schools with the intention of taking advantage of the new means of aerial loco-motion to put into practice their subversive theories." In several cases, he asked the police to look into the background of aviators, students, and employers "and to watch them attentively." From Beauvais came worries about two "suspect students," one German, the other Austrian, and that "certain revolutionaries" had attempted to find jobs there. There was no real reason for such suspicion, but the reports that reached high desks reflected the degree of fear gener-ated by the anarchist bandits at a time when new technology seemed to pose a potential threat for misuse while speeding up society. There is no evidence that Garnier, Bonnot, Callemin, or anyone else in the Bonnot Gang intended to fly anywhere; fancy automobiles remained their transportation of choice.[11]

As police aggressively monitored anarchists in Paris, on Febru-ary 3, 1912, *Le Libertaire* spoke for many: "The cops, kings for the moment, burst into the homes of comrades, searching everywhere, and in their rage at not finding anything just tear the place up. They track, they watch, they visit concierges, and they convince bosses to get rid of those who chance has put into their sight and under their claws. And the mass press sings the same refrain."[12]

Police pressure and the inevitable whispers of police spies with their hands out for payments eroded individualist and illegalist soli-darities. Victor believed that some *compagnons* were saving their skins and picking up some extra cash by tipping off the police about the activities of some of their comrades. To some extent, the mood had become *"sauve qui peut."*[13]

On February 15, Jouin ordered a search of Lorulot's residence near Buttes-Chaumont, not far from the former office of *L'Anarchie*. They found Jeanne Bélardi sleeping there. She was no longer with Édouard Carouy. That nothing suspicious had been found did not prevent police from closely monitoring the comings and goings of most everybody coming by to see Lorulot; nor did it prevent them from following him when he went out.

The next day, Jouin sent a summary report along to Xavier Guichard, his boss. In Jouin's view, a band of "dangerous anarchists" were at work. He insisted that police had found a base in Romainville where *L'Anarchie* had been published; then on rue Fessart, when the newspaper had moved back into Paris; as well as in the residence of Louis Rimbault in Pavillons-sous-Bois. In these places, Jouin related, plans for robberies were made, and booty from such coups divided up, designated as "taking back from the bourgeoisie." Jouin identified five members of "this formidable [anarchist] organization": Garnier, Dieudonné, Bonnot, de Boe, and "X," known as Raymond *la Science*. Carouy and Rimbault stood accused as accomplices in the theft of the Delaunay-Belleville automobile used in the event.[14]

Early on the day of February 27, a gray Delaunay-Belleville had been seen racing along rue de Rivoli. A policeman noted the license plate number, 878.8, but couldn't stop the drivers. The car, stolen in Saint-Mandé, knocked down the stand of a woman selling vegetables, scattering her wares on the street. Ten or fifteen minutes later, the Delaunay-Belleville came to a sudden stop on rue des Dames at the corner of rue Nollet. Jules Bonnot, who was as usual at the wheel, took out his tools; a gas leak was the problem.

Once the car had started up again, Bonnot drove toward the place du Havre near Gare Saint-Lazare, which was encumbered by that most Parisian of events: a traffic jam. The Delaunay-Belleville tried to maneuver through the cars, brushed a bus, and was pinned against the sidewalk by a truck. A policeman appeared, coincidentally named Garnier (François), demanding the driver's license and announcing that he would be drawing up a ticket. Bonnot got out of the automobile without saying a word, turned the crank handle and started the car up again. It began to move up the street, until a carriage and then a bus blocked its way.

The policeman jumped onto the running board of the automobile. Octave Garnier fired three shots. The policeman fell to the ground, fatally wounded. The Delaunay-Belleville raced off, crossed the boulevard Haussmann, and moved down the rue Tronchet and then the rue Royale. A soldier tried to follow them on a bicycle, as did two policemen who commandeered a sportscar from an astonished driver. That car crashed into a female pedestrian, gravely injuring her. Bonnot, Callemin, and Garnier were soon on the Champs-Élysées and then out of Paris.[15]

While Paris was stunned by the brutal murder of a policeman, Bonnot, Callemin, and Garnier prepared again to take their talents beyond the Parisian region. Callemin was in touch with Élie Monier, "Simentoff," who was in Alès, in the southeast. He had a robbery in mind for the gang. On February 25, a telegram had arrived addressed to Dieudonné from Alès with the cryptic message "This evening Mama's health is very good." It had been sent by Simentoff to indicate that everything was ready for the men to rob an employee who was transporting money from the silver mines near Alès. With this heist planned, Bonnot, Garnier, and Callemin and two others—wearing melon-shaped hats—began to drive to Alès, at the time at least a fourteen-hour drive from Paris, if not more.[16]

With Bonnot at the wheel again, on February 29 the car ran into a sidewalk in Pont-sur-Yonne, about eighty miles from Paris, damaging a tire. A nearby mechanic had the tools necessary to repair the car. Not long thereafter, the automobile broke down again, this time just outside Arnay-le-Duc in Burgundy, twenty miles northwest of Beaune. A rear tire had gone flat, and the men drove the car into town, causing considerable damage. The bad-tempered

Garnier went after Bonnot about his driving, suggesting that he had again been responsible for "their" car breaking down because he had clipped a sidewalk. Bonnot responded with anger. The men paid someone to drive them to Beaune, where they lunched. Their chauffeur noted to the police that "a large ruddy man," somewhat older than the others, appeared to be the organizer of the five. From Beaune they returned to Paris on the train. From photos, witnesses identified Bonnot, Garnier, and Dieudonné. The benevolent driver added that the leader appeared to be Bonnot.[17]

In the meantime, police surveillance of the anarchist typographer Léon Bouchet and of Jeanne Bélardi, as well as information divulged in an anonymous letter, led police to a rooming hotel on rue Nollet in the seventeenth arrondissement. The letter had denounced Dieudonné, indicating that he was staying in that lodging house. Jouin placed two policemen as lodgers in the building to monitor comings and goings.

On February 27, Jouin and his team interviewed Georges Rollet, who ran the lodging house. He said that a "Monsieur Aubertin" had come looking for a room in late December, having been sent by "Jules Comtesse . . . who had recommended our establishment to him." He had asked for room number 6, where Monsieur Comtesse had stayed. "Aubertin" left on January 12 and returned on February 2 with his spouse.[18]

Rollet's wife recalled that "Monsieur Comtesse" had been "presented" to them by David Bélonie, whom she had known four or five year earlier when she was concierge on rue Saint-Lazare near the railroad station, where she had lived with her first husband, who had subsequently passed away. At the time, Bélonie worked at a pharmacy on the same street.

As for M. Comtesse, he had first arrived on November 28 and stayed a fortnight. Several days later, Bélonie showed up to return the keys and take items that Comtesse had left behind, including a suitcase. Bélonie had come by to visit his friend several times. Comtesse had flashed large bills and "mentioned before his departure that he was going to work with a woman to start up a business and said that he had thirty thousand francs." Comtesse, of course, was Jules Bonnot, as the police now were convinced based on the description provided by Rollet.

Aubertin, then, was Eugène Dieudonné. He had introduced himself as an "*industriel*" from Nancy and taken a room with his wife, Louise Kayser, who had returned to her husband with their young son after the events on rue Ordener. The police settled in to watch the residence around the clock, hoping that Dieudonné and perhaps even Bonnot would return.

Dieudonné, who had lost his father at a young age, had started out as an apprentice cabinetmaker at the age of thirteen. He then began hanging around with a group of anarchists in Nancy. Dieudonné married Louise Kayser in 1907, the year he completed his military service. They had two children. Louise also became a passionate anarchist, and two years later the couple left Nancy for Paris, where in 1910 they attended anarchist *causeries* on rue du Chevalier de la Barre and nearby, on Wednesday evenings, in a small rented

Eugène Dieudonné, suspected of
participation in the Bonnot Gang.

hall on rue d'Angoulême. Dieudonné got a job through the efforts of Charles Bill, who was also from Nancy and who had written an occasional piece for *L'Anarchie*. In October 1910, Dieudonné stayed with the anarchist Dupoux, known as Rémond, in the nineteenth arrondissement and worked in a grocery store in Belleville. He had one arrest for carrying a prohibited weapon and another for making explosives. Dieudonné left the apartment in July 1911 when Dupoux was arrested. Someone came to move out his belongings.[19]

When Louise heard Lorulot speak, the object of her affection changed. Soon she was following the anarchist editor and orator to cafés and then hotel rooms, while Dieudonné worked. Gradually, when Dieudonné realized what was going on, he and Louise separated. He returned broken-hearted to Nancy, walking all the way because he had no money. Back home, he stole a bicycle and landed briefly in jail. Dieudonné returned to Paris in November 1911 in the hope of winning back his wife, who had become known in anarchist circles as the "Red Venus."[20]

The police outside the rooming house on rue Nollet on February 28 did not have to wait long. Jouin and his agents stopped "Aubertin" on rue Nollet and took him upstairs to the room he occupied, where Louise and de Boe's lover were talking. Police found maps showing ways of avoiding the customs post at the Belgian border, Browning pistols, bullets, and a ticket for something left in temporary storage at the Gare du Nord. They took Dieudonné into custody. Realizing that Louise Dieudonné's somewhat erratic personality and penchant for indiscretions might provide useful information, on March 1 they let "the Red Venus" go.[21]

The next morning, Jouin and Guichard got to work, believing that the key to the murder of the policeman on February 27 must be with "Comtesse" and "Aubertin." Again interviewing M. Rollet, this time in his office, Guichard, now the head of Security, showed him a photo of Jules Bonnot. Rollet quickly identified him as the "Monsieur Comtesse" who had stayed in his establishment and recommended it to "Aubertin"—Dieudonné. More important, witnesses at the place du Havre identified Bonnot from police photos. Guichard now concluded that Bonnot was the leader of the gang of bandits terrorizing Paris and its region. The police quickly found Bonnot's wife living in Annemasse on the Swiss border. She had nothing good to say about her husband, describing him as lazy, unwilling to work, and obsessed with money. Madame Bonnot had no interest in ever seeing him again.[22]

As the Parisian press expressed outrage that a policeman could be gunned down right in the center of Paris, Guichard and Jouin struggled with the enormous pressure of public opinion. The papers were doing detective work of their own. "A Policeman Killed!" screamed headlines in the papers of the next day. *Action Française* announced that the murderous shots came from Browning pistols, noting that the weapon was similar to those stolen from the store on rue Lafayette. *L'Excelsior*'s headline roared, "We Must Be Protected!" The newspaper organized a "Meeting of Public Safety" of leaders of banks, industry, and commerce to discuss the wave of crime that had engulfed the city. If France beyond its borders faced the challenge of an increasingly aggressive German empire, the country was threatened by bandits at home as well: "The hour of awakening has arrived. Just as the Agadir Affair succeeded in awakening our numbed sense of national pride, in the same way the hideous crimes of these scoundrels oblige us to defend ourselves against their attacks."[23]

About 3:00 a.m. on February 29, three men tried to burglarize the office of the notary Tintant, place de l'Hôtel de ville, in Pontoise, seventeen miles northwest of Paris. They arrived in an automobile and tried to enter with a "false key," but they could not do so as the notary had installed new locks inside the door after a recent theft. They went around to a garden wall and climbed over it. When they broke through a door into the house, the noise awakened the notary. He opened his window above, fired a revolver in the air, and yelled a warning to a neighbor. The men fired two shots in the direction of Monsieur Tintant and then fled in the stolen gray Delaunay-Belleville. A few hours later, passersby saw several men get out of the Delaunay-Belleville in a vacant lot in Saint-Ouen, douse it with gasoline, toss some straw into the car, and set it on fire. Tintant and his neighbor agreed that there had been three men, but they could not positively identify Bonnot, Garnier, and Callemin from photos.[24]

When Callemin ran into a friend, the man, who knew about the plans for the south of France, asked why he was back so soon. "We had a puncture (*Nous avons crevé*)," came the response. "A tire?" "No, a cop."[25] The prefect of police now informed his agents that they should not hesitate to draw their swords and puncture the tires of an automobile driven by criminals trying to flee the scene of a crime.[26]

On February 29, the police made their next move. They had discovered that "Deboit," who was identified by an anonymous letter more than a month earlier as having been involved in the rue Ordener heist, was Jean de Boe. Police arrested him at place de Clichy and found several pistols and chargers in his hotel room.[27]

Jouin was getting closer to Jules Bonnot. He brought Dettweiller and Louis Rimbault to his office. Rimbault was now suspected of having purchased the Brownings used in the holdup on rue Ordener. Other information continued to point to Garnier as having been one of the bandits. The second employee of the Société Générale branch, Peemans, identified Dieudonné from a police photo as one of the four men involved.

On March 2, the funeral of policeman François Garnier took place at Notre-Dame. In his eulogy, the president of the municipal council of Paris demanded increased resources for the police in their hunt for the bandits on the run. The council itself accused Lépine of using the police to monitor strikes while bandits went about their business. The National Assembly voted seven hundred ninety thousand francs for security, a sum intended for the purchase of more automobiles for the police in order to keep up with the Bonnot Gang.

The Parisian press, meanwhile, fretted even more about "the general state of insecurity," insisting that the bandits were anarchists. *Le Figaro* pleaded, "Protect us! Protect us!" Jean Jaurès's *L'Humanité* demanded that Louis Lépine be replaced by someone more competent. A Parisian newspaper editorialized hopefully: "This will be the end of the renaissance of big-time banditry, whose abominable exploits will only be found in popular literature in a time when, perhaps, the police will also have rapid automobiles at its disposition." However, Bonnot, Garnier, and Carouy were still at large. Their war on society continued without pause.[28]

Dieudonné, who had been in jail since February 27, continued to proclaim his innocence in the affair of rue Ordener. He had been in Nancy, seen there by several witnesses the afternoon of the holdup. Journalists raced to Nancy to interview Dieudonné's understandably frantic mother and others who claimed to have seen him there on December 21. Yet two days earlier, Callemin seems to have sent him a telegram with the message, "Don't wait, come immediately, Raymond."

Juge d'instruction Maurice Gilbert now suspected that Dieudonné was the man who had shot Ernest Caby. In his office on March 5, the investigating magistrate hurriedly organized a reconstitution of the holdup on rue Ordener, confronting Caby with Dieudonné. Gilbert made sure that no photo of Dieudonné appeared beforehand in newspapers, in order to not influence the outcome of the reconstitution of the event. Caby now formally identified Dieudonné as the gunman. Peemans seconded Caby's new selection of Dieudonné as the man who shot him, as did another witness. Caby had earlier designated Garnier as the gunman. Both men, to be sure, had piercing dark eyes and a mustache. Troubling for Dieudonné's case was the fact that one of the two revolvers found in his possession at the time of his arrest was the same caliber as the one that was used to shoot Caby, one of which had been originally purchased by Louis Rimbault. Moreover, the ticket for left-luggage at the Gare du Nord led to the discovery of a suitcase in which was found the surgeon's kit that had been stolen with the car in Ghent. Dieudonné's explanation: a friend gave him the suitcase, but he chose not to reveal the friend's name.[29]

Another break in the case came when the police learned the names and whereabouts of the two "brokers" who had tried in Amsterdam to sell the stolen securities taken on rue Ordener. A usurer with the appropriate nickname of "the Financier" and with a long police record had information that he was willing to trade for a break. He told the police that he knew two men who had been trying to sell the stolen securities from the rue Ordener holdup.

Using the Financier's tip, the police began to follow David Bélonie and Léon Rodriguez as they moved about in the eighteenth arrondissement. On March 12, agents watched as the two men left a package in the left-luggage at the Gare du Nord. The police swooped in and found fifty thousand francs in securities in the package. When Bélonie returned to the Gare du Nord to pick up the package, he was arrested. At first, he refused to reveal his name, but finally he began to talk. He had taken the train to Amsterdam, arriving on March 5. When he stepped off the train, he was carrying, as instructed, a copy of *Le Petit Parisien*. A man stepped forward, asking, "Have you seen our friends?" The connection was made. Soon Bélonie had one hundred thousand francs worth of the securities taken on rue Ordener; he strapped them to his body before returning to Paris. The next day, Bélonie met Jules Bonnot in the Métro station at place de la Nation, turning over some of the securities to him. Bélonie claimed that he had met Bonnot once a day for several days in the Bois de Vincennes, presumably to consider ways of unloading the securities.[30]

On March 12 police in Lille arrested Rodriguez, a thirty-four-year-old Parisian who described himself as a "traveling salesman." He was an anarchist who had served several prison sentences for counterfeiting, including one in London. His lover Anna Lecocq was also arrested. Rodriguez carried papers identifying him as Monsieur Lecocq. He also carried a loaded revolver and a pair of American brass knuckles. In Rodriquez's apartment, police found a suitcase full of well-crafted counterfeit ten-franc pieces, as well as some of the materials used to produce them. In The Hague, the automobile stolen in Ghent on January 24 was discovered. When Rodriguez returned to Paris in police custody, guards had to disperse an angry crowd—the Parisian press had already related his arrest and interrogation in

Lille—that descended on the prisoner as he was taken from the train at the Gare du Nord, some shouting, "Death! Death to the bandit!"[31]

On March 19, Rodriguez admitted to Gilbert that Bélonie had asked him for money to pay his way to Amsterdam to try to sell the stolen securities. In Paris they managed to sell some of them for about five hundred francs, presumably to the Financier, who then denounced them. They admitted to having met with Bonnot and Garnier in Clignancourt, on the northern edge of Paris near the fortifications that surrounded the capital. Rodriguez and Bélonie had found the two in a bad way, in tatters in a miserable place.

Unlike Bélonie, Rodriguez was willing to tell most anything he knew in order to avoid prosecution. He claimed Garnier told them that he—Garnier—and Dieudonné had fired shots on rue Ordener and that Garnier had "settled his score" with the cop on rue du Hâvre. Rodriguez insisted that he had seen about a dozen big revolvers stacked in the chimney, and that Bonnot had warned him not to play with "that thing there" or the same "accident" that had befallen "Sorrentino" might happen again, giving his version of the death of Platano. Rodriguez and Bélonie gave Bonnot one hundred francs, relating that he kept sixty francs and Bélonie had held on to 340 francs.[32]

In the meantime, anarchist friends of Dieudonné worked to prove that the former had been in Nancy the day of the bank robbery on rue Ordener. The police continued to insist that Dieudonné could have taken the train and been in Nancy late that same afternoon. An anarchist cabinetmaker and his wife constructed a false alibi for Dieudonné, claiming that he had been with the cabinetmaker's wife at the time of the holdup. They were denounced in an anonymous letter. A twenty-year-old friend of Reinert's, Charles Bill, suspected a man named Blanchet as the letter writer and early in May shot him dead. Charles Bill then fled, never to be seen again, at least by the police.[33]

Fearing Dieudonné would talk, Garnier sent a letter, addressed to Xavier Guichard "*chef de la Sûreté, et Cie*," to *Le Matin*. On March 21, *Le Matin* published the letter, written two days earlier. In his missive,

Garnier began as follows: "Since thanks to your mediation the press has put my modest person into the headlines, to the great joy of all the concierges of the capital," the police had announced that his capture was imminent. As for an informer or others who would be betray him, he warned that "me and my friends will know how to pay him back with the reward that he deserves." He mocked the police and the reward of ten thousand francs offered for information leading to his arrest, saying that if they considerably increased the amount, he would deliver himself to the police "feet and arms tied up, along with guns and baggage!" Garnier asserted that Dieudonné had not been the one who shot Caby on rue Ordener, contradicting Rodriguez, who had assured the police (hoping for a deal) that the cabinetmaker was guilty. He, Garnier, had been "more guilty than anyone else." He added that he had for a moment considered giving himself up, but changed his mind: "Ultimately I will fall into your hands but you should be certain that I will defend my skin until the end." He signed with "Awaiting the pleasure of meeting you!"—but not before warning Guichard, "Like Jouin, you're going to get it. Await your glorious death and you will be decorated with a cross— Rejoice, filthy cow!" At the bottom of the letter, Garnier took care to leave the prints of the four fingers and thumb of his right hand, along with the message "Idiot Bertillion, put on your glasses and have a look" ("*Bille de Bertillion mets tes lunettes et gaffe*"). Bertillon proudly identified the fingerprints as indeed being those of Garnier, but that wasn't particularly helpful to Guichard and Jouin. With dangerous bandits still at large, Jouin seemed on the verge of resigning, before Lépine convinced him to remain at his post and plough forward.[34] As two thousand five hundred copies of posters with photos of Bonnot, Garnier, and Carouy circulated through Paris, on March 20 *Le Petit Parisien* reassured its readers that nine members of the "band" were behind bars. The newspaper counted Victor Kibaltchiche among these "*malfaiteurs*."

Procureur de la République Théodore Lescouvé now formally declared the existence of an *association des malfaiteurs*, listing thirteen crimes allegedly committed by thirteen people: Bélonie, de Boe, Dettweiller, Dieudonné, Kibaltchiche, Henriette [Rirette] Maître-jean, Metge, Rimbault, and Rodriguez (all of whom were in custody), along with Bonnot, Carouy, Garnier, and Valet (whose name had not yet appeared in newspapers). Thus, although Victor and Rirette were specifically accused of receiving stolen weapons from the burglary of guns stores, they were lumped together in this *association de malfaiteurs* as therefore also responsible for the holdup on rue Ordener, among other crimes.[35] In the meantime, Rirette pleaded in *L'Anarchie* for those anarchists arrested and not really charged with anything specific. Caught in an "intolerable situation," they suffered "the lack of air and light, suffering the moral torture of handcuffs and cops." Victor—"Le Rétif"—was among them.[36]

In late March, for the first time (besides occasionally with reference to the earlier thefts in Lyon), the name "Bonnot Gang" (*la bande*

Jules Bonnot, Octave Garnier, Édouard Carouy, and the Bonnot Gang reach the headlines of the mass Parisian press.

à Bonnot) began to appear in the Parisian press. Gradually, Jules Bonnot's name had been placed in the context of a gang—on March 28, the "Bonnot–Garnier Gang." "Band of Murderers" had been used, along with "Bonnot, Garnier, and Consorts," "The Balance Sheet of Carrouy [*sic*], Bonnot, Garnier, etc.," and "Bonnot and his People." The first direct mention of "The Bonnot Gang" seems to have been in *L'Humanité*, March 30, 1912.[37]

However, it became increasingly obvious that the Bonnot Gang was not a finely organized group, but rather a band in flux, benefitting from a network of solidarity and assistance. Although the gang became identified with Jules Bonnot, in part because he was the oldest and drove the getaway automobiles, his name had been one of the first to reach Jouin's desk from various informers, and because of the Platano affair there was no "leader." Yet if there was one, Garnier probably assumed that role. Decisions were made after discussion, always reflecting anarchist individualism. What made it even more challenging and probably more dangerous to find Bonnot, Garnier, Valet, Callemin, and others is that they moved from place to place, finding hospitality with anarchists who did not even know their names. The police now considered Raymond Callemin particularly dangerous, because he was "gifted with an extremely lively intelligence that is particularly adapted to evil, excoriating all authority."[38]

So how were Jouin and his colleagues to find the Bonnot Gang? One possibility was someone on the inside providing useful information. For his part, Léon Rodriguez was now even more ready to talk in exchange for leniency. He wrote Jouin that, more than anyone else in the anarchist milieu, if freed he could discover the hiding places of Bonnot, Garnier, and the other members of their gang within two weeks. He implored Jouin to show his plan to the prosecuting attorney. His past meant that he, more than anyone else, could pull it off. Rodriguez would require only "relative, partial freedom . . . a freedom to act." He was not "so much compromised in this affair" that his offer could be rejected out of hand. Jouin himself would profit from such a coup, and he could be assured of "my entire good faith." Rodriguez received no reply. On the same day, he wrote the prosecuting attorney that in order to obtain a pardon he was "ready to do anything."

The killing in Étampes almost two months earlier of a policeman who had surprised anarchist burglars—one of whom immediately committed suicide—had led to the arrest of Joseph Renard but not the other killer. Both Rimbault and Renard had "worked" together in Belgium and knew Carouy and Garnier. Renard had stayed at passage Clichy, where Lorulot sold *L'Idée Libre*, and after his departure Garnier and Marie *la Belge* had shared a room. Moreover, Renard was in possession of a revolver when arrested; it had been stolen from the arms store on rue Lafayette. And so had the two Brownings found in the apartment in Belleville where Victor and Rirette were living. This put Rirette under even closer police surveillance.[39]

When Jouin again summoned Rirette for a fourth interrogation on March 25, she showed up the next morning as instructed to see Maurice Gilbert. Rirette denied that the offices of *L'Anarchie* had served as a meeting place for an *association des malfaiteurs*, adding reasonably enough that she did not ask those arriving in the office if they were members of such an association. Likewise, Victor, brought next into Gilbert's office, insisted that he had never in the offices of *L'Anarchie* heard of any planned crime and that he had certainly never profited in any way from any such criminal activity.[40]

Rirette's protestations were of no use. After the interrogation, she was arrested and sent to Saint-Lazare prison, once an institution for lepers. There Rirette was generally treated well by the Sisters of Marie-Joseph, even by the intimidating Sister Léonide, responsible for discipline, who was feared by most of the inmates, and who waged war on the enormous, ravenous rats who also resided in the prison. There was more to eat than Rirette had in her apartment—"If anarchy could not nourish its men, it nourished even less its women," as she put it. Moreover, Rirette knew that trusted friends were taking care of her girls. She was able to avoid the larger prison dormitories, whose residents, including many prostitutes, were forced to work. The prisoners benefited from an improved situation (*"en pistole"*) thanks to five *sous* a day paid for Rirette by donations from anarchist friends. They benefited, too, from the proximity of a stove. The spiders were left alone to spin their webs, and the omnipresent rats pillaged any food not eaten by humans.

Rirette was the only anarchist there. Her colleagues included bourgeois women who for whatever reason had shoplifted, other thieves, women condemned for "crimes of passion," and more. But most were ordinary working-class women who had for some reason fallen in disfavor with the police. During her incarceration, Rirette helped Barbe Le Clerch, Marius Metge's Breton girlfriend who was also imprisoned at Saint-Lazare, begin to learn to read. The prison chaplain came to visit Rirette, brought her books, advised her that "idleness is a poor adviser," and asked her if she wanted to learn Latin. She dared not refuse, and the course began. On one occasion, her daughter Chinette was allowed to come for a brief visit, which went very well once her mother convinced her that a well-meaning guard was not a "cop." Rirette suffered enormously from the forced separation from her daughters and from Victor.[41] While in prison, Rirette soon learned that Octave Garnier and her old friend André Soudy were almost certainly involved in the crimes.

An editorial in *L'Anarchie*, which had moved to a new address with Émile Armand taking over as editor, commented bitterly on Rirette's arrest: "It's natural. No judge would ever pardon her proud attitude and her disdain for the magistrature." "Le Rétif" had been arrested because of his propaganda for anarchist individualism, and Rirette by virtue of "her haughty refusal to play the role of an informer." Both were victims of the Scoundrel Laws that allowed them to be considered as belonging to an *association des malfaiteurs*.[42]

In the prosecution's case against Victor and Rirette, the only tangible piece of evidence that could possibly place them in an *association des malfaiteurs* was the two Browning pistols found in their apartment when it was searched on January 31. Yet clearly their role in the editing and publication of *L'Anarchie*, for which Rirette was legally the director, would play a role. They would be accused of being intellectuals who encouraged illegalist criminality.[43]

Chapter 13

THE BONNOT GANG'S MURDER SPREE

With accounts of carjacking prevalent in the press, those possessing luxury automobiles now had reason to fear for their cars. Quality locksmiths did a brisk business in securing garages. Wealthy owners readied their revolvers. Indeed two bold, violent attacks added to the anxiety.

Having failed to snatch a car in Chatou west of Paris with another coup or two in mind, Bonnot, Garnier, Monier, Callemin, and Soudy decided to steal one as it motored along a road. As usual, they were very well armed for the occasion, with Brownings and with a Winchester repeating rifle carried by Soudy.[1]

On the morning of March 25, a driver was en route from the Dion-Bouton car dealership on the Champs-Élysées to Cap Ferrat on the Riviera to deliver the expensive automobile to its purchaser, a retired colonel. A young employee, a mechanic who worked for the wealthy Riviera resident, accompanied the chauffeur. Bonnot had been tipped off by a *garagiste* acquaintance. About 8:30 in the morning, as the two men traveled through Seine-et-Marne, about fifteen miles southeast of Paris, a man waving a white handkerchief implored the driver to stop in the forest of Sénart. Then three other men sprang forward from nearby bushes. When François Mathillet, at the wheel, refused to get out and turn over the vehicle to them and appeared to reach in his pocket, Garnier shot and fatally wounded him. The professional driver staggered out of the car and collapsed. The mechanic, named Cérisole, who was also hit, played dead and survived. Hearing the shots, people in the vicinity began to arrive on the scene. The bandits waved pistols in their direction and then drove off. When the mayor of nearby Montgeron tried to alert the police by telephone and provide a description of the stolen automobile, the phone call did not go through.[2]

Now Bonnot drove the stolen car, packed with his colleagues, to Chantilly, north of Paris. About 10:30 a.m., they stopped in front of another branch of the Société Générale. They had checked it out the previous week, and they knew that its proximity to horse-racing tracks invariably meant there would be lots of cash around. The men were wearing caps and large automobile glasses that covered part of their faces. Bonnot remained at the wheel, and one of his colleagues stood guard, armed with a rifle. Three others burst into the bank, shooting dead two employees (a seventeen-year-old and a sixteen-year-old), and leaving another seriously wounded, as people dove under tables. One bandit, wearing a long raincoat and a melon-shaped hat, pointed a carabine in the direction of passersby, warning, "Get back, get back or I'll kill you," in argot ("*Caltez, caltez ou je vous canarde*"). The robbers emptied a cash drawer and an open safe. Several of them went down to the basement to open another safe but could not do so. The bandits left the scene quickly, guns blazing, wounding one passerby in the heel and lodging another bullet in a horse. They carried with them thirty-five thousand francs in bills, ten thousand francs in gold pieces, and four thousand francs in coins, leaving behind securities that they now knew would be too difficult to unload. The entire operation took but five minutes. A gendarme lamented that his office in Chantilly did not have a telephone and that thus his colleagues in the vicinity could not be notified.

The bandits returned to Paris through Épinay-sur-Seine and then Asnières, where they were followed by two unarmed policemen riding bicycles, whose pursuit quickly ended. At the Asnières train station, the bandits abandoned the car (which seems to have failed them—they were seen looking with concern under the hood). In the car, which had served its purpose, police found a *Guide Michelin* and maps of France.[3]

In Paris, the shocking robbery and murders in Chantilly accentuated growing fear—indeed, panic. Authorities were now sure they had identified Bonnot, Garnier, and Carouy as three of the bandits. Police offices everywhere in France received twenty-five hundred copies of descriptions of "Jules Bonnot, born October 14, 1876, in Pont-de-Roide (Doubs), son of Jules-Joseph Bonnot and Hermance Montot. [Bonnot] is a mechanic, unknown address. 1.59 meters tall, clear yellowish eyes, dark blond hair and a reddish-brown beard, with a scar on his upper right ear." Bertillon identified fingerprints on the steering wheel as those of Bonnot, and fingerprints on the windshield as belonging to Garnier. From police photos, witnesses in Chantilly recognized Bonnot and Carouy as two of the robbers. Witnesses described a smallish man wearing spectacles; this corresponded to Raymond "*la Science*," Raymond Callemin. René Valet may have been another of the passengers.

The press became obsessed with "*l'homme à la carbine.*"[4] *Le Petit Parisien*, among the other major Parisian dailies, expressed certainty that the weapons used in the murderous attacks in Montgeron and Chantilly had been among those Winchester rifles stolen on the night of January 9–10 from a store on boulevard Haussmann. The royalist newspaper *Action Française* was quick to add that "the Russian Nihilist Kibaltchiche and the woman Maîtrejean, recently arrested, had been involved."[5]

For his part, Victor, in jail and suffering from "constant hunger," heard "only distant echoes" of these murderous events. Yet he "recognized, in the various newspaper reports, faces I had met or known. I saw the whole of the movement founded by Libertad dragged into the scum of society by all sorts of madness; and nobody could do anything about it, least of all myself. The theoreticians, terrified, headed for cover. It was like a collective suicide."[6]

A letter sent to the police identified André Soudy as the *homme à la carabine* in Chantilly. Moreover, the letter indicated that Soudy was staying in the Channel spa town of Berck.[7] On March 30, police indeed found Soudy in Berck-Plage, as they had been tipped off. Soudy may have been betrayed by an anarchist and his girlfriend, whom Rirette had suspected of working with the police. The anarchist had also asked Victor to keep some counterfeit money that he had brought by, thus setting Victor up for a possible later arrest. (When Rirette became aware of this, she panicked, realizing that they may have been set up, but Victor, perhaps with what Rirette referred to as "Russian fatalism," merely shrugged his shoulders.)[8]

Soudy was receiving treatment for his tuberculosis and staying with the unemployed railroad man Barthélemy Baraille, who was well known to local police, in a small wooden house near the dunes. Baraille, a friend of Lorulot, probably did not know Soudy, but he would have respected the anarchist "*droit d'asile*" (right to asylum, refuge, or sanctuary). "*Pas-de-Chance*" Soudy said to the policemen who arrested him that "the bullets in my revolver were for you and prison is for me." On the way to Paris he told his guards, "To die of tuberculosis or to die on the scaffold, it's the same thing. I am condemned to death and have only a few months before I meet Deibler." Diebler was the famous executioner who had succeeded his father on the scaffold in 1899 and who did his best work in public.[9]

Police found on Soudy 969 francs, two Brownings, two chargers, and a vial of potassium cyanide. He refused to answer questions when interrogated in Paris by Guichard. The next day, Soudy's sister committed suicide, anguished by her brother's most recent arrest and the fact that their parents had forbidden her to marry.[10]

Soudy denied being involved in any way in the events in Chantilly. This despite being identified from photos by several witnesses who remembered his coat, his hat, his long, pale face, and that he spoke with an accent from the working-class faubourgs, using argot ("*Caltez, caltez, ou je vous canarde*"). Rirette, who had become close to him, remembered him "only speaking argot." A policeman who read of Soudy's arrest wrote from a sanatorium north of Paris, where he was being treated for tuberculosis. He had overlapped with Soudy in another a sanatorium, when Soudy was using the name "Colombo" and bragging about being an anarchist. And "this person very often spoke argot and the word *caltez* is really him." The policeman asked that his name not be revealed. He, too, feared reprisals. When Guichard asked Soudy if the possessions seized *chez* Baraille belonged to him, he replied, "None of it is mine. You know very well that property is theft, as [the anarchist writer] Proudhon said."[11]

On April 3, it was Édouard Carouy's turn to be captured and jailed. He had been seen in the vicinity of Choisy-le-Roi, near Thiais, where the elderly man and his maid had been horribly murdered. Agents on a stakeout were sure they saw Carouy, who had dyed his hair, and another man on bicycles at five o'clock one morning, but the two had disappeared into the lingering darkness. Later that same day, police learned that Carouy had found refuge with Granghand, a bookbinder in the village of Lozère, south of Paris. Granghand had quickly betrayed him, going to the police, undoubtedly in exchange for cash. He set up Carouy to go to the train station there, ostensibly to pick up a bed. Carouy noticed that his "friend" walked ten yards ahead of him on the way to the station. Five officers dressed as workers awaited in a nearby café. They subdued and arrested Carouy. He told arresting officers that he carried a Browning pistol because he had heard Garnier wanted "his head." Carouy said upon incarceration that he had no intention of trying to escape and that he would now finally have a good night's sleep. For reading matter, he asked for treatises on philosophy.[12]

Under interrogation, Carouy denied being anywhere near Thiais, rue Ordener, Montgeron, place du Havre in Paris, or Chantilly. When asked to explain where exactly he had been during those events, he fell back upon the classic anarchist answer: he would not say where he had been, not wanting to compromise comrades. Carouy became more and more depressed in jail, particularly after a young man serving a sentence for theft threw himself from the third floor of his block, the second suicide in a week. Carouy attempted suicide himself, swallowing what he thought was potassium cyanide. When it turned out to be something not at all lethal, he loudly denounced the pharmacist who had given him "little candies" instead of the powerful drug. After that attempt had failed, guards had to stop him from smashing his head against the cement wall of his cell. The *juge d'instruction* charged him with being part of the *association de malfaiteurs* that had been responsible for the theft of the automobile of M. Normand in Boulogne-Billancourt, a burglary in Maisons-Alfort in August 1911, murder and attempted murder in Mortgeron and Chantilly, and the burglary of the post office in Romainville. Those who feared reprisals had good reason: Two days following Carouy's arrest, a man who had been seen in Lozère the previous night fired at Granghand and his son as they returned home from work, wounding the younger man.[13]

Garnier and Valet were still on the run, with the police in full pursuit. The gang's string of successes, as it were, appeared to have reached an end. Most of the securities had not been sold, the burglary in Pontoise had been bungled, and they had not made it to Alès. Moreover, Dieudonné seemed on the verge of telling all he knew.

Valet's sisters claimed to have no knowledge of their brother's whereabouts. Like his parents, they insisted that he was an antimilitarist pacifist, nothing more. The police assumed that Anna Dondon, Valet's anarchist girlfriend, would be somewhere with him. Dondon, born in the small town of Decize in Nièvre in 1884, was "a little dumpling, very brown and somewhat creole, artistic-looking, with her hair in ringlets and wearing a bandana." She had been free since her release from prison in 1909 after a sentence for counterfeiting. The couple briefly lived in a room with an adjoining kitchen on the sixth floor of a bourgeois-appearing building on rue Ordener—only a couple of blocks from the Société Générale branch that Valet had helped hold up. The concierge recognized the renter from police photos. Her tenant had given a different name, of course, and told her that he worked in a nearby printing shop, but this had struck the concierge as unlikely, because he was seen at the times one would assume he would have been working. Leaving in haste, Valet had left behind a gray leather overcoat, three new rifles, and some burglary tools—by now classic illegalist provisions.[14]

The police noted the proximity of a furniture store owned by a woman who had anarchist sympathies. For a time, the store was run by the twenty-six-year-old anarchist printer named Bernard Gorodsky, the eldest of nine children. Gorodsky, whose father also had a furniture store, had worked as a printer for *L'Anarchie* and had been a *habitué* of anarchist lectures. He was known for his radical views but "was sober and hard-working" and had had a job in the municipal print shop. He and his girlfriend had left their apartment without paying the rent, "as is the custom in Paris," a policeman commented bitterly. Gorodsky and his girlfriend had then moved away from the furniture store to rue Cortot, a narrow Montmartre street, and the police found some stolen goods there. Rodriguez told police that Gorodsky had worked with Bélonie in trying to unload the securities. Moreover, Bonnot had received a letter addressed to him at that address. "Suspect" people came in and out of the furniture store, including Valet and Anna Lecocq, Rodriguez, and possibly Soudy, Carouy, and Bonnot. A couple, the man wearing a long gray overcoat, had stayed with Valet and Anna for several days—this was probably Garnier, along with Marie *la Belge*. But Gorodsky then quit his printing job at the Hôtel de Ville and simply vanished into the night.[15]

Garnier and René Valet had moved quickly from rue Ordener to avenue Saint-Ouen, not far away in the eighteenth arrondissement. However, early in the morning of April 23, fearing a police "descent," they suddenly left in an automobile. They stayed several nights with an anarchist in the nineteenth arrondissement. There, police found revolvers and cartridges.[16]

Chapter 14

PANIC IN PARIS

With the alleged leaders of the band still at large, Paris was in a full panic. The headline in *Le Matin* described the highway robbery of a car and the shootings in Chantilly as "the most terrifying in the history of crime." Newspapers called for the expulsion from France of all people banned from France and the obligatory registration of automobiles. They published accounts of disagreements between Xavier Guichard and his deputy-chief Louis-François Jouin. Henry Franklin-Bouillon, representing Montgeron's *département* of Seine-et-Marne in the Chamber of Deputies, questioned the readiness of the authorities to protect citizens, noting tensions within Sûreté and between branches of the police. The Chamber voted additional credits to hire and train new policemen in the struggle against "perfected banditry." In *L'Humanité*, an editorial suggested that France was becoming a new California, "where the revolver was king." Thanks to the automobile, the bandits were feared well beyond the region of Paris.[1]

Following the murderous attack in Chantilly, the bandits, in the words of Louis Lépine, "vanish like the wind . . . all the tracks disappear." A telegram went out to all police offices in the Paris region ordering policemen to carry loaded pistols night and day. Once again, police turned their eyes toward Montmartre.[2]

The attacks carried out so audaciously by the Bonnot Gang marked the culmination of public fears about crime, which appeared as an unprecedented threat to social order. Cities, in particular, were again perceived—as in the 1830s and 1840s—as dangerous places. Criminology developed as a field of study, with Alphonse Bertillon the rising star.[3] The mass press devoted an increasing amount of space to crime, often under the rubric "*faits divers*" (miscellaneous news in brief, increasingly emphasizing crime). *L'Excelsior* noted in October 1911 that the Sûreté Générale had accumulated three hundred thirty thousand dossiers, including thirty-one thousand photographs "of disreputable men about whom one must be concerned, and who are watched, or else known bandits who are behind bars."[4]

Crime continued to push troubling international affairs to the back pages. By 1908, 12 percent of the columns of the wildly selling *Le Petit Parisien*—1.5 million copies each edition—was devoted to the coverage of crimes, and a third of the covers of *Petit Journal* were devoted to crime. Specialized newspapers covering the police began to appear, such as *Le Passe-Partout* and *L'Oeil de la police* (1908). This was the golden age of the police novel in France. Maurice Leblanc's novels featuring the "gentleman" burglar Arsène Lupin had great success, reflecting public fascination with—and fear of—crime. Sherlock Holmes was already enormously popular, as were the memoirs of policemen. *Crimes et criminels étranges* ("Strange Crimes and Criminals") appeared, as did "Illustrated Violence." Illustrated supplements presented color portraits of notable criminals. The enormous success of police novels during the *fin-de-siècle* period may well have contributed to journalists merging criminal investigations with reporting. Journalists for Parisian newspapers elbowed each other out of the way in the frenzy to get the next "scoop." Reporters emerged as "modern adventurers," going after every possible story. By the time Bonnot, Garnier, Callemin, and their band entered the scene, the newspapers were primed to capitalize on their crime spree to sell papers.[5]

Indeed, violent crime had become more common. The number of murders rose between 1901 and 1913. The eighteenth and nineteenth arrondissements easily led the way in murders in 1911, followed by the equally plebeian twelfth and thirteenth arrondissements. Juvenile delinquency increased in scope and visibility, manifest in what appeared to be a growing number of bands, particularly on the edge of Paris—based in the "zone" around the fortifications.[6]

Newspapers sounded the alarm about a disproportionate number of crimes committed by these groups of adolescents and young men. They were nicknamed *apaches,* after the American indigenous people. Most Parisian apaches were between fifteen and twenty years of age, cared about their appearance and their physical strength, and were proud of their reputation as thieves. Bands of apaches—such as the Bande de la Goutte d'Or, the Bande de Belleville, and the Bande à Milo du canal Saint-Martin—were seemingly omnipresent in the first years of the new century, but they were still around when the Bande à Bonnot was named. They maintained a strict code of honor. In La Chapelle, apaches organized their own tribunals and condemned one of theirs for spying for the police. *Le Matin* demanded judicial action against the apaches—"the whip or the rope." The popular newspaper even blamed the persistence of the apaches, viewed as the "new barbarians," on antimilitarist propaganda, particularly in view of a number of incidents between apaches and soldiers. This representation of the "bad boys" and apaches contributed to the new view of delinquency as "a social phenomenon."[7]

A poem by Maurice Rollinat captured the dark side of Montmartre:

Accomplices of clever prowlers,
Stalking the monsieur with expensive tastes,
Gas lamps on the nasty corners,
Lighting up the crooks in rags,
And slashes of knives and blows of fists,
Aggressive whistles, suspect shouts,
Hideous ghosts, outrageous informers,

And as sole witnesses to this mystery
The gas lamps of nasty corners.[8]

Elite anxiety about the *apaches* had taken off in 1902, with the wildly followed affair of the Casque d'Or in Belleville, when two rivals and their bands battled it out in a Parisian suburb for the love of a prostitute named Amélie Élie—a blonde woman, thus "the golden helmet." Women, some of them prostitutes, played a prominent role in these bands. The police considered related incidents to be of no great significance, but the Parisian press remained fascinated with the apaches, portraying the associated neighborhoods as a "hotbed of crime and sex."[9]

The apaches and, later, the Bonnot Gang helped sell books and newspapers. The *Fantômas* novels, which began to appear in 1911 with enormous popular success, followed the "exploits" of the criminal of the same name. The first *Fantômas* film and those that followed during the next few years reflected the influence of Jules Bonnot.[10] The "*faits divers*" in the daily newspapers emphasizing crime also helped confirm the image of these stereotypes.

Le Petit Parisien, for one, attracted readers with articles on "the kings of the pavement." On behalf of the "*parti des honnêtes gens*" (the party of the "honest people," with a strong sense of "men of property"), *La Libre Parole* screamed, "Thirty thousand apaches are masters of the streets of Paris: they kill, they pillage, they rape." During the subsequent four years, six theater pieces appeared with "*Le Casque d'Or*" or "*Apaches*" in the title. For Parisian elites, the apaches embodied all forms of urban crime committed by young men. And while elites staunchly condemned the apaches, they could still be relied upon to buy books and newspapers and attend plays and now films that dramatized apache exploits.[11]

Thus, the press helped orchestrate this veritable psychosis, even though the band terrorizing Paris seemed to be common criminals—however much they were identified with illegalist anarchism—and not apaches, despite their young age. Moreover, the Bonnot Gang was not identified with a particular part of peripheral Paris. Still, the police focused on such neighborhoods in their investigations, and when others were caught up in the police dragnet, no one in power protested.

The increase in violent acts, some associated with the apaches, had contributed to an intense debate on the death penalty in 1907. The public worried increasingly about the high rate of acquittals; the previous year, only 34 percent of those accused of murder or attempted murder had been found not guilty, and only 30 percent the next year. Clearly, the majority of the French public supported the death penalty. It remained in place, and executioner Anatole Deibler's job would be safe.[12]

Jules Bonnot and his friends played into existing fears about the marauding apaches, but they had left them far behind. They seemed like a new and scary kind of bandit, carrying out their attacks in broad daylight, their Brownings firing away, and escaping in fast-moving luxury automobiles: "Banditry in automobiles!" *L'Auto-Journal* seemed almost proud to feature a photo of fancy automobiles with bullet holes in them, a drawing of the attack on rue Ordener, and a photo of Bonnot.[13]

These bandits were decidedly modern. One of those implicated in these events later would relate: "Let's go back to the progress of Science. Nothing very grand can be accomplished without it. Automobile, telephone, telegraph, automatic weapons—here are the veritable means." An article in the legal journal noted that "the industry of evil-doers" had evolved following the rules of the progress of science, "Only the police has remained basically stationary."[14]

Le Matin published a giant photomontage with map of France and the itinerary of the Bonnot band, so far as it could be known. *L'Excelsior* published "the double murder of Thiais in five photos," including the house, the rooms in which the victims had perished, and Bertillon closely examining fingerprints. Other films included two reconstitutions of the "exploits" of the Bonnot Gang. In 1912, the municipality forbade showing of the film *Bandits en automobile,* calling it "a demoralizing spectacle." *Le Browning* would appear on screen the following year. The first of five *Fantômas* episodic films, which followed by two years the beginning of the wildly popular series of thirty-two small volumes about the criminal underworld, appeared that same year, clearly reflecting public fascination with and fear of the Bonnot Gang.[15]

The bandits and their getaway cars seemed another sign that society was speeding up—indeed, spinning out of control.

Bicycles had already become "the little queens." Although still relatively expensive—and thus frequently stolen—there were one hundred fifty thousand bicycles in France in 1893, two years after the newspaper *Le Vélo* first appeared; by 1913 there were 3.5 million. The automobile, airplane, and even the submarine followed. The first aeronautic salon was held in Paris in 1908. Louis Blériot piloted a plane that flew across the English Channel through fog and wind in July 1909. Roland Garros traversed the Mediterranean without a stop in September 1913. Gatherings of airplane enthusiasts became common.

Gradually, middle-class people of means began to purchase automobiles. In 1898, Parisians owned 288 of them. Two years later, there were three thousand registered automobiles in France, a year after a driver's license was first required. By the end of the first decade of the new century, a second generation of automobile manufacturers was at work. In Lyon, the Berliet Company purchased machine tools from abroad—principally from the United States, Great Britain, and Germany. Berliet's factory was divided into specialized units, all under his personal supervision, where he was assisted by his foremen. By 1913, Berliet employed two thousand workers and turned out three thousand automobiles a year. By 1914, well over one hundred thousand were on the roads of France.[16]

The first taxi took to the road in 1904. Three years later, the iconoclast novelist Octave Mirbeau published an account of his—the first—journey across Europe in a car. In these early days of automobile travel, people in France owned half of the automobiles in the world.[17]

In these early days of automobile travel, the driver of a car had to know more than a little something about motors, as garages were then relatively few and far between. The first *Guide Michelin* appeared in 1900, selling thirty-five thousand copies. It listed garages in cities and towns and provided information for travelers, such as emerging rules of the road. It highlighted—not unexpectedly, given the guide's source—information on Michelin tires. Soon Michelin added the names of convenient, decent restaurants to the *Guide*'s entries for each town.[18]

The Michelin Company successfully pressured the government to place markers (*bornes*, as the Roman had used) to indicate the distance to the next town. These were of sufficient size so that drivers could see them without having to stop to get a closer look. The goal was to encourage travel for tourism, indicating beautiful routes, thus encouraging the sale of automobiles and therefore tires. Michelin also lobbied successfully to have the names of towns at the entry and departure points along, first, national and, then, departmental roads. By 1911, ten thousand towns had asked for them. Three years later, thirty thousand had been set along French roads.[19] Automobiles captured the public imagination. Races started up, attracting new customers.

However, automobiles generated anxiety as well as smoke, as they raced by at increasingly greater speeds. A car that went out of control killed a small boy during a race in 1901, and Louis Renault's brother died in a crash during the first Paris–Madrid competition two years later. The polemicist Henri Rochefort, for one, did not like what he saw: "the satisfaction [of drivers] who have run over dogs [and] old people and children who are crushed without even seeing the machine that has wiped them out." A journalist warned drivers that beginning on that day he would "walk with a revolver in my pocket and I will fire on the first of these enraged dogs who, having gotten into an automobile . . . will flee after having flattened me or mine." A doctor warned—already!—about the harmful effects that the carbonic acid exuded by cars was having on human beings.[20] A senator direly predicted that France would have to establish "special cemeteries for *automobilistes* along the roads."[21] Yet slowly but surely the automobile was transforming life in France. One critic saw this as sort of a "social Darwinism . . . adapted to the struggle between unequal old and new species within the space of Paris." Denunciations of "the automobile evil" became something of a staple for observers of the Parisian scene.[22]

In their early years, such moving machines were only for the wealthy. Custom-made automobiles, like the Delaunay-Belleville car used by the bandits in the holdup of the Société Générale on rue Ordener, could cost well over ten thousand francs each, and up to several thousand francs a year to operate. Tires went for as much as one thousand five hundred francs a year, the equivalent of many workers' annual income (assuming work could be found)—also the equivalent of fifteen years rent for a working family—and several thousand francs a year to run. Victor Kibaltchiche and Rirette Maîtrejean would probably never have occasion to ride in a car, unless it would be in an automobile operated by the police. The first two generations of automobiles were purchased by industrial barons, bankers, financiers, wealthy *propriétaires*, and *rentiers*.

The Michelin Company increasingly identified tires and thus cars with the bourgeoisie, with French nationalism (thus campaigns were mounted to discourage the purchase of German or British-made tires), and with masculinity (leaving women in a subordinate role as coy passengers). "Bibendum," the multi-ringed white tireman who still stands as an icon of Michelin, stood at the center of a very modern advertising campaign. Bibendum represented French civilization, contrasted with Africans or South Asians who had been annexed into the French Empire, which had expanded dramatically in the 1880s and especially the 1890s.

Many well-heeled Parisians took the plebeian origins of the assumed members of the Bonnot Gang as a sign of the danger the lower classes potentially posed to their riches. The Bonnot Gang were workers who—pushed by the lack of work and the police—traveled from place to place. That they were anything but sedentary made them seem even more frightening. Their young age compounded the danger. Morever, the fact that several of the members of the gang were Belgian added an international dimension to the crimes. To many wealthy Parisians, socialists and all anarchists were not much better than the bandits who were terrorizing the capital. That Jules Bonnot and his gang were illegalist anarchists in action—defying society, its laws, and the police—made social anxiety even worse. The elite still expected deference from the lower classes, even in a Republic.[23]

The press whipped up demands for dramatically increased security and vigorous repression. A reporter in 1907 insisted, "Insecurity is *à la mode*, it is a fact." *L'Éclair* worried aloud: "We are overwhelmed and surrounded by a troop of apaches, most of whom are repeat offenders and lower-life types," yet because of "the weakness of the courts, the lack of prisons and official tolerance," they were allowed to "obey their own pernicious principles while essentially retaining immunity." The public demanded action. Parisians signed a petition calling for more severe penalties, and merchants on the *grands boulevards* demanded more police searches of residences. Even the prefect of police called for more. Lépine proclaimed that "a virile repression" was desperately required to protect society. The first step was clear.[24]

Chapter 15

POLICE DRAGNET

Protecting society meant putting an end to the Bonnot Gang. Guards monitored the city gates of Paris and soldiers patrolled the main railroad stations. The Société Générale offered one hundred thousand francs for information leading to the arrest of the robbers, who had struck their banks twice in a matter of several months. "Suspicious" automobiles generated panic and police mobilization well beyond Paris, among other places in the Nord, Pas-de-Calais, and in Chartres.[1]

The police went after anyone vaguely associated with anarchism. Aggressive roundups (*rafles*) in working-class neighborhoods came more frequently. Police searches and arrests of random anarchists continued in the Paris region. In *L'Anarchie*, Victor Méric noted on March 14 that each day the public feasted on "previously unpublished details" and the attacks continued, after which the bandits simply disappeared: "The police arrest, release, and arrest again." For his part, the anarchist Jean Grave mocked the frantic chorus for defending bourgeois society: "Let's come up with more great laws and build more prisons!" Who were the people really responsible for these attacks? It was stated that amid the misery and suffering of ordinary people, "As long as you have not taken by the throat these odious criminals who are Luxury, Wealth, Indolence, and insolent Good Fortune, you the bourgeoise, you can fortify your police, increase the numbers of your defense forces, and continue to insult us, but there is nothing you can do."[2]

In the anarchist press, *Le Libertaire*, which had ignored the events on rue Ordener and in Thiais, noted that the victims of the crimes of Montgeron and Chantilly were ordinary people doing their underpaid jobs. An editorial refused to condemn the perpetrators, suggesting that social inequalities were behind the acts. The members of the Bonnot Gang were minor figures compared to those pillaging the colonies, "legal bandits" who were even more guilty. An editorial regretted that Bonnot had not put his "*heroisme*" and energy into "the emancipatory cause of the oppressed class."[3]

On March 21, *L'Anarchie* saluted the "four or five determined and audacious men who held the police, gendarmes, and magistrates at bay. . . . They managed to escape a powerfully armed organization, an entire dragnet closely linked. . . . Let's imagine a thousand men with the same courage as this handful of resisters and tell me if you do not see this "dying society" really in danger?[4] During a meeting of the Groupe de la Fédération Révolutionnaire in the thirteenth arrondissement, an individualist stated what was painfully obvious: "Those who possess great fortune have never backed away from any means to enrich themselves and similarly the 'illegalists' have done the same thing in acting as they have." In his view, the bandits' actions were good for anarchist propaganda and could bring "only good results."[5]

L'Anarchie continued to publish, although magistrates were taking copious notes of editorials for further use. From the point of view of the authorities, it was preferable to allow the anarchist newspaper to continue, because it provided a constant source of information on anarchist meetings, *causeries*, and other events that could easily be monitored.

Denunciations and letters containing "information" continued to deluge the office of Guichard, arriving by the thousands in response to the hefty reward offered by Société Générale. Each item had to at least be read. One citizen advised the police to investigate all the people who lived in a building next to the bank. A cuck-olded husband claimed that Carouy was his spouse's lover. A citizen boldly offered to find Bonnot and his gang within four months; he would need only an automobile, and he generously offered to give Xavier Guichard a quarter of the reward once the bandits had been captured. A Parisian sent along the address of his neighbor, who happened to have the surname Bonnot. His first name was François. A Parisian suggested that "aviation" be used to find the gang, asking only for employment as a secret agent in return for his brilliant idea. Another similar suggestion also reflected the influence of airplanes on the public imagination: a plane would follow the bandits, once their location has been identified, and drop messages to police below indicating the direction taken by their automobile. The helpful citi-zen even suggested dropping explosives from the air on anarchist targets, if such targets could be found. Other ideas included stretch-ing chains across roads to stop speeding bandit-mobiles, the way that chains had centuries earlier blocked the entry to ports. Another proposed covering over the new Michelin road signs to confuse the gang as they drove to their next coup.[6]

A resident of Lyon assured authorities that he had had "commer-cial relations" with Bonnot, and offered to help capture him. This relationship would make it possible for him to approach the bandit "without too many difficulties." A Parisian who lived in the same neighborhood as relatives of Garnier related that rumor had the bandit returning to see them. He added that he did not want to sign his name, fearing reprisals from the bandits. Another resident of the capital advised that if Guichard wanted to find the bandits, he should have a look in an orange house in the second arrondissement. He assured Guichard that "the owner hides anarchists," and he described this owner as "just as unsavory as the bandits you are after." A deaf mute simply denounced a neighbor as "dangerous."[7]

Reports of sightings of the bandits proliferated. A female day laborer related that as she carried lunch to her husband near the porte de Vitry close to the fortifications, she observed a small man with a *casquette jockey* running toward the railroad tracks. Four other men were running about sixty to eighty meters behind him, followed by a thin woman of about thirty years of age.[8]

Despite the vast judicial arsenal provided by the Scoundrel Laws of 1893, the Sûreté and the Paris police seemed at a technological disadvantage in trying to arrest bandits moving at fairly rapid speeds in automobiles. Gendarmerie posts and most police stations in Paris did not yet have telephones. In 1909, a member of the General Council of the *département* of Seine-et-Oise had suggested that gendarmerie brigades be equipped with telephones. The state had balked at sharing the cost of Alexander Graham Bell's invention with *départements* and towns. Only nine of the ninety-two gendarmerie brigades in Seine-et-Oise, which then covered a considerable part of the region of Paris beyond the walls of the capital, had phones. Now officials announced that beginning April 1 the central police office in each of the twenty arrondissements of Paris would be equipped with a telephone. The minister of the interior assured legislators that the police of Paris would soon have eight new automobiles that could match those now being stolen by the Bonnot Gang, and that they would be equipped with weapons.

Prefect of Police Lépine demanded funds to pay off informers, whom Guichard sent into action. While the police scrambled, the press criticized them for their failures. They mocked Xavier Guichard's preferred nickname of "*Guichard-Coeur de lion.*"[9] And *L'Humanité* published a poem that poked fun at Guichard and, here, Lépine:

The Ballade of the Fantome Bandits
Lépine, illustrious waster of time.
Ah! What disgrace and what grief,
If in this uncertain chase,
Guichard arrives dead last!
It's you, the most famous captain!
But where are Bonnot and Garnier?[10]

The police seemed inadequately organized, and they lacked coordination between sectors. Police offices, despite the recent call for funds to back the Bonnot investigations, were strapped for cash. Salaries for policemen remained low, even as the cost of living continued to rise. Agents earned between six and twelve francs per day. On one occasion, seemingly reliable information had two suspects dining in a Montmartre restaurant. Two police agents were sent there, but they did not have the twelve to fifteen francs necessary to order lunch there so that they could better observe their prey. While they stood outside, the suspects slipped out of the eatery by another door.[11]

Following his flirtation with the young Russian woman in Brussels when he and Victor Kibaltchiche were inseparable friends, Raymond Callemin had come to believe that falling in love was incompatible with true anarchism and, if anything, he had become a misogynist.[12] But now Raymond had become infatuated with Louise Dieudonné, and they were staying together with Pierre Jourdan on rue de la Tour-d'Auvergne in a *quartier populaire* in the ninth arrondissement, just below Montmartre. Jourdan, who had a sizable police record, now sold textiles for furniture in markets in the Paris region, notably that of Levallois-Perret three days a week. He knew many anarchists in and around Paris, probably including Carouy and Simentoff. The director of the market in Neuilly told the police that Jourdan was honest but that "the old redhead" who accompanied him "would not inspire me with confidence."[13]

The "old redhead" was Louise Clément, born in Marseille and formerly married to someone called Hutteaux. She was considerably older than Jourdan, who sometimes introduced her as his mother.

Louise Clément Hutteaux was a former midwife who had given up her profession because she could not bear bringing babies into such an unjust world. She accompanied her lover Jourdan as he sold cloth at markets in the near suburbs. Although he had paid the rent for one lodging, they had been booted out because people kept coming and going, disturbing other residents.

While living with Jourdan, Raymond and Louise Dieudonné went on walks and attended several classical music concerts. One day they realized that they were being followed. Louise assured Raymond that the man was too well dressed to be a policeman, suggesting that it might be one of her former lovers. Callemin relaxed. The man, wearing his ever-present glasses and with his rose-colored young face, "gave the impression of a friendly tourist out for a stroll."

On April 6, undercover police followed Louise Clément Hutteaux from a bar on boulevard Saint-Michel to the place where she and Jourdan lived in Montmartre. The concierge said that the couple had come there recently and announced that their profession was in sales and they traveled frequently. The police showed the concierge photos of Bonnot, Garnier, Valet, and Callemin, and she recognized Raymond *la Science,* who had been staying there for a fortnight. Waiting for the right moment to make their move, the police continued to watch the building.[14]

The next morning, April 7, Raymond *la Science* was arrested as he was carrying a bicycle down the stairs. He resisted, but he had no time to use the two loaded Browning pistols in his pocket. When asked why he was carrying loaded pistols, Raymond retorted with his usual cynicism, "The streets are not very safe!" Taken to jail, he recognized the man who had been following him the evening before. He asked a guard about him. It was Jouin. Callemin told the police, "It is too bad that you took me by surprise before my pistols had the chance to speak!"[15]

A search of that apartment turned up a tan leather suitcase that Jourdan claimed belonged to a friend. Another suitcase, which Louise Clément Hutteaux had purchased for Callemin at Bon Marché on April 4 and which contained clothes for him, had been seized at Gare Saint-Lazare. Jourdan said Callemin had given him the revolver, although it seemed more likely that it was the other way around. Indeed, the Browning pistol had been sold to Jourdan the previous January 21 for eighty-five francs. A gray overcoat was also there, seemingly belonging to Callemin "because of his small size."[16]

The arrest of Raymond "*la Science*" Callemin.

Interrogated by the *juge d'instruction* Gilbert, Callemin claimed not to have been at Montgeron, and he refused to say where he had been on the day of the now-famous holdup on rue Ordener. Gilbert insisted that he clearly had participated in both attacks. Raymond sarcastically retorted, "I observe that you admirably make deductions!" He refused to say where he had bought his pistol, and he explained the sizable sum he had been carrying as having been won at the racetrack. Callemin denied knowing Garnier, Bonnot, or Valet—he claimed to know only Carouy. When Gilbert returned to the subject of Montgeron and Chantilly, informing Callemin that Marie *la Belge (femme* Schoofs) had related that her lover Garnier had placed Raymond in both places, Callemin replied, "I have nothing to respond to the calumnies of a woman paid to denounce me!"[17]

André Soudy holding a rifle during
the reconstruction of the Bonnot
Gang's holdup of the Société
Générale in Chantilly.

On April 11, *juge d'instruction* Gilbert ordered a confrontation between André Soudy and witnesses present outside the Société Générale in Chantilly who had identified him as *"l'homme à la carabine"* who had shouted *"Caltez, caltez, ou je vous canarde."* The director of the Société Générale's branch formally identified Soudy, who was then given an unloaded rifle and told to repeat *"Caltez, caltez, ou je vous canarde."* Soudy insisted that the banker was in error, but the damage was done.[18] The Parisian press soon knew that he had lived in what *Le Petit Parisien* referred to as the "phalanstery" that *L'Anarchie* had established the past summer in Romainville. Once more, this seemed to link Victor and Rirette to the Bonnot Gang. *Le Matin*, now that all three were in prison, was quick to denounce the Belgian connection, or "Belgian Trio," of Callemin, Carouy, and Victor Kibaltchiche.[19]

Bonnot, Valet, Garnier, and Monier *dit* Simentoff were still at large, but the police were closing in. Still, each burglary or robbery brought assertions in the press that the Bonnot Gang was responsible. In Belgium, the manager of a railroad station, thinking he recognized members of the Bonnot Gang, fired shots in the direction of a group of travelers. The *Titanic* went down in the Atlantic Ocean on the night of April 14, drowning more than fifteen hundred passengers, but the Bonnot Gang stole the headlines.[20]

Chapter 16

ANTOINE GAUZY'S VARIETY STORE

The Corsican anarchist Pierre Cardi, thirty-seven years old, emerged as a person of interest in the search for Jules Bonnot. It was Cardi, of course, who had probably first suggested the Société Générale, located across the street from his old wine shop, as a dandy potential target for a big heist. Cardi had published several articles in *L'Anarchie* and founded "*La Chaîne*," a short-lived newspaper that he claimed to be "the response to the sycophants of bourgeois order, [which is] maintained by the sword, prison, and the guillotine." The infamous "anarchist millionaire" Alfred Pierre Fromentin had subsidized Cardi's store, as he had earlier Cardi's brothel at 46 rue Lamartine, a house purchased by Fromentin.[1]

Cardi had tried to sell some stolen securities, including some of those lifted from the Société Générale in the daring heist, but now needed another source of income. He now lived with his mistress in Alfortville, a suburb southeast of Paris. Invariably wearing a velvet suit, he opened a store selling "novelties" in Alfortville. Pierre Fromentin subsidized the store, paying the 130 francs annual rent. Cardi's wife, meanwhile, washed clothes there.

Cardi seemed a likely person to offer hospitality to Jules Bonnot, whom the police suspected would be running out of possibilities.[2] So on April 17, police followed Cardi from Alfortville to a store on rue de Paris, in the quartier of Petit-Ivry in Ivry-sur-Seine, about five hundred meters beyond the southeastern walls of Paris. The shabby houses that lined the rue de Paris were barely in better shape than the shacks that stood even closer to the fortifications and gate into Paris, where the lowest of prostitutes went about their work ("A girl from the fortifications! That says it all!"). Petty criminals would go out to the edge of Paris to count up their take.[3]

The shabby shop Cardi visited on rue de Paris, the "*Halle populaire d'Ivry—nouveautés et confection—vêtements du travail*" was quite similar to his store in Alfortville. Yet an anonymous letter to the police had signaled the store as suspect. The store offered cheap clothes, ribbons, and other inexpensive items. It was owned by Antoine Gauzy, another anarchist to whom Fromentin had advanced money so that he could start up the business. Thus Gauzy, like Cardi, had been subsidized by the anarchist millionaire.

As police discretely observed the comings and goings of customers and visitors, they recognized Monier *dit* Simentoff, the illegalist who had been at Romainville, suspected of having been involved in burglaries around Paris and in the Gard in the south. Monier had been seen several times in the offices of Lorulot's *L'Idée Libre*, as well as at an anarchist bookstore. Police watched Monier's every move, following him to his mistress's apartment on rue Cloys, which parallels rue Ordener. He had been working at the Halle Populaire and returned to Gauzy's store on April 18. Monier had taken a liking to Marie Besse, a sixteen-year-old who worked in Gauzy's shop and who had worked for six months for Pierre Cardi. The young woman had become influenced by anarchist ideas and had left her family to work for Cardi.

That day, Monier disappeared into the crowds going down the stairs; the police lost track of him. But Jouin knew well that he would return to the Halle Populaire, where he could easily be arrested. Still, his principal goal was to find Jules Bonnot. Police observed Monier as he went to several textile shops on boulevard Sebastopol to order goods for Gauzy's store. He then met up with Cardi at Châtelet, already one of the capital's busiest Métro stations. The police lost track of Monier when he disappeared into the crowds going down the stairs. On April 21, police followed Lorulot, Jeanne Bélardi, and Monier out to Levallois-Perret. There they lost them.[4]

At six in the morning of April 24, Jouin and his agents burst into Monier's room as he slept in a small hotel at 129 boulevard Ménilmontant in Belleville. They were on him before he could grab the Mauser pistol under his pillow or the Browning loaded with eight cartridges by the chimney across from the door. The police found letters Monier was writing Cardi, a military record book (*livret*) in the name of a printer from Marseille, an electoral card of a resident of Levallois-Perret, a hundred francs, and also a sweet note Marie Besse had written him. When police asked for Monier's identity card, he refused, but added that if they were arresting him, they must surely know who he was. And they did.[5]

Something the police found in Monier's room when he was arrested suggested that Jules Bonnot might well be staying above anarchist Antoine Gauzy's store.[6] The police had done their homework on Gauzy.

The anarchist Antoine Gauzy was small, thirty-four years old, and had been born in Nîmes, the accent of which he retained. His father was employed by the town hall. In 1902 Gauzy had married Anna Uni, seven years younger, known as Nelly, whom he had met in their hometown and who shared his anarchist convictions. The couple then moved to Paris, where Gauzy worked delivering barrels of wine for a wholesale merchant in Charenton. His boss there had no complaints about him. Gauzy then found work in a foundry, but with four to five hundred workers there, no one remembered him and his foreman had recently passed away. Someone at the company told the police that it was quite possible that he might have been injured at work and thus left, "because in this industry there are injuries almost every day." Then Gauzy took a job in a yeast factory in Maisons-Alfort, earning seven and a half francs a day until there was no more work to be had there. Gauzy then managed in April 1910 to start up the "store of novelties," the Halle Populaire.

Gauzy and his wife lived above the store with their two children—a third had died of meningitis several years earlier—and frequented *causerie populaires* in the fifth and thirteenth arrondissements. Neither had ever been arrested yet police knew that anarchists frequented the store, especially Monier.[7]

When the police questioned Monier about Bonnot and his ties to Gauzy, he refused to provide any information. But it now seemed certain that Jules Bonnot might well be staying above Gauzy's store. The question remained whether Gauzy knew of the identity of his temporary lodger. The police learned that a family of Russian immigrants lived in an apartment above the store, but that they were on vacation. Was the apartment empty?

At 10:15 in the morning April 24, a few hours after they had arrested and questioned Monier, Jouin and the policemen entered Gauzy's store. They came upon Cardi and Gauzy in the back of the store. Gauzy's wife and children were away in Nîmes, where the couple still had family. Jouin showed Gauzy a police photo of Monier *dit* Simentoff and asked if he knew him. Gauzy readily admitted that he worked in the store, but that he had not seen him for eight days, which was clearly not true. They also pulled out a photo of Bonnot. Did Gauzy know him? Not at all, came the reply. Was there someone living in the apartment above? Not at all, he replied. It is empty.[8]

Jouin and two officers, Inspector Colmar and Inspector Prosper Robert, followed Gauzy up to the second floor and unlocked and opened the door of a room. It was indeed empty. They then opened the door to a darkened second room with the curtains drawn.

Suddenly, a man hidden behind the door jumped on Jouin, who, armed only with a cane, grabbed him by the throat. Inspector Colmar tried to help but in struggle the canes of Jouin and inspector Colmar were broken, leaving them without means of defense. Inspector

Prosper Robert pushed away Gauzy, whom he was guarding, and also jumped on their attacker—Jules Bonnot.

The bandit had a Browning and managed to fire five times. Colmar was wounded in the chest, emitting "Adieu, my old friend Robert, it's all over for me" ("*je suis foutu*"). A bullet hit Jouin directly in the head and he fell dead. Bonnot lay motionless on the floor, as if he too was dead. Robert helped Colmar downstairs, and returned in time to see Bonnot jump up and escape through a window, bumping into and threatening a neighbor lady who, hearing the commotion, had stepped onto an exterior landing. Without a weapon, Robert could do nothing but watch as Bonnot jumped onto the roof of a garden shed and down into a courtyard, quickly climbed a wall, and disappeared.

Gauzy made a break for it, but was caught by policemen and struck by people outside, coming close to being lynched by a small crowd that had quickly assembled. The crowd watched as police arrived at

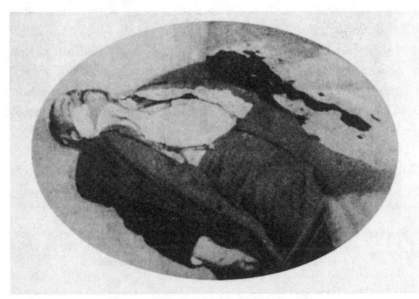

The body of Louis Jouin.

After shooting dead Deputy Security Chief Louis Jouin, Jules Bonnot escapes from the apartment above Antoine Gauzy's variety store.

As he is led to jail, Antoine Gauzy is confronted by a hostile Parisian crowd.

the scene, carted off the gravely wounded Colmar, and collected the body of Jouin. Gauzy was taken in for questioning.

Xavier Guichard was furious and needed answers. Although he later denied it, he struck Gauzy in the face while policemen were holding him in Guichard's office. He warned Gauzy that his store would be closed and his children forced to beg in order to survive, telling him that his wife was pretty enough to be a whore. Gauzy categorically denied knowing that he had lodged Bonnot, falling back on the anarchist insistence on solidarity and the *droit d'asile*. When Gauzy was interrogated, he admitted only that he had met Monier in Nîmes two years earlier "as a propagandist for revolutionary ideas." Some journalists supported him. Anatole France and Octave Mirabeau signed a petition in his favor. Yet others told stories about Antoine Gauzy's store being frequented by "men and women appearing very suspect."[9]

Nelly Gauzy was stopped by the police after returning from Nîmes. Now she learned of what had transpired and the arrest of her husband. Nelly claimed that she did not know under what conditions

Monier had been hired. She also insisted that she had never seen Bonnot and had no idea if her husband knew Cardi and the Besse girl, although she had worked in the store for four or five months.[10]

With no revelations from Gauzy or his wife forthcoming, and a high-ranking officer dead and another wounded, the public wanted answers. Guichard, Gilbert, and other top officials launched a vast police operation and decided that the police officials would carry pistols, not merely canes. After all, as the bandits demonstrated, it was easy enough to get guns in Paris, with virtually no control of their sale. The two break-ins to arms stores had provided the Bonnot Gang with a daunting arsenal.[11]

Le Matin was indignant: "To avenge Louis Jouin: the hunt for anarchists. They are arrested in the morning and go free that very evening. And Bonnot still cannot be found!"[12] Torrents of denunciations poured into police offices, as teams of officers scoured the suburbs of Paris, particularly those offering forests as potential hiding places. Other missives arrived purporting to have been sent by the bandits. One that was nicely written—often not the case—was signed "Bonnot" and informed Guichard that he and his friends were on the Côte d'Azur: "Please forgive me for having left Paris without having notified the police, who are so costly and who serve so little purpose." The author sent along fingerprints, "in place of the flowers of Nice."[13]

Chapter 17

BESIEGED IN CHOISY-LE-ROI

In the wake of the killing of Louis Jouin, Xavier Guichard ordered a flurry of more searches and interrogations in working-class neighborhoods in Paris and its industrial suburbs. Victor Kibaltchiche and Rirette Maîtrejean were among the most prominent of those taken in because they had associated with members of the Bonnot Gang. A number of anarchists who had avoided military conscription were arrested. Searches of the residences of "illegalists" were only modestly fruitful, turning up counterfeit money and items stolen in burglaries—the usual. The crackdown made it less likely that Victor and Rirette, two of the more well-known anarchist intellectuals in prison, would be released. They remained incarcerated.

As for Jules Bonnot, he moved from place to place in Paris and its region, never staying anywhere for more than one night. Those with whom he lodged may or may not have suspected whom they were putting up—the "right to asylum" remained sacred in anarchist circles. More denunciations and letters containing information about possible hiding places for Bonnot and the others arrived in huge quantities at Security headquarters. Almost all were useless. One letter led police to a quiet street in the fourteenth arrondissement where a Russian lived. They showed photos of the suspects to the concierge, who assured them that the man living in the building was not one of them. He was Vladimir Ulyanov, later to become known as Lenin. Yet another letter suggested that the properties of the "anarchist millionaire" Fromentin should be sought in Choisy-le-Roi just south of Paris. Ten years earlier, Fromentin had purchased a large tract of land there and had set up an anarchist colony, constructing small detached houses (*"pavillons"*) that he sold or rented out. The same man who had linked Gauzy and Cardi seemed, once more, to be leading the way toward Bonnot. Anarchists of any persuasion—anarcho-syndicalists, individualists, illegalists, or mere intellectuals—were targets for police and judicial action.[1]

A pharmacist reported that on April 24 a man wearing a raincoat and a melon-shaped hat, a description that could well fit Bonnot himself, had been seen at the garage of Joseph Dubois. Dubois was a Russian-born anarchist to whom Fromentin had also loaned money to start a business, and he knew Bonnot as well. Dubois did not approve of Bonnot's crimes but had vowed to defend him if necessary. Indeed Bonnot and Platano had apparently planned to stay with Dubois after they arrived in the Paris region several months earlier. Platano, of course, never made it. The police had learned that Dubois had sold a car that Bonnot had stolen in Lyon, making him even more suspect.[2]

The pharmacist had treated the wound of a man who corresponded to the descriptions and photos of Bonnot that were everywhere in the press. The man had threatened him with a pistol. Information gathered the same day indicated the presence at the garage of Joseph Dubois.[3]

Early in the morning on Sunday, April 18, Guichard and a number of policemen went to Choisy-le-Roi to interview twenty-four-year-old Juliette Frémont, who worked in a nearby rubber factory. She insisted that she knew nothing of Bonnot or his friends, but she enraged her interrogators by proudly stating that she would be pleased to shelter the bandit. This led to a thorough search of her apartment. Police found nothing the least suspect. A bar next door was also searched, in vain.[4]

The police squad, about twenty men in all, then descended on the Dubois garage, which was surrounded by vacant lots, not far from the Seine.[5] It was a clumsy structure built of cement blocks on the ground floor, a brick second floor, and a roof of red tiles. By that point, Dubois had begun his workday. When the police arrived, he was hunched over the motor of a motorcycle, as a young boy watched with fascination and handed him tools as necessary. Inspector Arlon announced the police presence and Dubois suddenly saw what he was up against. He quickly dried his hands on the back of his workcoat and yelled to the boy to run away.

Dubois retreated into his garage. The police yelled out, "Hands up! Don't shoot! Hands up and we won't hurt you!" Dubois quickly returned with a pistol and began to fire, aiming at the police. He ducked back into the garage when the police fired at him, then stepped out again, firing at the police and lightly wounding Inspector Arlon. Dubois then retreated behind a car in the garage and, having been hit by at least one police bullet, collapsed.

From the second floor, a man wearing dark pants and a white shirt, with one arm wrapped in a bandage, began to fire at the police. He pulled back, and then began shooting again, wounding another policeman amid a barrage of bullets flying in both directions. The police recognized Jules Bonnot. The now famous bandit then began firing from a window, wounding another police inspector.[6]

Bonnot was trapped above the garage; the only access was by the exterior wooden staircase. Guichard, sporting his tricolor sash, called in gendarmes and policemen as reinforcements, having no idea of the number of men and weapons above the garage. He considered asking the army to provide machine guns and maybe some artillery to use against the man firing from the second-floor window, but Guichard already had an imposing armed force at his disposal. Requisitioned tramways brought more official reinforcements.

Republican guards stepped out of taxis. They took up positions in ditches around the garage. Wearing his top hat and carrying a cane, Louis Lépine emerged from his limousine and announced that he would command police operations. The prefect of police was always eager to be photographed.

As news of the drama quickly spread, residents of Choisy-le-Roi hurried to the garage, many armed with aged rifles and pistols as if they were going off to war. Thousands of gawkers came to witness the spectacle on a warm and sunny day, some arriving in cars causing a traffic jam. Couples arrived with small children and babies and picnicked with sausages, bread, and wine. The siege was transforming into a festival. By ten in the morning, at least five thousand people had turned up, held back by policemen. The crowd applauded as police and soldiers fired at the garage. From the building, Bonnot kept on firing back. The mayor of Choisy-le-Roi arrived, resplendent in his tricolor stash, and began to fire his hunting rifle in the general direction of the shooter assumed to be Bonnot. A nearby bar served as headquarters

FIN D'UNE TERREUR — LA TRAGÉDIE DE CHOISY-LE-ROI
La Fusillade

Local residents and others join the siege of Dubois's garage in Choisy-le-Roi.

for the "forces of order." A hundred policemen, a company of *Gardes républicains*, a detachment of gendarmes, a recently formed brigade of police with the goal of combating anarchism, and firemen stood ready. Surrounding the building, they began to fire, riddling the structure. Then the bugles of the firemen called out a ceasefire.

At this point, Guichard decided to blow up the garage with dynamite. The authorities requisitioned a peasant's cart, complete with bales of straw and an attached horse to pull it. A first attempt to move the cart toward the building was greeted with a volley of shots, most absorbed into mattresses that had been arranged on the cart to protect Lieutenant Paul Fortan, a *Garde républicain*, who was pushing it. Fortan lit the fuse for a stick of dynamite at the base of the northwest corner of the garage. Nothing. It did not ignite. Fortan tossed a second stick of dynamite at the house. It exploded, but did little damage. The third time was the charm. Fortan lit a fuse and placed the dynamite against the wall of the garage. A powerful explosion took out some of the western part of the building, which was then enveloped in thick smoke as a fire spread on the roof. Finally, a major assault began on the garage and its residents. The huge throng of onlookers roared its approval.[7]

Guichard, his deputy, his younger brother Paul—who was also a policeman, overseeing the great market of Les Halles[8]—and Lieutenant Fortan charged into the garage. They came upon Dubois's cadaver, his left hand still clutching a pistol with two unused bullets. Then, protected by a mattress they carried in front of them, the assault team went up the outside staircase to the rooms upstairs. Armed with revolvers, they forced open the door to the first room. It was empty. Rushing, albeit cautiously, into the second room, Paul Guichard shouted, "Bonnot is here! He is still alive!" Bonnot's face and body were riddled with bullet wounds. He had rolled himself up in two mattresses.

Bullets littered the floor. Two large Browning pistols were on the floor, along with a smaller revolver. A box of twenty-five cartridges lay under Bonnot's head. In a small container, police found a white chemical that they believed to be potassium cyanide. The bandit

Jules Bonnot, wrapped in a mattress, is mortally
wounded in Choisy-le-Roi.

was still alive and fired at least one more shot, which struck a wall, shouting, "You bunch of bastards!" when he was unable to fire any more. He would die as he had lived, in utter rage and violence. Surrounded by hundreds of police and soldiers, he knew it would end that way.

Policemen carried Bonnot, still barely alive, out of the building, fending off people from the crowd who rushed forward to strike Bonnot, despite the fact that he was obviously gravely wounded. A few people charged into the garage and began to kick Dubois's lifeless body. Bonnot was carried to an ambulance for the trip to the Hôtel Dieu. He died there at 1:15 p.m., with eleven bullets lodged in his body, including three in his head and two in his chest.

After six hours, legions of police and soldiers had managed to finally finish off two men besieged in a garage in a vacant lot. Although some might have noticed that the "forces of order" had used dynamite, the chosen weapon of anarchists Ravachol and Émile Henry two decades earlier, in the end it was guns, not the explosive, that killed Jules Bonnot. As soon as the police had carried Bonnot out, a crowd stormed into the building to nab souvenirs, including Dubois's tools and most anything else they could carry away.[9]

Bonnot left behind a notebook, in which he had written: "I am a famous man. My renown trumpets my name to the four corners of the globe. The publicity awarded to my humble person by the press should make jealous all those who go to so much trouble to have anyone speak of them and who don't manage to pull it off." One might wonder to what extent the publicity generated by the

The crowd moves toward the garage where Bonnot has been mortally wounded. Some would carry away souvenirs to sell or to keep.

mass Parisian press pushed Bonnot to continue his "exploits." He had achieved renown.

Bonnot's note went on: "Should I regret what I have done? Perhaps, but I have to continue and despite any regrets, I will do so . . . I have the right to live. Everybody has the right to live and because your imbecile and criminal society intends to get in my way, too bad for you all."[10]

In his note, Bonnot insisted that his lover Judith Thollon and her husband were not involved in his acts, nor were Antoine Gauzy and Eugène Dieudonné, both of whom were in jail. He ended with "I die." And signed it "Bonnot." He left a small trunk containing various military papers and drivers' licenses, all in other names, as well as a capsule of potassium cyanide.[11]

The press went wild. Newspapers doubled and tripled their normally large print runs in this their golden age. *L'Excelsior* offered four pages of photographic reproductions of the siege, the final assault, and the capture and death of Jules Bonnot. Men and boys selling newspapers in the streets jacked up their prices as the number of copies available diminished. The recent rage for postcard photographs also contributed to the public's fascination with Bonnot's demise. News photos were quickly transformed into postcards for sale, complementing reporting in the press. Even more than before, crimes, and especially bloody crimes, sold big. An increasingly insecure public wanted to know what might be next for them.[12]

Le Matin insisted that Xavier Guichard had himself pumped a bullet into Bonnot's head. The Parisian press, often critical of the police, sanctified the men of Sûreté and the brave Lieutenant Fortan. *L'Excelsior* demanded stronger means of police action and the right-wing, anti-Semitic *La Libre Parole* called for the expulsion of "cosmopolitan anarchists"—Jews—from France. Many of the policemen who participated in the siege asked to be decorated for their efforts and a good many were. They had, after all, helped hundreds of gendarmes and troops overcome two men.[13]

The very first trains of the next morning carried Parisian newspapers and photos into the provinces. "*La Bande Tragique . . . Les*

Assassins de la Rue Ordener, Chantilly, Ivry, Choisy-le-Roi," an "*édition de luxe*," went for sixty centimes and included photos of the body of Dubois and of his garage blowing up.[14]

The bodies of Bonnot and Dubois were tossed into a common grave—the "*Champ de Navets*" ("Field of Turnips")—in Bagneux, just south of Paris. Xavier Guichard and his brother Paul, meanwhile, received gold medals, and Xavier Guichard was decorated with the Legion of Honor eight months later, along with Lieutenant Fortan and inspector Arlon, as well as another of his colleagues. Over the next few days, tens of thousands of residents of the Paris region went out to Choisy-le-Roi to have a look at what was left of the site of Bonnot's last stand. On May 13, an auction of the "historical" items in the garage and house that had not been carried away by the crowd at the end of the siege attracted hundreds of people, some of whom bid on possessions damaged by the fires. They took away boards shattered by bullets and stained with blood as souvenirs. Jules Bonnot's last bed went for five francs, the sheets for six.[15]

The memorial service for Louis Jouin took place on April 29 at Notre-Dame Cathedral. His death at the hands of Jules Bonnot catapulted him from an occasional target of derision into a hero. Théodore Steeg, minister of the interior, saluted Jouin's courage "against terrifying adversaries seeking to panic the popular imagination with the sinister novelty of their organization and their weapons." The president of the municipal council of Paris loudly lamented rampant criminality. The events in Ivry-sur-Seine dramatically increased the collective psychosis as well as the demands for better coordination between the various policing authorities. Commentators insisted that if gendarmes had surrounded Gauzy's store, Jouin would not have been killed. They also decried the fact that the "forces of order" lacked the weapons available to these modern bandits

Louis Lépine's eulogy quickly turned political. The prefect of police reminded those assembled that in five years, thirteen policemen had now been killed in the line of duty. He insisted emphatically that society had the right to defend itself and that the courts did not deal harshly enough with criminals, finding "attenuating circumstances" and excusing crimes because the perpetrators were young "and were just beginning their criminal careers."[16]

Le Matin succeeded in finding and interviewing Sophie Bonnot, who lived in Annemasse on the Swiss border with the son she had born with Jules, whom she had not seen in five years: "Very quickly I knew the torments of betrayal, the revolting brutality of the miserable person to whom I had given myself." She insisted that he never liked work, and that money was his single passion and that he would do anything to have it.[17]

The few dissenting voices could be found in the anarchist and syndicalist papers. In *L'Anarchie* in April 1912, Mauricius, who had been editing the newspaper under the pseudonym "Lionel" since Rirette's arrest, wrote indicating his approval of the crimes of Bonnot and his gang: "Bonnot, with his revolver in his hand, going out to take back bourgeois gold in the saddle-bag of the Société Générale, and defending himself with bullets from his Browning, was an anarchist." He saluted Bonnot's anarchism, depicting him as "alone against an army of cops, soldiers, magistrates and the rabble of *honnêtes gens.*"[18] *La Bataille syndicaliste* adopted the same tone, but with a telling difference: "Bonnot and his acolytes are impatient for social justice. Bonnot is a monster, but what can one say about [Xavier] Guichard?" Mauricius was indicted for apologizing for a crime and sentenced to five years in prison, but the conviction was overturned on appeal. In *La Guerre sociale*, Gustave Hervé wrote the equivalent of a eulogy for Bonnot, saluting his courage as a "wild boar tracked" by the police, who, before being killed, somehow found a way "to kill one of the pack of dogs who were tracking him." The newspaper defended the right to asylum and announced a collection for the families of anarchists arrested in the police round-ups for which the acts of the Bonnot Gang had served as a pretext.[19]

The novelist Léon Bloy was not alone in sarcastically highlighting the "glorious victory of ten thousand against one. The country is in great joy and several bastards will be decorated." Cynics noted that it was the first victory of the French since Austrian troops were defeated at the Battle of Solferino in 1859.[20] At least for some, Bonnot's death transformed him from a vicious bandit into a martyr and a hero.

Chapter 18

SPECTACLE IN NOGENT-SUR-MARNE

On May 14, fifty armed detectives led by Guichard and Lépine headed out to Nogent-sur-Marne where they believed Garnier and Valet might be hiding. The decisive tip possibly could have come from a resident of the eastern suburb, a bank employee who had agreed to convert stolen securities, but who then called the police after recognizing Garnier and Valet. But it is more likely that the information was provided by Alphonse Kinable, who went to the quai des Orfèvres to relate that two suspicious young men and their girlfriends had been living in the "Villa Bonhoure," a house that was considerably less stately than its name would suggest. Kinable thought that the men's hair had been dyed and noticed that they remained inside almost all the time. The woman who did their shopping had a Belgian accent and from police photos he recognized Marie *la Belge*. In the meantime, the earlier presence of Anna Dondon could now be confirmed by nearby residents, but the presence of Valet or Garnier could not.[1]

The house had most recently been a weekend recreation site on the river, near an open-air café, Le Petit Robinson, which had opened in 1906 next to the viaduct stretching across the Marne River for the train heading east to Mulhouse and Bâle. The large park had been subdivided into small properties and paths bordered by hedges. The Villa Bonhoure stood one hundred meters from the river, the closest to the Marne of seven similar houses, and it was isolated by several rows of trees and accessible by several paths. The viaduct towered over the house and its gardens.

Garnier had rented the house on May 4. "A tall, large woman" went out to do the shopping, while the two men were scarcely to be seen, except while exercising in the villa's garden. Another neighbor also identified Marie *la Belge* from police photos. At 3:45 on the afternoon of the day Guichard and his men showed up, a police inspector was interviewing a nearby grocer when the Belgian herself walked into the store. But arresting Marie on the spot would merely have served to tip off Garnier and Valet that the police were on to them. The police had confirmed in the meantime that Anna Dondon, Valet's girlfriend, had been seen there a few days earlier, but now she was in Garches, to the north of Paris.[2]

Inside the villa, Octave Garnier was writing his own account of the now famous holdup on rue Ordener. Garnier was in many ways the real leader of the Bonnot Gang. Although Rirette would describe him as never speaking, he always thought ahead, planning the next coup that would bring the Bonnot Gang the cash they needed. Guichard was bent on finding Garnier, even if it meant organizing another massive police operation just a few weeks after Bonnot's death. He had to catch the man who had sent him the threatening, mocking letter, complete with his fingerprints and a warning.[3]

At about six in the evening, the police surrounded the villa and its gardens, placing agents in the adjoining streets. Several policemen carefully approached the house wearing protective vests and their tricolor sashes. They came upon a woman in a dressing gown standing in the garden. Nearby stood a man who resembled René Valet. The police announced their presence and called out to the woman, whom they recognized as Marie *la Belge*. The man took out a pistol and began to fire in their direction, one bullet striking a police officer's protective verst.

Garnier, who was in the house, began firing at Marie because he believed that she had betrayed them. He hurled insults in her direction as she was taken into police custody: "If they kill you, it will be good for your bones!" The police managed to get her safely out of Garnier's range as an angry crowd of observers gathered beyond the garden to shout at Marie, some calling for her death. The police informed her that she was under arrest and took her to a nearby house. She told them, "I followed Garnier everywhere he went, even though I was terrified of him," even knowing he was a criminal. "I love him," she added simply.[4]

The "forces of order" continued to exchange shots with Garnier and Valet, who fired through the windows while protected by mattresses, sometimes with a pistol in each hand. Bonnot's friends were clearly not about to give up, although besieged by about four hundred armed police, gendarmes, and soldiers. Two sides of the villa were vulnerable to an attack: from the rue du Viaduc and from the garden. There were so many policemen and soldiers firing that it seemed likely that they would shoot each other by accident, particularly because some had climbed up on the railroad viaduct and now were firing down at the house. Police officers dropped huge stones on the roof of the villa, doing little more damage than taking out a few tiles. Lépine, again presiding over a hastily organized headquarters, called for more gendarmes, as well as Zouaves—a light-infantry division whose baggy red pants and open shirts were more suited for their usual service in North Africa—from the nearby fort of Nogent-sur-Marne.[5]

The standoff at the Villa Bonhoure drew an enormous crowd of perhaps as many as twenty thousand people all gathered in the vicinity. Police worked to hold back the crowds pushing forward to see the action up close, as if they would be beholding the Wild Bill Cody Western extravaganza that had recently thrilled Paris and other European capitals. Mothers carried babies in their arms. Hundreds of carriages and taxis on the grand boulevards offered their services for hefty sums to carry the curious out to watch the spectacle. Couples dressed in "smokings" (tailcoats) and evening gowns turned up, some having earlier attended shows in Paris before hearing about the police action, others having just finished a champagne banquet for the seventy-fifth anniversary of a literary association. An improvised restaurant, safely away from the besieged house, soon ran out of sandwiches and beer.[6]

After a meeting of the top authorities present, the commanders of the operation again decided to use dynamite, as they had done at Choisy-le-Roi. Sticks were dropped from the viaduct twice, the first at about 8:00 p.m., but they did little damage. A third stick of dynamite was placed against the house by a courageous soldier, but the explosion yielded no better result. In the meantime, flares of acetylene merely served to provide Garnier and Valet better light with which to see their targets. The siege risked turning into a humiliating fiasco.

Finally the commanders ordered four sticks of the powerful explosive melinite from the nearby forts of Rosny and Vincennes. They also requested two machine guns from Vincennes, but those never arrived. Before long, a car drove up carrying one hundred sticks of the explosive. Following a brief ceasefire at about 1:45 in the morning, the melinite was used and did its job, creating a breach in the villa's walls. Garnier and Valet continued to fire. A policeman and an inspector from Security entered the garden, wearing shields that offered some protection, but not enough. The inspector fell wounded. The garden was now "full of imprudent shooters." An officer outside apparently inexplicably yelled for a ceasefire. Another officer shouted, "You ordered a cease-fire and I see them there in the room." The officer outside yelled back "Very well! Then move in!"

About twenty policemen and Zouaves poured into the villa through the garden at about 2:15 a.m. Thick black smoke provided protection for the attackers. Garnier and Valet, both shirtless and wounded but still alive, continued to fire from behind mattresses at the approaching policemen and soldiers. A corporal, "with the butt of his rifle," and policeman Paul Guillebaud finished them off, although it's possible Garnier ended his own life, despite the policeman's claims. Valet, following Garnier to the very end, fell mortally wounded, his head riddled with police bullets. He died after being carried into the courtyard. It was 3 a.m. when the fighting finally stopped.[7]

In Nogent-sur-Marne, as in Choisy-le-Roi, the crowd, so pleased to have observed a real-life battle, raced into what remained of the villa to grab souvenirs, encumbering the police as they attempted to carry Garnier and Valet out of the house. Two sheets were found to cover the bodies. Eight hundred fifty francs had fallen from Garnier's wallet. Garnier and Valet left behind a considerable cache of weapons, as well as some recently burned letters. Dry vegetables, pasta, macaroni, and the formerly forbidden coffee were on a shelf. A peddler sold macaroni, now quite toasted by the fire, advertised as the last meal of the bandits. The next day, the bodies of Garnier and Valet were tossed into a common grave in Bagneux.[8]

Octave Garnier, as Jules Bonnot before him, left sort of a "testament" behind: "Let's reflect: our women and children are piled into hovels while thousands of villas remain empty. We build palaces and we live in miserable dumps." He called on all workers to develop their intelligence and their strength: "You are a sheep, the cops are the dogs, and the bourgeois, the shepherds. Our blood pays

The crowd engulfs the Villa Bonhoure in Nogent-sur-Marne where Octave Garnier and René Valet have been shot dead.

for the luxury of the wealthy. Our enemy is the master. Long live anarchy!"[9]

Unlike the siege at Choisy-le-Roi, the "victory" of the "forces of order" after a siege that lasted nine hours failed to draw the enthusiasm of most of the big Parisian newspapers. Seven hundred policemen, gendarmes, and Zouaves had fought against two men amid confusion and shots fired in every conceivable direction. Two of the three policemen wounded had been hit by bullets fired by Zouaves from the viaduct above the villa. A police inspector was wounded by a rifle shot—yet Garnier and Valet had only revolvers. With the modern military technology at the disposal of the police, the results seemed almost laughable. Would this transform Garnier and Valet into martyrs? Guichard found himself on the defensive, arguing strenuously that the vast majority of troops and police—four hundred Zouaves and police officers—who had been sent to Nogent-sur-Marne were there to keep the crowds in line and maintain order vis à vis the civilians, not the bandits.[10]

The one-sided sieges in both Choisy-le-Roi and Nogent-sur-Marne played a role in bringing about greater centralization and coordination between branches of the police. They could not afford another episode in which gendarmes, the Republican Guard, municipal police, and soldiers were all involved in what was invariably described as another example of "tactical bricolage" and an "indescribable chaos."[11]

Thus one of the results of the Bonnot Gang's string of robberies and the virtual obsession they generated in and around Paris was greater coordination within Security, as well as an enhanced role for the gendarmerie.[12] In addition to this "Sacred Union" organized between branches of the police, the number of policemen increased dramatically. In 1911 there were 531 men working in Security, by the end of 1912 there were 650, and two years later 738, with its budget considerably augmented. Under the leadership of Célestin Hennion, who succeeded Lépine as prefect of police and who had earned his reputation as a professional policeman who had reorganized Security, the Parisian police became more efficient and more powerful.[13]

The Bonnot Gang, now that it had been defeated, generated a modicum of public sympathy. Like Victor and Rirette, other intellectuals as well as more ordinary people may have rejected the bloody crimes and loss of life, but they also placed these events into the context of a society marked by incredibly glaring social inequalities, the sheer arrogance of the wealthy and privileged, and the power of the state and its police, even if at times the police had looked rather bumbling in the process of taking down the Bonnot Gang. By the end of the Bonnot affair, some fifteen hundred people had been subject to searches and interrogations, which had begun in May 1912, including men whose only crime was operating a garage.

L'Anarchie, for its part, continued to find excuses for the bandits: "Misery rules everywhere . . . What is astonishing about these men—the so-called 'bandits'—battling with a massive organization which is every single day trying to annihilate them . . . All along these tragic events, can one deny the energy displayed by those who are being called bandits?" The viability of "illegalism" was still being hotly debated in *L'Anarchie'*s pages, sometimes depending on who was writing. On September 5, 1912, an editorial noted, "The bourgeoisie assumes the right to theft . . . why cannot it be ours as well?" Yet in the same newspaper, Émile Armand now suggested that one could not have imagined how "illegalism could end up there." Individualism had led to an impasse.[14]

Jean Jaurès's *L'Humanité* was not at all for the bandits, but could not help commenting, "One must affirm and repeat, the police authorities became engaged in an abominable and bloody parade, which never lacked the ridiculous and impotence."[15]

La Guerre sociale equated the Bonnot Gang, for whom the newspaper had no sympathy—at least for their crimes—with "the robbers and murderers of Morocco." Yet the anarchist journalist Victor Méric saluted Garnier and Valet, "[the] prodigious vanquished . . . By your origins, you are ours . . . For the crowd, you are bandits. For us, you are victims." Méric condemned the crimes of the bandits while recognizing the atrocious social conditions which he viewed as being in part responsible: "Garnier, Valet . . . [Yet] you have not understood that the battle has to continue against the conservative forces of ignorance, methodically, in the general interest, towards a common goal, the end of the servitude of the people."[16]

Hundreds of letters, some signed, many not, arrived at the prefecture of police or in Xavier Guichard's office. These letters expressed support for the bandits and, above all, hatred for the police. One simply stated, "Garnier will be avenged." Another, sent to the commissariat of the twentieth arrondissement, read, "Bonnot, Garnier, Valet . . . all our comrades are still good citizens . . . Long live Garnier, Long live Bonnot, Long live Ravachole [sic]." Another, "Filthy cop . . . We have decided to kill you. Watch out! Your days are numbered."[17] One to Guichard read, "You are a coward of a bastard" for having killed "a poor man who was also the father of a family . . . Bonnot." The letter warned, "we are going to take care of you!" It was signed, "the avengers of Bonnot, Garnier, Valet and their consorts."[18]

In September, another killing by an anarchist illegalist helped keep the seeming threat of violence in the news. Perhaps illegalism was not finished off. On September 12, near the train station of Les Aubrais just outside Orléans, a certain Lacombe, known as "Léontou," or by some as "the Dog," killed a railway policeman, escaping on the policeman's bicycle. Lacombe then murdered a post office official in Bezons during a holdup. The preceding January he had stayed with a Swiss anarchist named Erlebach—who was then going by the name Ducret—on the passage Clichy, where, in a rented store, the latter had sold copies of *L'Anarchie*. Erlebach had also certainly lodged Garnier and Marie *la Belge*. Erlebach knew that the police were looking for Lacombe and probably denounced him to the police. And so Lacombe shot Erlebach dead on December 7. Arrested on March 11, Lacombe jumped to his death in the prison of La Santé. Another incident at the prison on January 13 made the headlines and reinforced fears of survivors of the Bonnot Gang. A prisoner managed to get into the room of an absent guard and put on his uniform before being stopped. He had with him a list of the numbers of the cells of Callemin, Soudy, Monier, and Carouy. Could an insidious escape place the survivors of the Bonnot Gang back on the boulevards of Paris?[19]

PART THREE

Chapter 19

ON TRIAL

Bonnot, Garnier, and Valet were dead. The long-awaited trial of the twenty remaining accused slowly approached in early February 1913, nearly ten months after the death of Garnier and Valet in Nogent-sur-Marne. Rirette was transferred with the other defendants to the Conciergerie, the tiny cells of which were beneath the Palais de Justice on the Île de la Cité. There were nuns there, too, but unlike at Saint-Lazare prison they did not serve as guards. Real prison guards searched prisoners morning and night. A bare light bulb hanging from the ceiling made sleep extremely difficult, as did the opening and shutting of the little window in the cell door every ten minutes or so, so a guard could peek in. Republican guards escorted the prisoners up narrow stairs to a lateral door that led into the grand courtroom at the Palais de Justice, the scene of so many famous trials in the City of Light, with its polished wooden walls, rows of seats, and large chandeliers hanging from the ceiling.

Juge d'instruction Maurice Gilbert began his interrogations on February 3. Marie *la Belge* calmly related that Garnier and Bonnot had been involved in all the incidents, noting the tensions between them. She stated flatly that Garnier had shot the courier Caby on rue Ordener and had killed the policeman (also named Garnier) at place du Havre. She placed Valet at Montgeron and Chantilly, but Marie said she did not know more than that and was unsure about Dieudonné's involvement in any of this, but repeated that he had not gunned down Caby. Marie explained that following the death of Bonnot, Garnier and Valet had watched her closely, fearing that she might talk. Marie said that she had asked Garnier about the packages he had left in his mother's apartment and that he had snarled that it was "not the business of women. . . . You have what you need, thus my business is none of yours." When he had left, she looked in the packages and had seen the burglary tools. Garnier had warned Marie not to talk to the concierge and to speak in only a low voice with "Julien" and with the younger comrade. She told the *juge d'instruction* that she had feared Garnier and that he had predicted he would soon be dead and Marie would be arrested. She claimed rather disingenuously that she had not believed Garnier to be guilty and had remained with him out of love and pity until the police surrounded the villa in Nogent-sur-Marne.[1]

André Soudy was next in line. When being interrogated, he denied being "*l'homme à la carabine.*" He said he had an alibi, but that he would not use it for fear that it would lead to his being prosecuted for another crime. But he had no fear of the scaffold, he insisted—he would prefer death to prison. Why did he have two revolvers when arrested? Because he had decided to defend himself to avoid arrest. And the 980 francs in his possession? The product of a theft.[2]

No evidence or testimony placed Carouy on the rue Ordener at the time of the holdup of the Société Générale courier, nor in the car when the policeman was killed at place du Havre. However, fingerprints taken of the murder victims in Thiais suggested that Carouy had been present in Thiais when the two elderly people had been slaughtered. A print of one of Metge's palms had been found there, as well. Indeed, police had found jewelry taken from the house at the residence of Barbe Le Clerch, Metge's girlfriend. Moreover, a woman testified that Metge and Carouy were the two men who asked how to get to their destination in Thiais, and that she heard Carouy lament the fact that it was broad daylight, or they might have robbed the woman, who might have been carrying funds from the

Singer Sewing Machine Company, where she worked. Indeed, she identified the two men when confronted with them, despite their dyed hair. Callemin also had dyed his hair, but when questioned on June 3 as to why, he replied that it was for his "personal satisfaction." He denied being at Montgeron or Chantilly as Marie *la Belge* had claimed, improbably replying that he had won the money found in his possession at the racetrack.[3]

The prosecution lumped Victor Kibaltchiche and Rirette Maître-jean together with the Bonnot Gang, particularly during the inter-rogation of Callemin. Neither Victor nor Rirette had had anything to do with the gang's misdeeds, and they were now well known for their opposition to illegalism. But they were anarchists—and for the prosecution, for the police, that was enough. Victor stood accused of approving of the crimes of the Bonnot Gang, and of serving as an "ideologue," pushing the gang members toward crime. In the political climate of 1912, it was easy to accuse Victor and Rirette of being part of a highly organized *association des malfaiteurs*, however little evidence existed to prove the claim. The indictment, commu-nicated to the press on November 25, 1912, insisted that the Bonnot Gang was an organized band, whereas as Rirette noted in retrospect, "what the band most lacked was precisely organization!"[4]

As the trial approached, Victor expressed hope that this "imbe-cilic and undeserved nightmare" would soon end. He and Rirette agreed perfectly about the lines of their defense. In particular, Victor believed that the courtroom would not be the place for him to speak against illegalism. If the prosecution tried to link him to crimes "that I find repugnant," he would have to explain himself, but he would do so carefully in a way to prevent the prosecution from turning his words against other defendants. He would refuse, no matter what, "to become an informer."

In *L'Anarchie*, Victor, the so-called "ideologue" of the Bonnot Gang, had done no more than insist that "the bandits are the conse-quences of causes well beyond them," while recognizing "the legit-imacy of all revolt." Victor still found it difficult to imagine how former comrades could have carried out "the butchery of Thiais." He would limit himself "to prove that I never encouraged nor was ever partisan of this theory." He began to second-guess himself: if at some point he had been "more firm," would his old friend Valet still be alive and "poor Soudy free. I only lacked combativity."[5]

The trial began on February 3, 1913, in the Palais de Justice in Paris. Along with lawyers and policemen out of uniform, there were highly placed personages with connections—even some ladies from high society, dressed as for a Parisian show, sat in the audience. The twelve jurors seemed on the elderly side, a variety of shapes and appearances.

There would be twenty-one sessions. The prosecutor, Attorney General Joseph Fabre, presented thirty-one different allegedly criminal affairs. Twenty people were accused of participation in an *association des malfaiteurs*. Barbe Le Clerch, who had been arrested on October 25 with 975 francs in cash and some items taken in the burglary in Pavillons-sous-Bois, and Marie *la Belge* stood accused of complicity in theft. Fifteen lawyers would defend the accused. Fabre was resplendent in his bright red robe with fur trim, leading Rirette to admire "without reservation the majesty of his appearance" and his "sober and cool elegance." Rirette had the impression of standing helplessly before "an amazing force, prodigious, against which the paltry theories of illegalism could never prevail." Victor was less impressed by the bench, "composed of short or fat old men, drowsy or nearsighted." The court president, whose role was to interrogate the accused, referred reverentially to "society" as he stood before this group of anarchists who did not accept its laws. He began by insisting that this was not a political trial, but rather one considering serious crimes. Yet inevitably the presiding magistrate admitted that during the trial it would be impossible, given the circumstances, not to consider the doctrine of anarchism.[6]

The twenty men and women accused stood and then sat in the dock. Charges included murder, armed robbery, assault and battery or grievous bodily harm, theft and possession of firearms, being part of an *association des malfaiteurs*, or assisting in criminal acts. Some seven hundred pieces of evidence were displayed on tables, including suitcases, burglary tools, and, safely within a glass case, rifles and Browning pistols. During the month-long trial, 239 witnesses testified. Some related the most improbable tales, contradicting one another, reflecting pressure from the police, as had happened during previous testimony before the investigating magistrate.[7]

L'Anarchie—which proclaimed in February that the "only crime is to judge!"—provocatively listed the names and occupations of the forty jurors initially convoked and then the twelve jurors ultimately selected to decide the fate of the accused, potentially putting them at risk. Of the twelve jurors and two alternates, there was not a single worker. A notary's clerk, a clerk for a stockbroker, and another white-collar worker would certainly feel a bit out of place among men of means, including, appropriately, an automobile manufacturer.[8]

As the trial began, *L'Anarchie* once again defended the bandits, who had been "brought up in misery" without "the care of a family." How could one be surprised that they revolted against society in a country in which "misery grows each day"? Ordinary workers, who earned so little money when they could find jobs, could only watch as "their masters live in sumptuous palaces and the bourgeois class revels in gold and joy. They see millions and hundreds of millions pile into the safes of financiers, industrialists, politicians, and speculators."[9]

The Parisian dailies feasted on the proceedings. A prominent lawyer was scathing about the role of journalists, who provided all possible information not only on the accused but also on the lawyers for the defense. The press had become a "supplementary and extra-legal but overwhelming and imposing judge." The Parisian press covered the trial, reporting what had occurred, based on the accounts of those actually in the courtroom—but with a strong bias against the anarchists, whom they believed threatened society. Coverage of the trial dramatically increased the number of copies of each edition published, as readers impatiently awaited details of what was transpiring in the courtroom.[10]

Rirette was the first summoned to face judge and jury, which suggested that she was the leader of the band. Dressed in a black smock with a high collar and with her hair cut short, she appeared severe, described in one of the thirty or so newspapers closely covering the trial as "a schoolgirl, lively and mischievous, holding her notes in her hands, with a notebook for her homework, and at the end of her fingers a small pencil on which she gnawed the lead." Rirette's calm and reasonable replies to questioning during the trial impressed even hostile onlookers. She later recounted having the impression of being in "sort of a fog that prevented me from seeing the court and [making] out the jurors." Her voice seemed to her "distant, strangled, strange. I had an incredible difficulty swallowing."

Rirette rejected the prosecution's attempt to present her as one of the leaders of the Bonnot Gang by virtue of her legal capacity as managing director of *L'Anarchie*. As she explained, someone had to have that legal status in order for the newspaper to publish. She was simply a "comrade," like all the others who worked on the newspaper, and she insisted that the newspaper provided a means of bringing together men and women who wanted to study and learn. Certainly, the anarchist newspaper condemned social inequalities and bourgeois morality, she allowed, but it had never incited anyone to crimes and murder. Rirette denied that she had benefited from thefts committed by illegalists. The proof was that they had remained poor and had never had enough to eat. They had always lived honestly. Neither she nor Victor had stolen stamps from post offices, even if they had used them to send out their newspaper. When asked about stolen identity and military papers found in the offices, she explained that they had been left by comrades, but that "[anarchists] never ask a comrade his name or where he is from." And what about the two revolvers police found in their apartment? "I am not a thief!" Rirette sharply replied. She had no way of knowing that the weapons had been stolen by another anarchist.[11]

Rirette made clear that she had not asked Garnier, Valet, or de Boe to come to Romainville. Indeed, they were already living there when she and Victor arrived. When the court president asked her about earlier crimes allegedly committed by Callemin, Soudy, and Carouy, Rirette insisted, again, that it was part of the culture—indeed, the morality—of anarchism that one never asked newly arrived comrades to discuss their lives. Anarchists came and went. After Rirette testified and returned to the benches reserved for the defendants, Raymond Callemin assured her that she had done very well. Even the hostile royalist *Action Française* newspaper admitted that Rirette had defended herself "with considerable strength."[12]

Victor, the second to face judge and jury, wore the shirt of a Russian peasant for the trial. He spoke easily, softly, and clearly, with "a vocabulary even better than proper." The court president began his interrogation by stating, "You appear to have never been previously convicted." The defendant replied, "I don't just appear to have never been! I have never been convicted." Like Rirette, he rejected the idea that he and *L'Anarchie* were in any way responsible for the crimes committed by the illegalists. He stated, clearly and unequivocally, "You are confusing Madame Maîtrejean and me with comrades who do not share our ideas. . . . You refuse to distinguish between *L'Anarchie* of Romainville and that of rue Fessart." He insisted, "Between those who are sitting on the [courtroom] bench and us, there are enormous differences. Rirette Maîtrejean and I, we are neither criminals nor thieves." None of the illegalists at Romainville had gone with them to rue Fessart. Most of the crimes, Victor reminded the jury, had occurred when he was already in jail. He found himself on trial, he argued, because "I am an anarchist."[13]

Speaking calmly and with composure as always, Victor made clear that he had indeed been friends with Callemin, Carouy, and de Boe, but they had gone their separate ways because of their ideological differences. He insisted that most anarchists were not illegalists. Moreover, Victor, like Rirette, was not the director of *L'Anarchie*; there was no real director—everyone was a comrade. The anarchist intellectual Sébastien Faure spoke in defense of Victor and Rirette, providing a brief history of anarchism and making clear that the very term *anarchism* glossed over absolutely significant differences between anarchists, making preposterous the term *association des malfaiteurs* used by the prosecution. As the first day of the sensational trial came to a close, most journalists concluded that Victor would be acquitted.[14]

Eugène Dieudonné came next, on the second day of the trial. He defended himself awkwardly, particularly when asked if his separation from his spouse Louise was mutual. Although she had run off with Lorulot, he tried to explain, they had remained on good terms. Any attempt to prevent her from leaving would have run counter to his "social ideas." "What morals!" interjected the court president, shocked at such an affirmation. Dieudonné admitted having received a telegram from Raymond *la Science* on December 19 while in Nancy, telling him to come to Paris immediately. Yet Dieudonné insisted that this missive was related to his attempt to work out a reconciliation with his wife. He asserted that he was not an illegalist and was appalled by Bonnot's acts. Moreover, he claimed that he had never met Garnier, despite the fact that his name turned up in the latter's notebook, nor had he met Bonnot. He told the court that it was a coincidence that he took a room on rue Nollet just after Bonnot had departed. As for the surgeon's tool kit, it had been left by a comrade whose name he would not reveal.

Dieudonné made a point of not invoking any other anarchists, for fear of compromising them. It was like that in the anarchist world. He had been "an anarchist, as one is Christian, Jewish, or Muslim."

After denying the assertion of witnesses that he had been in Arnay-le-Duc, he also rejected the idea that he had ended up with a stolen bicycle. Where did he get it? Again, he refused to give the name of the comrade who had given it to him. To the court president's scathing comment, "Too bad for you," Dieudonné's attorney replied, "A man has the right to say, 'I don't want to hand over another.' That in itself is beautiful."

The most serious charge against Dieudonné was that he had shot the courier Ernest Caby as he approached the Société Générale branch on rue Ordener. Victor realized that witnesses had confused Dieudonné with someone else because of "a resemblance between his dark eyes and another pair of eyes, still darker, which were in the graveyard"—Octave Garnier.[15] Several people from Nancy testified to Dieudonné's presence in that Lorraine town on the day of the now-famous holdup and getaway. The court president attempted to undercut such testimonies that Dieudonné had been in Nancy that day by dismissing one of the witnesses as an anarchist. That Dieudonné clearly was right-handed, not left-handed, posed a problem for the prosecution. One of Dieudonné's former employers testified that he could not loan his own tools to Eugène because he—the boss—was left-handed. Dieudonné found himself facing Caby in the courtroom. Again, Caby insisted that it was Dieudonné who had shot him on December 21—although from a police photo on an earlier occasion the courier had identified Garnier as having wielded the pistol and almost killed him. And when the court president reminded Caby that what he said could cost the head of a man, he again swore that Dieudonné had shot him. Peemans, the other employee of Société Générale who had gone out to meet Caby, also insisted that Dieudonné had fired the Browning.[16]

Callemin followed Dieudonné on day two of the trial. The charges against Raymond *la Science* were the most serious, including several murders. He had been identified by two witnesses—but others had their doubts—at Montgeron. Callemin answered the questions with sarcasm, occasionally scribbling notes on a pad. He sneered when the clerk read from the indictment a witness's testimony that he had "the look of a rosy baby." Callemin told the court president that the magistrate was carrying out his duties "in bad faith," and at one point he interrupted to say that his interrogator was "monologuing." He would reply to his questions only when he felt like it. What did he do upon first arriving in Paris? Well, he worked. Where? He would rather not say. He repeated the assertion he had made when he was first questioned: the money he was spending had been won at the racetrack. As for the guns found in his possession when he was arrested, well, he needed them for a counterfeiting job. Rirette watched as "he got all tangled up in his sentences, became confused about dates, and in the end just mumbled." In the end, Callemin denied all the accusations against him. When the judge asked if he had an alibi for March 25, 1912, the day of the events in Montgeron and Chantilly, he scoffed and replied, "I don't keep a datebook." Comparing Callemin's performance to that of Dieudonné, *Le Petit Parisien* assessed that, "Callemin was without question the most mediocre. . . . He wanted to be ironic, insolent, but soon he realized that it was not working . . . far from showing himself to be brilliant, he was only ridiculous."[17]

When Callemin faced the court for the second time, the judge again asked if his name was Raymond Callemin. Raymond *la Science* replied that he had not changed his name since the previous day. At one point, he told the court that after being accused of one crime after another, he had written the investigating magistrate, "As you seem to take quite seriously . . . despite my assertions—[my role in] the murder of Charlemagne, I want to announce to you that I strangled Louis XVI with my own hands."[18]

Three guards testified that they had heard Raymond *la Science* admit to several of the crimes of which he stood accused. He had even assured the guards that because the robbery on the rue Ordener had not brought in enough money, they had to "do" Chantilly. He now claimed to have been kidding when he bragged about his responsibility for various crimes, although he admitted telling the guards that his head was now worth one hundred thousand francs, the reward offered by Société Générale, but that each of theirs had a value of seven centimes, the price of a bullet. A guard standing outside Callemin's cell declared that he needed only one revolver to defend himself, to which Callemin had boasted, "Unlike me you have not used hundreds of cartridges to get to know Browning pistols." He also told a guard, presumably the same one, that after the coup of the rue Ordener, the bandits had decided that if ever they were on the verge of arrest, they would enter a shop and defy a siege. That was why they carried so many guns and bullets. He had apparently added that the coups at Montegeron and Chantilly had been acts of desperation, although he had formally denied being involved in these two events.[19]

When interrogated by the court president, *Pas-de-Chance* Soudy denied any participation in the murders in Montgeron and Chantilly. And he rejected the right of the court to judge him at all, while denying the assertions of witnesses that he had been the now-infamous *"l'homme à carabine"*—a man described as tall with a narrow, pale face and wearing a big coat that reached the tops of his shoes—who had fired his gun during the holdup at Chantilly in order to keep onlookers away. Some witnesses claimed that it was not the very thin Soudy who held a rifle, but rather someone much heavier. Marie *la Belge* told the president of the court that her lover Garnier had insisted it was Soudy who had carried the rifle. Soudy's response was that her lawyer had put her up to saying that. Where did he get the 980 francs found in his pocket when arrested? From a theft, came the obvious answer. Why did he have pistols in his possession when arrested? To defend himself against arrest: "Banned from France, I decided to defend myself to the end." Had he not been surprised by the police when taken, there would have been one more cadaver "because I have had it with spending my life in prisons and hospitals."

Soudy described, rather incoherently, his disadvantaged childhood and adolescence. He defended individualism and illegalism, adding, "If I had been given a situation compatible with my tastes, I would not have been reduced to illegalism." After contracting tuberculosis upon being released from prison, he told the court, he had turned to illegalism in order to survive. To the end, Soudy remained childlike, someone who could not say no when a comrade requested something of him, even if it led him to meet *"La Veuve"* ("The Widow"), the guillotine.[20]

When Monier *dit* Simentoff took the stand, the court president made a point of calling out the "bad company" he kept, in that one of his friends had been guillotined a week earlier in Vincennes. Monier replied, "It's true! Not everyone can hang out with investigating magistrates." He claimed that the telegram he had sent Dieudonné on February 28 ("This evening Mama's health is very good") referred to the fact that he had taken a train without a ticket and had arrived without any problem. That witnesses, including the wounded mechanic in the former attack, unanimously placed him at Montgeron and at Chantilly left Monier without much hope for an acquittal, despite his denials. In the end, he would admit only to having stayed with Antoine Gauzy before Bonnot arrived.[21]

Carouy, more effective than the others, vigorously denied being involved in any way in the murders in Thiais. He had been identified as being there by a woman to whom the police presented but one photo—Carouy's—and he added that given his prominent nose, it was unthinkable that she had not made note of that. When asked why he had stopped working in Paris in July 1911, Carouy replied, reasonably enough, that as an anarchist, he could not find any work. Why had he gone under the name of Maury? It sounded more French than Carouy, he explained, and he had used it in an effort "to make myself more French. I love France very much!" This brought laughter to the solemn court.

Carouy's lawyer insisted that Bertillon could be wrong in claiming that Carouy's prints were on the armoire in the house in Thiais where the double murder had been committed; he reminded the court that Bertillon had been disqualified as a reliable witness during the Dreyfus Affair in 1894 because he had been unable to identify the *bordereau* (the sheet of paper containing detailed military secrets, the discovery of which had led to the Jewish captain's arrest). The evermore-famous Bertillon, who later testified, modestly admitted that the chance he could have misidentified the fingerprints was about "one in two billion." Carouy had evoked the uncertainty of science, but not convincingly. At the end of his interrogation and testimony, Carouy seemed a beaten man.[22]

Metge, accused of involvement in the theft of the car used on rue Ordener, also denied participation in the savage murders of the two elderly people. He admitted to only one burglary, that in Pavillon-sous-Bois, and to giving thirteen hundred francs and some earrings to his Barbe Le Clerch. His explanation was that "a friend" had given him that amount. Who? He refused to say. He insisted that the weapons, burglary tools, and stolen tools found in the residence in Garches belonged to Valet.[23]

Antoine Gauzy claimed he knew nothing about the identity of his lodger, who had been sent his way by Monier *dit* Simentoff. Gauzy insisted that earlier that morning Bonnot had told him he was leaving, and that he did not know that Bonnot was still upstairs. Policeman Colmar, badly wounded by a bullet in the chest, contradicted Gauzy's assertion, saying that a nervous gesture upon their arrival made Colmar sure in retrospect that Gauzy knew Bonnot was still there. Moreover, Gauzy had not attempted to aid the wounded policeman; instead, he had tried to flee. Inspector Robert firmly asserted that Gauzy was responsible for the death of Louis Jouin. Gauzy's only break came during Xavier Guichard's testimony, when Guichard was forced to admit that he had intimidated Nelly Gauzy, shouting, "You are young. You could be a whore! We will put your kids into an institution!"[24]

Before Léon Rodriguez was interrogated, the prosecution read out a long list of his previous brushes with the law. Rodriguez was indignant: "Excuse me, that's not right. I have many more convictions than that!" At one point, he drew the laughter of the audience by saying that he was "in a state of inferiority here."[25]

Once the prosecution had laid out its case, it was the defense's turn. Relations between most of the defense lawyers and the accused then became almost cordial. On February 18 and 19, fourteen lawyers wrapped up the defense. For the most part, the defense lawyers spoke effectively and sometimes brilliantly. Dieudonné's lawyer defended him with eloquence and passion, warning jurors to beware of public opinion: "Get rid of it, this prostitute who pulls the judge by his sleeve!"[26]

During breaks in the trial—which Soudy dubbed the "entr'actes"— the accused were grouped together in two small, adjoining rooms. Callemin had not changed—he gave little sermons and criticized the other defendants for things they had said during questioning. As the trial approached its end, Raymond *la Science* became "sentimental and lyrical," remarking that "for a woman" he would cease to be "scientific." He added, "It's sad at my age to be reduced to marrying 'the Widow'"—the guillotine. When given the chance to speak during the summation, he spoke vaguely, unconvincingly, finally saying, "I am not an orator. Indeed I have sort of lost my train of thought."

Care had been taken to keep Rirette and Victor apart, but they exchanged letters when they could. Victor sent a message to Rirette: "I ask you on behalf of both us to resign yourself in advance to the worst outcome . . . and we know that whatever the outcome is we will find each other again one day."[27]

On February 18, Attorney General Fabre boomed out his closing speech for the prosecution. He presented anarchism as the "vague appearance of a social and philosophical system," behind which was "an association having no other goal but theft and murder." The goal of all anarchists, Fabre argued, was to destroy society. The accused were proud of their crimes. The time had come to reassure the public with judicial condemnations. He told the jury, "You have before you vulgar criminals, but of an audacity and entitlement without precedent, and with a criminal organization without equal." The next day, Fabre asked the death penalty for Callemin, Soudy, and Monier for the murders at Montgeron and Chantilly; for Carouy and Metge for the murders in Thiais; and for Dieudonné for having shot Caby. For most of the other accused, the prosecution demanded lesser but still harsh penalties, as prescribed by existing laws, including prison sentences and labor camps for life for those with prior convictions. Fabre insisted that "any indulgence toward such guilty people would neither be justified nor understood." At the same time, he insisted that Gauzy was more than an accomplice in Jouin's tragic death and that he knew perfectly well whom he was lodging in the rooms above his store. Perhaps because a municipal councilman from Ivry-sur-Seine and a deputy from the Gard testified to his integrity, the prosecution proposed extenuating circumstances for Antoine Gauzy.[28]

Following Fabre's summation, the defense lawyers did what they could. The defense for Monier *dit* Simentoff and Soudy suggested that the witnesses had been influenced by photos of the two accused that had appeared in Parisian newspapers. Gauzy's lawyer admitted that his client had lodged the anarchist Bonnot, but that he had done so because for him anarchism was a "generous" ideology and comrades were always welcome. He could have had no idea about the man staying above his garage. Carouy's defender noted his client's simple tastes, his love of nature, and his association of anarchism as an ideology for poor people such as himself. He had not been at Montgeron, place du Havre, nor Chantilly. Soudy's defender again insisted that Soudy had not killed anyone and evoked his burden of tuberculosis, then an incurable disease.[29]

The jury began deliberating at three in the afternoon on February 25. They had 383 questions to consider, and they spent the rest of the day determining the fate of the accused. The twenty men and women waited nervously in their tiny cells. A nun brought Rirette tea with a little rum in it to help ease her nerves. At about eleven in the evening, the defendants were brought into a large room and informed that the verdict would be delivered at about dawn. They waited among the strewn debris from the meal of the fifty municipal guards until five in the morning, their every movement closely observed. They talked in loud voices about nothing in particular. Waiting to be led into the courtroom to hear their fate at four in the morning, Callemin boasted: "I will die when I want to!"[30]

A guard suddenly summoned Madame Maîtrejean. Rirette blew a kiss to Victor, and then was led into a corridor. There she found Marie *la Belge* Vuillemin, Barbe Le Clerche, and Léon Rodriguez, who at five in the morning had been taken away from where the defendants were awaiting their fate. Rirette knew immediately that she had not been found guilty and that she and the other three would be released. Rodriguez had benefited from having provided useful information to the police.[31]

Raymond *la Science* was condemned to death for his role in the crimes of rue Ordener, place du Havre, Montgeron, and Chantilly. The jury found André Soudy guilty of being *"l'homme à carabine"* in Chantilly as well as being involved at Montgeron, and Monier was found guilty of the same crimes. Both were also condemned to death. And so was Eugène Dieudonné, who clearly had been misidentified by witnesses on the rue Ordener. When Dieudonné's sentence was read, Callemin shouted violently, "Dieudonné is innocent, I was the one who fired!" He later wrote the prosecutor to insist again that it was Garnier who shot Ernest Caby on rue Ordener, adding that Monier was innocent of the robbery and murder in Chantilly. Édouard Carouy and Metge were condemned to life sentences of hard labor for their participation in the murder in Thiais, yet the absence of a death sentence revealed some doubt as to the conclusions of Bertillon. Victor despaired for Carouy, whom he believed innocent of the atrocious killings, suspecting an unidentified third man wearing gloves as having strangled one of the victims. Upon hearing the sentence, Carouy muttered, "Prison for life? Death is better!" Jean de Boe was sentenced to ten years of hard labor for having gone with the bandits to the Netherlands to try to unload the securities, Bélonie to six years in prison, Dettweiller four years, and Gauzy eighteen months. The fact that Gauzy had already spent ten months in jail may have played a role in Fabre's decision to be somewhat lenient in the sentencing. Improbably, Victor Kibaltchiche was convicted of the murder of Louis Jouin, but with "attenuating circumstances." He was sentenced to five years in prison, in part because he had refused to testify against the others on trial.[32]

Following the reading of the sentences, "the cold in the courtroom engulfed everybody." The condemned men were led from the court, stopping at the sign from an official, who asked, "To what have you been condemned?" "To death" came several replies. Guards inventoried their possessions. Policemen escorted them in a wagon for the final ride across Paris for those condemned to death. At La Santé prison, they were stripped down to make sure they had no poison with them: "You are to die at the guillotine, and not in another way," they were told.[33]

Victor resolved to survive. He found himself next to Raymond, and, probably because of his resolution a few seconds earlier, murmured, "You live and learn." Callemin had not long to live, and Victor immediately regretted his words. Raymond replied, laughing, "That's exactly right. Living is just the problem!" "Forgive me!" Victor replied. Raymond shrugged, "Of course! My mind's set."[34] That evening Victor wrote a note to Rirette, expressing joy that she would be free and promising to return: "Retain for me the affection of Chinette. Profit from sunshine, flowers, good books, all that we love together." And, he begged her, "Never, never return to that milieu."

Later that evening, Victor heard sounds of monstrous breathing from the adjacent cell. Carouy had swallowed cyanide that he had hidden in the heel of a shoe. He died in agony. Carouy left a letter to his lawyer. He had relived, all through the night, "my entire little life." He had had little joy, little happiness. To be sure, he had made some errors along the way. But "all my dreams of happiness collapsed at the moment I believed that they could become reality. This is why, not having known the joys of life, I am leaving this kingdom of atoms without regrets." And as for the fingerprints found on the armoire in Thiais, he wrote, "Oh, Science! You have hit me with a dirty blow."[35]

Most of the leading Parisian newspapers proclaimed their pleasure at the death sentences, and also of the sentence given to Victor Kibaltchiche. Yet *La Bataille syndicaliste*, for one, wrote optimisitically, "It is impossible that a pardon will not be given."[36] It never came.

L'Anarchie reflected on "the bloody verdict." It lamented that neither the judge nor the jurors had managed to find pity for the accused, even though Callemin had, without question, killed. The anarchist newspaper saluted Carouy's disdain for those judging him and Callemin's "noble gestures" in the face of "the mighty bourgeoisie who believed they could humiliate and devastate all anarchists in striking this man." Of Soudy they wrote, "His sarcastic defiance demonstrates his proud contempt for those who condemned him." Yet in an editorial on April 24, Lorulot asked rhetorically if the newspaper had some indirect responsibility for what had transpired—not because it had preached illegalism, but rather "in calling for struggle, for revolt."[37]

For their part, the major anarchist associations limited their energies to defending Gauzy, among others, who had been convicted of having lodged illegalists on the run. A Committee for the Defense of the Right to Asylum went to work. Gauzy emerged for anarchists as a hero of the "right to asylum," despite the fact that he had lodged a murderer, whose identity he may well have known.[38]

Chapter 20

THE WIDOW (*LA VEUVE*)

In the prison of La Santé, those convicted in the trial, including the four who were to be executed, seemed generally in good humor. As during their trial, they remained for the most part reserved, demonstrating the same sangfroid with which they accomplished their acts. The prisoners impressed their guards with their attention to being clean, reflecting their obsession with hygiene and diet. It could be very cold in their cells, but they continued to wear only shirts and leave them unbuttoned, to spite the chill.[1]

None of the prisoners expressed any resentment of the investigating magistrate, the trial judge, or the jury, using expressions like "*un brave homme.*" It had been war between them and society. Society had won, and that was that. The perhaps understandable targets of their hatred were the informers who made a profession out of reporting to the police.

Émile Michon, a psychologist, was granted frequent access to the prisoners; he wanted to understand them, see what they had in common, and write a book about them. He found them intelligent and articulate. They spoke calmly and philosophically, despite having absolutely no illusions about their future. They were not afraid, and they took bad news with indifference. Michon contended that the only way to get them out of that calm was to contradict them. During a visit, one of them became angry, pounding his fist on the table and denouncing bourgeois society, pacing like a caged animal, his hand ready to grasp an imaginary Browning. It was an old song.[2]

One of the prisoners insisted to Michon that he had never liked carrying out burglaries and had never killed. He had used his pistol only once, to knock down with a blow to the head a "*bonhomme*" in their way. But he would have used the weapon to shoot to kill if he had been surrounded and on the verge of capture.[3]

Yet another of the bandits told Michon, "We settled an old debt with Society. No hesitation. . . . If one day we are on the point of being captured, well, they won't take us alive and we will make them pay very dearly for our skin!"[4] For his part, Victor had his own sense of how members of the Bonnot Gang were dealing with their fates: "When they knew that they were lost, they decided to get themselves killed, not accepting prison. 'Life is not worth that!'" One prisoner—insisting that he never went out without his Browning—told Michon, "'Six bullets for the guard-dogs, the seventh for me.' You know, I am at ease. It's difficult, to be light-hearted. The doctrine of salvation which is inside of us led us, in the social jungle, to the battle of one against everyone else."[5]

On the last days of his young life, Raymond Callemin tried to win guards over to anarchism. He alone did not sign a request for a pardon and remained insolent to the end. Raymond *la Science* offered no regrets for what he had done. In his cell he wrote a piece he titled "My Memoirs: Why I burgled. Why I killed." Like Bonnot, he proclaimed that everyone is born with "the right to live," which stems from nature. He asked why on this earth there were people who managed to have all the rights. No one has the right to impose "his will under any pretext." Why could he not eat grapes or apples found on the property of M. X.? He had the right "to take them according to his needs." He asked why "this minority who possess so much is stronger than the majority who are dispossessed?" The majority of people were "ignorant and without energy. . . . These people are too cowardly to revolt." It was "for all these reasons that

I revolted." Raymond wanted to live, but not in the kind of society in which he had suffered.[6]

He said of Ernest Caby, "Even wounded, this courier of funds maintained his sense of duty to defend the money of his bosses." Callemin insisted that he and his friends were not any more bloodthirsty than "the financiers who often drive their clients to misery and suicide."[7]

Soudy seemed more or less indifferent to his fate. He told a guard that during the trial he had hidden some prussic acid, which could kill someone in two seconds, and that he had kept it when he heard the sentence. On April 5, he wrote Rirette:

> Rirette, do you remember,
> Buttes-Chaumont,
> The park in the sunshine, the suspended bridge,
> The very shallow lake,
> And the temple of love
> Where lovers having escaped the factories
> Return, embracing
> Going over the red-brick bridge?
> I put in rhymes more feet than were necessary.
> It's better.[8]

On April 9, he again picked up a pen, writing that Billy the Kid had died at the age of twenty-two, adding somewhat mysteriously that the American outlaw had killed twenty-one men, but had never "pillaged banks. Or at least it appears that way. It's disappointing."[9]

Soudy wrote a testament, leaving to the minister of war his burglary tools "to help him open the door of militarism thanks to the Law of Three Years." He left his brain to the Medical School; his skull to the Anthropology Museum, hoping that an entry fee might go toward the soup kitchens; his hair to the union of hairdressers; and his signature to "Anarchy . . . so that the priests and apostles of philosophy can use them for the profit of their cynical individuality."[10]

On April 18, a policeman named Moutard came upon this threatening poem on a Parisian boulevard, promising that very soon:

The Tragic Bandits will be avenged,
[by] the death of the executioners and
the principal men responsible
[for] multiple executions.

These would include President Poincarré [*sic*], if the executions take place, Lépine, Guichard [having taken part in the exploits against Bonnot].[11]

The Montmartre anarchist poet Paul Paillette sang the praises of Jules Bonnot:

Conserving Family and Property
How can one hope to live in freedom?
Keep the laws and the gendarmes
To vanquish us ready your weapons.

. . .

Leaving, under your fist, women in servitude,
The perverse masters have an attitude.
And you, clairvoyant—without contradiction—
Caltez! Caltez! Soudy would say.[12]

The early morning hours of April 21 were overcast and humid. Cavalrymen lined the boulevard Arago. Taxis brought journalists to the executions, scheduled to begin at 4:05 a.m. An old lamp in the wall of the prison of La Santé cast some light on "The Widow," who awaited her victims.

At about 3:30 a.m. guards shouted, "Okay, get up!" to awaken Callemin, Soudy, and Monier. When a guard offered Callemin a drink of rum, he predictably refused. He wrote a short message to his lawyer, drank a glass of water, and noted the obvious: "It's a day without a tomorrow." Upon being escorted from his cell, he muttered, "Finally I am free." Monier thanked his guards, related that he had had a "dream of love," and said he wished he could kiss the young Marie Besse, who had attended the trial. He smoked a cigarette and drank a cup of coffee. The prison chaplain was there, as always; Monier shook his hand as a friend, not as a priest, as he was led to the scaffold. Émile Michon was there, carrying a *laissez-passer* issued by the Prefecture de Police. One of the men to be guillotined finished a conversation he had had with Michon and told him what he thought of the press.

Pas-de-Chance Soudy, whose life had been marked by abject poverty and constant illness, asked for a *café au lait* "without alcohol!" and two croissants with "the joy of a *gamin de Paris*." Yet as it was so early, neither cream nor croissants could be found. "No luck to the end," Soudy wryly noted. He told the guards that he was ready and that he had no "human life on his conscience. It's a sad ending, but I will have courage until the final moment." When he saw a policeman from Security, he shook his hand and said, "It does me good to see you worthy men." He sang a line of "Salut, oh my last morning," from Gounod's *Faust*. An officer told him, "Above all, no fanfare," and he responded that that would be the case. Executioner Anatole Deibler cut the hair of those about to die, so that nothing would impede the rapid fall of the blade.

The wagon arrived to take the chained men to meet "The Widow." In attendance were about two hundred "privileged" observers with access to the best seats near ringside, including the investigating magistrate, as well as other magistrates, and Xavier Guichard, in quiet triumph.

The executioner Diebler picked the order of the heads to fall, beginning with the youngest, *Pas-de-Chance* Soudy. The hands and feet of the three men had been tightly bound. As he stood before the guillotine, Soudy noted audibly that he was trembling because it was a cold morning: "It's the best possible end, better than prison." He addressed a few words "to conscious and liquored-up workers," then yelled to the crowd below, "*Au revoir!*" before his head was placed through the little window. Callemin's turn came next. Raymond *la Science* nodded toward the throng that had assembled—some having taken prized places as early as midnight—to watch the executions: "It's beautiful, eh? The agony of a man!" Monier then followed, saying, "Adieu to you all, *messieurs*, and to society." The three executions took four and a half minutes. Only Soudy had someone come to claim his severed body.[13]

While the others were being led to their death, Eugène Dieudonné's lawyer had gone to his cell to tell him "They won't have your head." President Raymond Poincaré had pardoned Dieudonné upon appeal by his lawyers, if "pardon" could somehow be defined as being sentenced to life at hard labor in French Guiana. The evidence that Dieudonné had not shot the courier Caby was overwhelming. Moreover, Bonnot in the testimony he left behind and Callemin during and after the trial insisted that Dieudonné was innocent. Diedonné managed to escape twice from the prison in the roasting hellhole of Guiana but was recaptured each time, returned to the harsh conditions, and denied even the right to speak to anyone. He finally escaped to Brazil, where he survived incredibly brutal conditions before finally receiving authorization to return to France in 1927 after his story became known and supporters organized a campaign on his behalf.[14]

The trial of the Bonnot Gang, and the wave of illegalist violence these particular bandits represented, had a chilling effect on French anarchists. Rirette remembered: "Our ideas were beautiful. Unfortunately, these neophytes, these kids . . . killed . . . and the blood they shed engulfed us."[15]

In the prewar period—the Belle Époque that never was—French anarchists were undercut by the wave of illegalist violence. Victor referred to this as a "collective suicide." The notoriety of the Bonnot

Gang had attracted other marginal characters who now flaunted their admiration for the bandits, further contributing to the association in the mind of the public of anarchism with illegalism and banditry.[16]

The split between individualist anarchism, a decided minority, and the "communist anarchists" became starker after the trial. More than ever, the "communist anarchists," like Victor, Rirette, and the other intellectuals, insisted that the individualists, and particularly the illegalists, had cast a shadow on anarchism by saluting "destructive egotism as an ideal," and thus being responsible for the little progress made by anarchist ideas. Individualists fought back against these attacks and remained convinced that the communists' ties to Syndicalism was corrupting "the true conception of anarchism." The latter wanted to identify individualism with illegalism and banditry, although there were some "illegalists and bandits among the communist faction."[17]

The anarchist André Girard went further, accusing the bandits of being "among impatient pleasure-seekers who, without any legal means—capital—of being able to 'live their lives' in complete security have recourse to an illegal instrument—the revolver." Thus they were "quite worthy sons of the bourgeoisie," obsessed with living well, worthy of the French statesman François Guizot when, in the 1830s, he had advised the upper classes to "get rich!" (*"enrichissez-vous!"*). With their "appetites" for bourgeois luxury, they were not anarchists at all; they abused property as did the bourgeoisie, taking lives as did the bourgeoisie and its state. "Purely egoistic" acts, like theirs, he argued, had to be rejected, as those in the time of "propaganda by the deed," 1892–1894.

Because of the Bonnot Gang, and thanks in no small part to the press and the newly reinforced police force, virtually any crime could be blamed on anarchists. Any anarchist could be portrayed as "a violent man, without reason and uneducated in his fury, the dangerous neighbor, the unsociable being, the bandit."[18]

The influential Italian anarchist Errico Malatesta shared the revulsion of most anarchists for what the Bonnot Gang had done to damage the cause of anarchism. But he also placed the blood they shed in the context of the society against which they had waged war:

> Several people stole, and in order to steal, they killed. They killed at random . . . killed people they did not know, workers, victims like them and even more than them of the evil existing social organization. . . . They are the bitter fruit that ripens on the tree of privilege. When all social life is stained by fraud and violence and those who are born into poverty are condemned to all sorts of suffering and humiliations, and when money is absolutely indispensable in order to live and achieve respect and when for so many people it is impossible to find honest and worthy work one could not really be astonished [by the result].

Malatesta had noted the obvious. The police and the ruling upper classes seized upon the crimes of the Bonnot Gang as an excuse to denounce anarchism. Now, the "forces of order" had the power and the public support that were needed to intensify a violent war against those who opposed the existing regime.[19]

Anarchism was now largely discredited in France, although it remained strong in Spain, both in Andalusia and on the docks of Barcelona in Catalonia, for the next two decades. Anarchism was betrayed in the Spanish Civil War of 1936–1939, then by Joseph Stalin, and finally it was crushed by General Francisco Franco's nationalist hordes.

In sentencing Victor to five years in prison, Rirette said, French magistrates "had destroyed her youth and her love." She took a job with a company that purified water. With her two daughters, now six and seven, she moved into a tiny apartment in Belleville, where she still felt at home. She was briefly arrested when police took in a young friend of hers whose residence was full of stolen goods.[20]

Between August 19 and 31, 1913, *Le Matin* published some of Rirette's memoirs, which offered unflattering accounts of the "*bandits tragiques*," as newspapers began to call them. In her writing, Rirette attacked illegalism as "ridiculous" and "grotesque." She probably hoped to influence an appeal of Victor's sentence, and she denounced Lorulot for not admitting the clear position Victor had taken against illegalism. In response, some anarchists now denounced Rirette. Her former lover Mauricius insisted on his obligation to "publicly express his disgust and contempt for a woman who [earlier] had shared his life." Rirette stopped attending anarchist *causeries* and maintained friendships with very few of her former anarchist comrades.[21]

Victor now seemed a broken man: "The very roots of our mind plunged into despair. Nothing could be done. Man is vanquished, lost. We were destroyed in advance, no matter what we did." After a brief incarceration at La Santé prison, he was transferred to a larger prison situated on an island in the Seine in Melun. Victor spent nights in solitary confinement; during the day he worked ten hours in the printing shop as a typesetter and then as a proofreader. No newspapers were allowed. At first he was allowed only one book a week to read, and he had to choose "from among the idiotic novels found in the prison library." Gradually, understanding guards began to bring him books. No visitors were allowed—"My solitude was painful." Victor tried his best to remain healthy, fearing diseases, especially tuberculosis. He did exercises in his cell, walking the equivalent of ten kilometers a day around his tiny space. On one occasion, he fell so ill because of the lack of food that for the first time, "I feared to be on my way to the little cemetery." Bouillon and milk in the infirmary brought him back to reasonable health in a fortnight, but he was still in prison.[22]

From prison, Victor began to consider the illegalists' legacy and roots. The illegalists' desperate and, to be sure, self-absorbed tactics against the state and capitalism (and organized religion and the armies that supported them) had failed completely. Victor compared their acts to the period of "propaganda by the deed" in the early 1890s, when Ravachol, Émile Henry, and Cesario killed: "The same psychological traits and the same social elements were present in the two episodes. . . . They felt themselves in an impasse, fought, and succombed [*sic*]." The economy and society had achieved "a structure, so durable in appearance that one can't really see any possibility of real change." This had carried the masses along with it.

The harsh conditions of working-class life had improved ever so slowly since the 1890s, "with no resolution for the immense majority of proletarians," while "insolent riches accumulated with pride far above the crowd." Strikes and criminality followed, "these crazy battles of one against everybody else." Ideologies had failed the people and "the decline of anarchism in the capitalist jungle [had become] evident." It was now increasingly difficult to believe "in the renovating power of science," for clearly science had worked "to increase the possibilities of the development of a traditionally barbaric order. We feel that an era of violence is approaching; no one can escape it."

Victor looked even more to the Russia of his family's origin for hope and a possible alternative to what he had witnessed in France. There, the revolutionary movement had "directed these errant energies and carried them along through the paths of sacrifice toward great possible victories wanted by peoples."[23] From his prison cell, Victor tried to imagine the fall of tsarist Russia.

Chapter 21

THE VIOLENCE OF STATES;
THE CLOUDS OF WAR

Europe—at least the old, more reassuring Europe—would soon disappear in a wave of unprecedented destruction. The violence unleashed by the Bonnot Gang was horrendous. But it was nothing like the violence generated by modern states, both autocracies and republics. Anarchists rejected state power, capitalism, and concomitant aggressive nationalism. Theoretical, observant, and informed anarchists such as Victor and Rirette certainly got it right. States had become ever more powerful, controlling the means of violence with huge armies and increasingly modern weapons. For now, the French government used its strength to quash dissent within its borders, but before long that same power would be used against its neighbors.

Long before the outbreak of war, anarchists had been critical of the professional armies of nation-states.[1] All anarchists were opposed to armies, which represented the force of states. Anarchist propaganda had increasingly denounced the professional armies of nation-states. Victor referred to colonialization as the "same as banditry" ("*synonym de banditisme*"), the imperialists protected by powerful armies ready to kill anyone who got in their way.[2] The same armies attacked strikers domestically as well. French troops had massacred demonstrators in Fourmies on May Day, 1891; gunned down a striker in Limoges in 1905; and fired into crowds during le Révolte du Midi (the demonstrations and indeed insurrection of wine producers in the south) two years later. Not all anarchists agreed on strategies and tactics in the struggle against militarism. While just about everyone supported the right of conscripts to avoid military service by fleeing to Belgium or Switzerland, or simply by hiding, others believed that comrades should work against the army from within.[3] In Zola's *Paris*, published in 1898, the main character, Abbé Pierre Froment, believes that anarchist bombs could ultimately lead to the annihilation of armies and "the nations forced into general disarmament."[4] He was wrong about that.

The Association Internationale Antimilitariste had been founded in 1904. That same year, the CGT had asked workers "to remain absolutely away from conflicts between nations." The rise in international tensions in Europe was episodic rather than hydraulic in the period following 1905, the year when Germany and France, during the First Moroccan Crisis, seemed dangerously close to hostilities over influence in North Africa. In January 1906, when the international conference was held at Algeciras, Spain, to try to resolve the tensions that had brought Germany and France close to war, the CGT called for an increase in an increase in antimilitary and "antipatriotic" propaganda. The Fédération Communiste Anarchiste (FCA), founded in November 1910, made antimilitarism an essential part of its program.[5]

In June 1909, army officers badly beat a twenty-two-year-old soldier, Aernoult, who, coincidentally, was from Romainville. He had been forced into the army after being arrested while participating in a strike of road workers. Aernoult died from his injuries. Only one brave soldier publicly denounced what had occurred. The incident again cast the army in a bad light and provided fodder for the cause of anarchist antimilitarism.[6]

In April 1911, a new outbreak of discord between Germany and France in North Africa led to the Second Moroccan Crisis. Tensions heated up and Italy claimed Libya, bringing war with Turkey. Serbian and Bulgarian troops now invaded Turkish territory. Many nationalists wanted war, which they assumed would lead to the liberation of Alsace-Lorraine, annexed by Germany after France's defeat in the Franco-Prussian War. The great composer Claude Debussy, who had emerged as a fervent nationalist, refused to attend a program of French music held in Munich the following year. A police spy reporting on an anarchist meeting held in Paris noted that "everyone there showed that they are for stopping the war by all means, including insurrection and a revolutionary General Strike." Anarchism, at least in the eyes of the police, began to be seen as a threat to national strength, and in the new climate of war, there was less tolerance for it than ever before.[7]

L'Anarchie kept up its barrage of denunciations of militarism. The newspaper offered scathing commentaries on military life and the role of soldiers, who were described as hanging around bars, smoking and drinking, "a worker who will wear a ridiculous costume" so that his comrades from the atelier will obey the bosses. In one editorial, "The War and the Anarchists," the newspaper wrote: "And everybody, patriotic parrots or socialist 'voters,' class conscious proletarians or groveling fatalists, all of them will go off to war, without a doubt" upon a declaration of hostilities.[8]

Beneath the slick veneer of the *fin de siècle* and the first years of the twentieth century, the embrace of violence and the anticipation of war took on wider cultural dimensions as well. Futurist artists in France and other countries, attracted by technological innovations and speed, eagerly looked forward to war. Likewise, the emergence of mass sports, including soccer and rugby, also manifested martial concomitants and the growing obsession of nationalists that French soldiers be fit and ready for a war against Germany. Proliferating gymnastic clubs echoed patriotic themes. Their members were expected to be ready to fight.[9]

War-like patriotism became a regular theme even in music hall reviews. Patriotic themes filled the Moulin Rouge in January 1912. Films reflected the growing obsession with war, including *Honor the Soldier* and *Don't Touch Our Flag*! Frenzied cheers greeted *To the Glory of the French Army* at the Gaumont-Palace cinema on the first day of 1913. That year, a man assumed for some reason to be German and thus a German spy was chased by thugs near the theater. Newspapers reflected the increasing obsession with German saber rattling. Ernest Psichari's *L'Appel des armes* published that year celebrated patriotic Catholicism and the virtues of war—the enemy was clearly the (largely) Protestant Germany.[10]

In January 1913, a soapy theatrical piece called *Alsace!* opened at the Réjane Theater on rue Blanche. Taking place in Thann, near Colmar, the central point of the play was that Alsatians could never really be assimilated into the German Reich, but would always be French. Excited audiences cheered frenetically.[11]

In November 1913, German soldiers—not from Alsace, whose residents were not trusted in Berlin—insulted Alsatians in the Saverne/Zabern Affair (the names of the town in French and in German). Both the German and French governments reacted with fury, before things calmed down. Yet the idea of *"Revanche"* remained in the air in France. The Michelin Company offered a prize for aviators capable of dropping practice bombs on a target. The French were not alone. German nationalists, too, seemed eager for war.[12]

At the time Victor had written in *L'Anarchie*, "The possibility of a war preoccupies everyone, thinking about the sheer horror of battlefields and burned villages, bodies along every road and entire regiments decimated." He predicted, "All of Europe is moving toward solutions of violence. We are breathing the oppressive air of *l'avant-guerre.*"[13]

Anarchist propaganda during the Balkan Wars in 1912 and 1913 reiterated the call for insurrection against an eventual war. (The first Balkan War was fought by Bulgaria, Montenegro, Serbia, and Greece against the Ottoman Empire in 1912. The Second Balkan War, a year later, pitted Montenegro, Serbia, Greece, and Romania against Bulgaria.) The Fédération Communiste Anarchiste readied plans for sabotage. A *Revolutionary Manual* explained how to make bombs. Circulars included propagating instructions about how to destroy rail lines and viaducts, telegraph lines, and even how to sabotage an airplane. Anarchists encouraged desertion from the army and counseled acts of sabotage if mobilization was declared, to make it more difficult to marshal troops in military centers. With the Second Moroccan Crisis, the CGT insisted on the necessity of insurrection in the case of war. Protest meetings took place, including one bringing together as many as twenty thousand people at an "Aéro Park" outside of Paris, where speakers denounced the government's seeming plans for war and proposed a general strike to protest a move toward hostilities with Germany. France had ordered thirty planes for military purposes the year before and now purchased sixty more, holding its first military air show. In June 1912, *Le Libertaire* had complained of the cost of building planes for army at a time when "We can no longer live with our miserable salaries."[14]

In December 1912, *L'Anarchie* noted with accuracy that "rumors of war are in the air. . . . The coalition of five powers . . . arms and mobilizes in secret and newspapers heat up public opinion; alarming news circulates and we are so close to an inevitable butchery. . . . Everywhere an intense fervor reigns." Three months later, in March, diplomatic tension increased again. Clearly, "the slightest incidence would be transformed into a matter of national honor and make a war inevitable," one that would "bring dreadful results."[15]

Anarchists joined the widespread campaign against the Three Year Law, proposed to the Chamber of Deputies in May 1913 under the stewardship of Poincaré. The law, approved in July, increased the term of military conscription, which had been reduced from three to two years in 1905, back to three years. The principal reason was clear: there were sixty-seven million Germans and only thirty-nine million French, and the Reich had a standing army of more than eight hundred thousand men. The Three Year Law brought French service in line with several other allies and enemies. The Fédération Communiste Anarchiste printed a hundred thousand brochures, "Against Three years, Against all Militarism." Enormous protests against the law coincided with anniversary of Bloody Week during the Paris Commune.

One month before the protests, Callemin, Monier, and Soudy were executed. The anarchist newspaper *La Guerre sociale* drew a clear connection between the Bonnot Gang and the war that was sure to come: "The crimes of these tracked wild animals, as revolting as they may be, are far from equaling the horrors that society is now committing."[16]

Still, there were other things to distract Parisians in 1913—and not just the trial of the Bonnot Gang's surviving members. On May 29, despite several years of success of his Russian ballets, Serge Diaghilev's *Le Sacre du Printemps* (*The Rite of Spring*) shocked and angered the decidedly upper-class audience at the sparkling new Théâtre des Champs-Élysées, a recently constructed cement palace on avenue Montaigne that combined a classic style with emerging Art Deco. Most of the outraged crowd whistled at the choreography of the great dancer and Diaghilev's young lover, Vaslav Nijinsky. The complicated and somewhat violent avant-garde keys of the young Russian composer Igor Stravinsky found admirers, but to traditionalists, the performance provided further affirmation that contemporary life was spinning out of control. Many in the audience expressed their disapproval, and here and there fights broke out. A reviewer scathed, "It's not the Rite of Spring, It's the Massacre of Spring!"[17]

The first part of Marcel Proust's *À elle la recherche du temps perdu*, that classic of modernism, was published that same year. Proust's great novel takes place exclusively in the wealthy arrondissements of western Paris, where he lived on boulevard Haussmann. Proust presented anything but a *panoramique* view of Paris. He drew upon his memories of literary salons, banquets, and the interchanges of the Parisian elite, evoking the intimate details of privileged life, one that would have meant very little indeed to most ordinary Parisians.[18] Few who read Proust's novel when it first appeared could have imagined that war was drawing near.

The war that anarchists—and others—feared and that many nationalists wanted did indeed come to Europe. On June 28, 1914, Gavrilo Princip assassinated Archduke Francis Ferdinand and his wife in Sarajevo. The Austro-Hungarian government handed a devastating ultimatum to Serbia on July 23. The German Empire famously gave Austria-Hungary a blank check by indicating that it would fully support any Habsburg response to the crisis, including war. The French government frantically demanded Russian assurance that it would honor the military alliance between the two powers, leaving Germany and its Habsburg ally to fight a war on two fronts. Russia declared mobilization on July 30, an act tantamount to a declaration of war. German commanders believed that the planned invasion of France via Belgium would have to begin almost immediately so that their enemies across the Rhine could be quickly defeated. Attention could be then turned toward the east, to stopping the big Russian bear, whose troops would, they assumed, require as long as several weeks to be readied for war. The European alliance system's house of cards was quickly bringing on the Great War.

Yet during the dramatic international crisis, in France popular attention focused on the possibility of an income tax—approved by the Senate on July 25—and on the murder trial that began on July 20 of Madame Henriette Caillaux, the wife of Joseph Caillaux, former minister of finances and of the interior and head of the Radical Party. On March 16, 1914, Madame Caillaux had shot and killed Gaston Calmette in his office—with a Browning, of course. Calmette was the editor of *Le Figaro*, and his newspaper had violently attacked Joseph Caillaux, never forgiving his support for an income tax. On July 28, one month after the assassination of Archduke Francis Ferdinand and his wife in Sarajevo, the jury found Madame Caillaux not guilty of this crime of passion by a vote of 11 to 1 after only an hour of deliberations.[19]

On July 27, *La Bataille syndicaliste*, under the headline "On the Brink of the Abyss," announced prophetically that "the unleashing of a cataclysm that will surpass in horror what men with the fullest imagination could never conceive of hangs by a thread . . . It is the burial, pure and simple, of humanity."[20]

Yet with hostilities now virtually inevitable, anarchists' determination weakened as the war approached. Six hundred demonstrators were arrested on July 27 protesting the onrushing war, some of them anarchists. For all their planning, anarchists posed no threat to the French state as it moved toward war.[21]

The great socialist leader Jean Jaurès went to Brussels on July 29 to participate in a massive demonstration against the war. He returned to Paris and on the evening of July 31; Raoul Villain, a young right-wing nationalist, shot Jaurès dead as he sat in the Café Croissant on rue Montmartre near the offices of *L'Humanité*. Jaurès had just decided on the next morning's headline, "*En Avant!*"—"Forward!"[22]

Germany declared war on Russia on August 1, 1914, and the next day Belgium rejected Germany's demand that the small, strategically important country allow Germany's troops to pass through Belgium on the way to France. Germany delivered an absurd ultimatum to France that same day and declared war two days later. Crowds of soldiers and civilians rushed to the Gare du Nord and the Gare de l'Est, shouting, "To Berlin!" In Berlin, soldiers and civilians rushed to the Hauptbahnhof shouting, "To Paris!"

Most of the leaders of the CGT were away from Paris when the war broke out. Mobilization against the war was decentralized and depended on local initiative. Although the mobilization was greeted with a lack of enthusiasm in France—particularly in the countryside, as the harvest approached—no general strike was forthcoming as anarchists had hoped. Internationalism disappeared. With the Germans invading France, possible movements against the war vanished into the air. The dire necessity of defending France created the Sacred Union, the unity of all political parties. That the government did not apply "Carnet B"—a list of socialist, syndicalist, and anarchist militants who were to be arrested upon the mobilization for war—contributed to the emergence of the "Sacred Union," even if it was then viewed as a short-term solution. The 1914 legislative elections had returned more than a hundred deputies—they rallied to the war effort as German forces approached France. Some anarchists accepted the "Sacred Union," while others left the struggle against war because of the repression and the shock of seeing former comrades enter the army. Most anarchist groups and public meetings and *causeries* simply disappeared into what would be an impossibly long night. Anarchist propaganda disappeared. The last issue of *L'Anarchie* had appeared on July 22, 1914. Workers went off to war as everyone else. War took over and there was nothing to be done.[23]

Most people in France believed that the war would be short and victorious. The fall of Mulhouse to German forces and massive losses in August (at least two hundred thousand casualties and twenty-seven thousand killed on one day, August 22) and in September at the Battle of the Marne—in which eighty-one thousand soldiers on both sides were killed—shocked all of France. The prison in Melun, where Victor was being held, was only twenty-four miles from the Battle of the Marne in September 1914, but the prisoners were deprived of any news about it, or about anything else about the war raging so near.[24]

Charles Péguy, who had written the minister of war that since 1905 war was "our only thought" and had loudly denounced the pacifist instincts of Jean Jaurès, was killed in battle at Villeroy near Meaux on September 5. Guillaume Apollinaire entered the war as an artilleryman, writing where he could in trenches and dugouts, working on battered wooden tables or slabs of cement. Cubism also went to war, its design techniques used to camouflage soldiers' uniforms.[25]

Victor Kibaltchiche and Rirette Maîtrejean took no comfort or solace in the fact that millions died during the Great War as states battled it out in total war.[26] The Great War destroyed Europe as they knew it, and they watched helplessly, Victor from prison and Rirette from her small apartment in Paris, as the continent disappeared in absolutely unprecedented, murderous violence. "You may not be interested in war," Léon Trotsky once said, "but war is interested in you."[27] The Great War unleashed the demons of the twentieth century.

Chapter 22

AFTERMATH

During most of the Great War Victor languished in prison in Melun. Friends undertook several attempts to obtain a pardon for him, supported by the director of the prison, but each time the Ministry of Justice turned down the request. Victor was one of rare few political prisoners at the time forced to serve out virtually his entire sentence. In the meantime, he witnessed "promiscuity, half-crazy (prisoners) and victims of all kinds" suffering "the lack of food and the rule of silence forced on life in common at all times, humiliating, torturous, and debilitating punishments, as well as the deprivation as much as possible of intellectual exercise."[1]

Rirette had officially divorced Louis Maîtrejean in November 1913 and she and Victor obtained permission to marry. The brief ceremony, with two prison guards as the witnesses, took place in the town hall of Melun on August 3, 1915. Guards allowed them to spend an hour alone together back in a prison office, and then that was that. During the time of Victor's incarceration, he sent Rirette 528 letters, each numbered by the controlling authorities.[2]

In their correspondence, they disagreed on what Victor should do once he was freed. Victor decided that he should apply for early release on the condition that he join a regiment of the Russian army stationed in France. Rirette, who had heard about the horrors of

life—and death—in the trenches, contended that he should serve
out his term.[3]

After almost five years in prison for having been convicted of,
in his words, "the triple crime of being a foreigner, being an anarchist, and not wanting to become a police spy," Victor was released
on January 31, 1917. He spent several weeks in Paris. After so many
years in a prison cell, "I filled my eyes with distant horizons and
my lungs with good air." He wrote, "The city is beautiful and
made a very good impression on me." But Victor found Belleville
even poorer than the last time he had been there. War had taken
its toll on the residents, too. A shop advertised enamel medallions
of soldiers. A funeral service announced: "Funerals in twenty-four
hours, moderate pricing, with an installment plan." With the war,
there was a lot of business to be had. Yet civilian life went on,
"Pigalle, Clichy, le faubourg Montmartre, and the great boulevards,
are teeming with people who amuse themselves, but after us, *le
déluge!* . . . the faubourgs sink into an intense darkness, but the well
lit center vibrates long into the night." Victor was absolutely without resources, so Émile Armand, who had taken over editorship of
L'Anarchie, organized a collection of funds for him, but this brought
in only 235 francs.[4]

After spending time with Rirette and her children, Victor took
a train in late February to Barcelona. Rirette followed in May, but
left a month later, unable to find work. Strains began to appear in
their relationship—after all, they had seen each other but once in
almost five years: the day of their marriage. Victor confided to Émile
Armand that from then on he and Rirette considered themselves
"entirely free so far as regards the one to the other."[5]

Victor did, however, feel obliged to respond to the furor in anarchist circles that the publication of Rirette's memoirs in *Le Matin*
had caused. In prison, he had heard nothing of this. Now he simply
noted that she alone had been responsible for what she had written.
She remained "my partner." They had been separated for five years,
even though being apart so long did not change "our life together . . .

especially such a past—of struggle and separation, [and] a tight ideological solidarity."[6]

In Barcelona Victor joined a veritable colony of deserters from French, Russian, and German armies, including individualists and revolutionaries. Here he took the alias or *nom de plume* of Victor Serge. He worried that "Le Rétif" would be known and that the reactionary Spanish press would attack him and associate all anarchists with prison sentences. He signed an article with "Le Rétif" for the last time on February 12, then used Victor or Victor K., then V. S. Le Rétif.

Yet Victor found no peace in the Catalan sun. The cafés were improbably full while millions were dying in the war. Moreover, he did not have a great impression of the people of Barcelona: "The Spanish [*sic*] are ten times less apt to take initiative than the French and a hundred times more sleeping." During the five months he was there, Victor worked in printing shops and collaborated with *Tierra y Libertad*, where he signed his first article Victor Serge. The failure of a general strike planned for July 19 disappointed him. He now fully accepted collective action.[7]

Following the Russian February Revolution of 1917, which overthrew the tsarist autocracy and led to a provisional government, Victor increasingly turned his attention to the dramatic situation in the country he had never seen. A change had come over him: "With my Russian background, I believed in revolution as a concrete reality."[8] In Paris years earlier, he had translated Russian modernists from the prerevolutionary period into French and had read widely about the French Revolution. Rirette remembered: "When the Russian Revolution burst out, it immediately seemed to him that he should go there, be there, participate, in it, and put great effort into it."[9]

Five years of suffering in prison had contributed to his changing conception of "our struggle." Victor Serge no longer believed "that the anarchist ideal could be limited to a single formula. Now I pay much less attention to words than to realities, to ideas than to aspirations, to formulas than to the sentiments." He was now ready to work with "all those whose good will becomes fraternal to me, without paying much attention to the secondary divergences in ideas."[10]

Victor was able to return to Paris on July 26 with a special visa that would allow him to join a Russian regiment. But Russian officers suspected that political refugees might join up in order to convince soldiers to desert. Not having money for a hotel, Victor went from anarchist to anarchist hoping to be lodged, without success, until finally he was taken in by a cabinetmaker and former contributor to *L'Anarchie*. He returned to Buttes-Chaumont for walks in the park with Rirette and her children. Victor found work in a printing shop, ironically close to the site where the guillotine had dispatched Callemin, Soudy, and the others, and then moved into the residence of a bookshop owner whom he had known before his arrest.

When Victor's visa expired, and with Clemenceau in power and waging war on all dissidents, the police arrested him on October 2, along with other anarchists. Victor wrote Chinette goodbye, telling her that once again he had been incarcerated and once again he had done nothing to merit it. He would "do the impossible to go to war" and asked her to remember him "even if I do not come back. And for your mother, also a goodbye and perhaps adieu." His final sentence may well contain a hint as to one of the reasons that their relationship fell apart. "I now feel more than ever," he wrote, "how total is the collapse of all to which I held. . . . Goodbye." It is possible that in the end Victor could not accept Rirette's ideas about free love and open relationships.[11]

In the meantime, the Bolsheviks had come to power in Russia by way of the October Revolution. Victor must have heard the news in prison in the Seine-et-Marne. In March 1918 he was transferred to another prison in Précigné in the Sarthe, a dumping place for foreigners who had been arrested, thieves, and anarchists and others with "dangerous ideas." The Treaty of Brest-Litovsk that month had officially taken now Communist Russia out of the Great War.

When Victor was imprisoned, Rirette loyally came to visit him and obtained books for him, and tried to mobilize some journalists and lawyers on his behalf. She had no success, and Victor became frustrated, writing Rirette angry letters, which she clearly did not deserve, and asking her to work more actively to try to achieve his freedom. From his cell, Victor wrote articles for the individualist newspaper *La Mélée*, signing them as Victor Serge. A quarter of the inmates in the prison were killed by the Spanish flu, a pandemic that killed millions of people worldwide from 1918 to 1920, but Victor survived. The Red Cross organized an exchange of French prisoners being held in Russia for Russians incarcerated in France. This finally brought Victor's release in December 1918, the month after the Great War ended.[12]

Before leaving for Russia, Victor sent *Le Libertaire* comments on the Russian Revolution, which were published as articles: he signed them "V. S. Le Rétif."[13] Victor and Rirette would be separated once again. He told her, "You understand, it is what my father hoped would happen. This is why he fought. I have to go there." She replied, "I don't have the strength to follow you. My life is here. Your revolution is taking place over there. I will work for mine here." Victor promised to return.[14]

Victor boarded a ship for Finland on January 26, 1919. Vladimir Lenin had arrived two years earlier, transported in a sealed railroad car. Lenin had been in exile from the country in which he had been born and organized a revolutionary movement against the tsarist autocracy. In contrast, when Victor arrived in Petrograd, it was his first time in the county of his family's origin. On the journey he fell in love with Liouba Roussakov, a twenty-year-old Russian woman who had lived in Marseille. She was the daughter of a veteran of the Revolution of 1905 who was making the same journey. Victor and Liouba married in Russia on August 13, 1919, even before he had divorced Rirette. Liouba gave birth to their son, Vlady, the next year, and a daughter, Jeannine, fifteen years later.

Victor's attraction to Russian revolutionary idealism had remained with him. In a letter sent from Petrograd he wrote that he would "join again with those who will fight the evils of the new regime."[15]

He broke with anarchism in 1919 and accepted Leninism, which led to angry disputes with anarchist friends. He joined the Communist Party that May, and at one time was given responsibility for looking after the archives of the tsar's secret police, the Okhrana. He worked for the Communist Third International, the Comintern, which had just been created. Victor readily admitted that "socialism itself contains seeds of reaction . . . an internal danger much more real at present than the external ones that are harped upon." To Victor, socialism could only triumph in the Soviet Union and the world "if it surpasses capitalism not in the building of tanks but in the organization of social life." Looking back, he believed anarchism had failed because anarchists were unable to organize a mass movement.

Victor explained his evolution in a letter to *Le Libertaire*: "We are past the time when someone can believe himself an anarchist because he is a vegetarian." Things had changed. Now it was necessary to accept "all the requirements of the struggle—organization, the use of violence, revolutionary dictatorship—that are part of the vast Communist movement." Anarchism had shown itself "incapable of any practical initiative through its divisions . . . its lack of organization and discipline. Whatever it enjoyed in the way of real capacities and energies [was] wasted in small chaotic struggles."[16]

Leninism, at least in the early days in the post-revolutionary period, seemed to Victor, among many others, far more capable of offering a "revolutionary elite, powerfully organized, disciplined, obeying a consistent direction, marching toward a single clearly defined goal." And, at least early on, discussion and debate took place, and dissension did not bring automatic exclusion—at least on minor issues. To be sure, Victor may have exaggerated the degree of democratic discussion after the Bolsheviks came to power with the October Revolution, a year before he arrived in Russia. And, as brutal repression of the insurrection of sailors at the Baltic port of Kronstadt in March 1921 demonstrated, workers' control quickly disappeared. Victor opposed the establishment of the Cheka Soviet

Victor Kibaltchiche, then Victor
Serge, later in life.

secret police and of the repression at Kronstadt. These factors probably led him to withdraw to a short-lived rural colony near Lake
Ladoga, not far from St. Petersburg. But Victor returned to militancy and in 1921 was named head of propaganda aimed at Central
Europe. In Germany between 1921 and 1923, he wrote articles on
the political situation there and elsewhere, continuing this work in
Vienna in 1924 and into 1925.[17]

Victor returned to the Soviet Union in 1925 and joined Leon
Trotsky and what became the Left Opposition to Stalin. At the end
of 1927, Victor was expelled from the Communist Party. Several
months after Trotsky's deportation to Kazakhstan, the secret police
arrested Victor as he was purchasing medication for his wife, who
was becoming increasingly psychotic. Imprisoned for thirty-six
days, he decided to devote himself to writing, believing it "a means
of finding harmony by offering our accounts of the vast life that is
racing by us and of which we attempt to establish essential aspects
for those who will come after us." Victor embraced what he believed
the mission of the Russian writer of fiction, "a means of expressing

to men what most of them live inwardly without being able to express, as a means of communion, a testimony to the vast flow of life through us."[18]

Victor's first novel, *Les hommes dans le prison* (*Men in Prison*), published in 1930, was "an effort to free myself from this inner nightmare and also to fulfill a duty to all those who will never be freed." He wanted to communicate the dehumanization of daily life in prison to people who had no idea what life was like in such places. He insists on the "multiple presence of death" in prison and "a total powerlessness that becomes even clearer with the passage of time."[19] The experiences Victor had had during the five years he spent in the French prison now came pouring out. He would soon see Stalin's even more horrifying institutions of incarceration.

In June 1933 Soviet police again arrested Victor. He and his son Vlady, who was then thirteen years old, were sent to the Gulag in Orenburg in the Ural Mountains near the border with Kazakhstan. Victor sent Liouba, his spouse who was in failing mental health, back to Moscow for psychiatric treatment. In France, a defense committee for Victor started up. In late 1936, Victor asked to be allowed to return to France, where the Popular Front was in power. French intellectuals—notably Romain Rolland but also André Gide, André Malraux, and Henri Barbusse—pressured Stalin to order Victor's release.

Victor was freed from the Gulag and returned to France in 1937, when his ban was lifted, along with Liouba and their two children. That year, he published on life in Stalin's Soviet Union and left the Communist Fourth International. However, Victor remained faithful to Marxism, about which he wrote "allows us to confer on our isolated lives a high significance."[20] Yet again, French authorities refused to allow him to stay in France. He went briefly to Brussels, where he had not been in at least thirty-seven years, and was reunited with Jean de Boe and Eugène Dieudonné. De Boe had been condemned to ten years of hard labor after the trial and had escaped to Belgium in 1922. In May 1937 Victor returned to Paris, living in Le Pré-Saint-Gervais not far from Rirette. Their divorce had been finalized on February 14.

The next month, Victor referred in a letter to "a large, dense and reflective book" he had written on *l'Affaire Bonnot*, but that it had fallen into the hands of Soviet censors. He believed that "the bastards are considering using it against me." But Victor indicated that he would write it again and "soon." However, no trace of such a book has ever been found.[21]

The French police, never letting up, identified Victor as a "suspect" in October 1938, on the occasion of an official visit by the king of Belgium to Paris. As a result, Victor managed to get a postponement of a year for his forced departure from France, which was renewed in January 1940.[22] In Le Pré-Saint-Gervais, Liouba had become increasingly ill, and was later transferred to an asylum in Aix-en-Provence.

With the German invasion of France in 1940, Victor left Paris for good on June 10, arriving in Mexico on a cargo ship in September of the next year. Victor traveled to Mexico with a new partner, Laurette Séjourné, his son Vlady, and his daughter Jeannine. Stalin's secret police continued to track him. It was in Mexico that Victor wrote his memoirs.[23]

Victor had remained loyal to Trotsky, despite their break over Victor's view that the Popular Front in France, formed in 1936, and other popular fronts, including that in Spain, could become an instrument of class struggle. Trotsky refused to give unconditional support to Spanish anarchist forces even though they were being undermined by Stalin. For his part, Trotsky denounced Victor as a "disillusioned pretty bourgeois intellectual," someone who "plays with the concept of revolution [and] writes poems about it but is incapable of understanding what it really is."[24]

Like Kropotkin, Victor was increasingly horrified that one kind of centralized state had been replaced by another, a totalitarian state, which had sent him to the Gulag, along with his young son. Victor's later "witness-novels" took readers across the Russian revolutionary experience, from before the war, through the Revolution, Civil War, the New Economic Policy (when in 1922 Lenin retreated somewhat from War Communism and permitted the coexistence of the private and state sectors in order that the return of the market to agriculture would increase food supply in the wake of the Civil War and subsequent famine), and the Stalinist period. Ever the idealist, Victor wanted to "rescue the honor" of the men and women who made the Russian Revolution. In January 1947, still in Mexico, Victor published "The New Russian Imperialism: Europe at the Crossroads: Renaissance or Totalitarianism?"[25]

Years of suffering had taken their physical toll on Victor Serge: "I suffered more than ten years in various prisons, was an activist in seven different countries, and have written twenty books. I own absolutely nothing." He had often been the victim of the mass press "because I tell the truth." Looking back, he had seen "a victorious revolution that then went wrong, several failed revolutions, and so many massacres that it makes one dizzy. And it is not finished." Yet until the very end, he expressed "more confidence in mankind and in the future than I have ever had before."[26]

Victor passed away on November 17, 1947, in Mexico, still optimistic that "the technical advantages of production, the sense of social justice, the newly found freedom would combine naturally to place the economy at the service of the community. . . . All is not lost since this rational and strongly motivated hope remains."[27] The last word Victor Serge wrote was "dazzling."[28]

Rirette's life went in a direction decidedly different from Victor's. After they parted ways, she remained in Paris, with no means of existence and two young children to feed. On May 4, 1918, she was arrested after a theft from a store. A magistrate sentenced her to two months in prison, but with a suspended sentence. After the war ended, Rirette earned her living as a proofreader for *France soir*. She continued to live in Belleville, and then purchased a small house in Crosne, near Villeneuve-Saint-Georges southeast of Paris. There she was able to invite friends to stay with her, as before, and gradually returned to attending anarchist *causeries*, although she was no longer a militant. Victor and Rirette had continued their relationship as friends. In 1959 Rirette wrote of their relationship, "Throughout this extraordinary odyssey, we never stopped talking to one another spiritually. I have quite a lot of letters from everywhere—Russia, Germany, Austria, Silesia, and finally Mexico."[29]

Rirette moved for a time to Lyon during World War II, where she became friends with Albert Camus. She returned to Paris after the war, moving into a small attic apartment near the Louvre. She worked for *Libération* until 1953. It was in the newspaper's office that she learned the devastating news that Victor had passed away.[30]

Rirette Maîtrejean lived to see the *révolution manquée* (failed revolution) of 1968, a year of hope in France for many, marked by massive student protests and widespread strikes by workers in Paris (and elsewhere in France and abroad) but also by frustration and disillusionment. Rirette passed away on June 14 of that year at the age of seventy-nine in the hospice of Limeil-Brévannes. Rirette had always rejected the pointless violence of "propaganda by the deed" that turned people away from anarchism. The battle, she felt, still had to be won with ideas. At the Sorbonne, anarchists observed a minute of silence in her honor. The newspaper *L'Aurore* made an obvious comparison: like the young of today, she wanted to "shake the very structures of society and overthrow the bourgeoisie of her fathers." To the end she conserved "the profile of a young schoolgirl," still insisting that "our ideas were beautiful."[31]

The Bonnot Gang remains in the collective memory of France. In 1915, a *Fantômas* film left no doubt that it was about Jules Bonnot and his colleagues. Subsequently, many accounts have appeared in French telling essentially the same story. Since World War II alone, a television series, a film in 1968 with the singer Jacques Brel playing Raymond *la Science*,[32] a song by Joe Dassin the same year,[33] and a comic strip published in 1978[34] have kept the story alive. In 1973, a man wrote the Museum of the Prefecture of Police offering to sell "some of the blood of the celebrated bandit Bonnot." His father, a policeman who claimed to have participated in the siege at Choisy-le-Roi, had hoped to capitalize on Bonnot's renown. With this in mind, he had "put this blood on a large sheet of white paper." The museum declined. Someone else contributed several locks of Bonnot's hair to the museum.[35]

Yet the Bonnot Gang should remain in our memory of France for other reasons. In 1926 the anarchist Victor Méric, who lived through the period and had at the time revealed sympathy for the bandits following the siege at Nogent-sur-Marne, published his reflections on the *Bandits Tragiques*. He now expressed no sympathy for Bonnot, Callemin, and the others. Looking back from the postwar period, he drew a conclusion: If in society one could ever find "a little equality in human relations, a little less savage inequality, more absolute certainty in the precarious lives of the humble and the laborious," Méric concluded that such events as the sheer brutality of the Bonnot Gang would be impossible. The Great War had had changed nothing in this regard: "The lamentable spectacle [of] 'the sumptuous arrogance of some and the sordid misery of others' remained, well after the Belle Époque that wasn't had been swept away by the violence of states."[36]

PRIMARY SOURCES

Archives of the Prefecture of Police

JA 15
JA 16
JA 17
JA 18
JA 19
JA 20
JA 21
JA 22
JA 23
JA 24
JA 25

EA140
EA141
77W 4255
BA 928
BA 1499

KA 74
KA 77

French National Archives

F7 13053

L'Anarchie
Le Matin
Le Petit Parisien
L'Excelsior
Figaro

National Library of France

Salle X, banque DOSS. FOL-LN1-232 (11228)

MEMOIRS AND SECONDARY SOURCES

Bancquart, Marie-Claire. *Images littéraires de Paris fin de siècle*. Paris, 1979.

Bancquart, Marie-Claire. *Paris "Belle Époque" par ses écrivains*. Paris, 1997.

Beaudet, Céline. *Les milieux libres. Vivre en anarchie à la Belle Époque*. Saint-Georges-d'Oléron, 2006.

Becker, Émile. *La "Bande à Bonnot."* Paris, 1968.

Bernard, Jean-Pierre. *Les deux Paris: les représentations de Paris dans la seconde moitié du xixe siècle*. Paris, 2001.

Bernède, Arthur. *Bonnot, Garnier et Cie*. Paris, 1930.

Becker, Jean-Jacques. *1914: Comment les Français sont entrés dans la guerre. Paris: presses de la fondation nationale des sciences politiques*. Paris, 1977.

Berenson, Edward. *The Trial of Madame Caillaux*. Berkeley, 1992.

Berlanstein, Lenard. *The Working People of Paris, 1871–1914*. Baltimore, 1984.

Berlière, Jean-Marc. *Le monde des polices en France*. Paris, 1996.

Berlière, Jean-Marc. *Le Préfet Lépine: Vers la naissance de la police modern*. Paris, 1993.

Boucabelle, Marius. *A propos de l'affaire Bonnot*. Paris, 1912.

Bouhey, Vivien, and Philippe Levillain. *Les anarchistes contre la République*. Paris, 2008.

Cannon, James. *The Paris Zone: A Cultural History, 1840–1944*. Farnham, UK, 2015.

Carco, Francis. *La Belle Époque au temps de Bruant*. Paris, 1954.

Caruchet, William. *Ils ont tué Bonnot: Les révélations des archives policières*. Paris, 1990.

Castelle, Pierre. *Paris Républicain 1871–1914*. Abbeville, 2003.

Charle, Christophe. *La crise des sociétés impériales (1900–14)*. Paris, 2001.

Chevalier, Louis. *Montmartre du plaisir et du crime*. Paris, 1995.

Chomarat, Michel. *Les Amants tragiques. Histoire du bandit Jules Bonnot et de sa maîtresse Judith Thollon*. Lyon, 1978.

Clavé, Florenci. *La bande à Bonnot*. Grenoble, 1978.

Davranche, Guillaume. *Trop jeune pour mourir: Ouvriers et révolutionnaires face à la guerre (1909–1914)*. Paris, 2014.

Delacourt, Fréderic. *L'Affaire bande à Bonnot*. Paris, 2006.

Deluermoz, Quentin. *Policiers dans la ville: La construction d'un ordre public à Paris 1854–1914.* Paris, 2012.

Depond, Dominique. *Jules Bonnot et sa bande*. Paris, 2009.

Dhavernas, Marie-Joseph. "La surveillance des anarchistes individualistes (1894–1914)," in Philippe Vigier, Alain Faure, et al., *Maintien de l'ordre et polices en France et en Europe au XIXe siècle*. Montrouge, 1987, 347–360.

Dieudonné, Eugène. *La vie des forçats*. Paris, 1930.

Girard, André. *Anarchistes et bandits*. Paris: Publications des Temps Nouveaux, 1914.

Gordon, Paul. *Vagabond Witness: Victor Serge and the Politics of Hope*. Washington, DC, 2013.

Grave, Jean. *Mémoires d'un anarchiste (1854–1920)*. Paris, 2009.

Guillaume, Marcel. *Mes grandes enquêtes criminelles. De la bande à Bonnot à l'affaire Stavisky.* Paris, 2005.

Harp, Steven L. *Michelin: Publicité et identité culturelle dans la France du XXe siècle [Marketing Michelin: Advertising and Cultural Identity in Twentieth-Century France]*. Baltimore, 2001.

Higonnet, Patrice. *Paris, Capital of the World*. Cambridge, MA, 2002.

Jacquemet, Gérard. "La violence à Belleville au début du xxe siècle," *Bulletin de la Société de l'histoire de Paris et de l'Île-de-France*, 1978, 141–167.

Jones, Colin. *Paris: Biography of a City*. London, 2004.

Juin, Hubert. *Le Livre de Paris 1900*. Paris, 1994.

Julliard, Jacques. *Clemenceau briseur de grèves*. Paris, 1965.

Kalifa, Dominique. *Les bas-fonds: Histoire d'un imaginaire*. Paris, 2013.

Kalifa, Dominique. "Belle Époque: invention et usages d'un chrononyme," *Revue d'histoire du XIXe siècle*, 52 (2016/1), pp. 119–132.

Kalifa, Dominique. *L'encre et le sang*. Paris, 1995.

Kalifa, Dominique. *Véritable histoire de la "Belle Époque."* Paris, 2017.

Kaluszynski, Martine. "Alphonse Bertillon et l'antropométrie," in Philippe Vigier, Alain Faure, et al., *Maintien de l'ordre et polices en France et en Europe au XIXe siècle*. Montrouge, 1987, 269–285.

Laux, James M. *In First Gear: The French Automobile Industry to 1914*. Montréal, 1976.

Lavignette, Frédéric. *La bande à Bonnot à travers la presse de l'époque*. Lyon, 2008.

Lépine, Louis. *Mes souvenirs*. Paris, 1929.

López, Laurent. *La guerre des polices n'a pas eu lieu: Gendarmes et policiers, co-acteurs de la sécurité publique sous la Troisième République (1870–1914)*. Paris, 2014.

Lorulot, André. *Chez les loups. Moeurs anarchistes*. Paris, 1922.

Lorulot, André. *Le crime de 1914*. Conflans-Sainte-Honorine, 1922.

Machelon, Jean-Pierre. *La République contre les libertés?* Paris, 1976.

Maitron, J(ean). "De Kibaltchiche à Victor Serge. Le Rétif (1909–1919)," *Mouvement social*, 47, avril–juin 1964, pp. 45–80.

Maitron, Jean. *Le mouvement anarchiste en France*. Vol. 1. *Des origines à 1914*. Paris, 2007.

Maîtrejean, Rirette. *Souvenirs d'anarchie*. Quimperlé, 2005.

Manfredonia, Gaetano. *Anarchisme et changement social: Insurrectionnalisme, syndicalisme, éducationnisme-réalisateur*. Loriol, 2007.

Manfredonia, Gaetano. *La chanson anarchiste en France des origines à 1914*. Paris, 1997.

Marchand, Bernard. *Paris, histoire d'une ville, xixe-xxe siècle*. Paris, 1993.

Marshall, Bill. *Victor Serge: The Uses of Dissent*. New York, 1992.

McAuliffe, Mary. *Twilight of the Belle Epoque: The Paris of Picasso, Stravinsky, Proust, Renault, Marie Curie, Gertrude Stein, and Their Friends Through the Great War*. New York, 2014.

Méric, Victor. *Les bandits tragiques*. Paris, 1926.

Merriman, John. *Dynamite Club: How a Café Bombing in Fin-de-Siècle Paris Ignited the Age of Modern Terror*. Boston, 2009.

Merriman, John. *Massacre: The Life and Death of the Paris Commune*. New York, 2014.

Micale, Mark S., "France," in Michael Saler, ed., *The Fin-de-Siècle World*. New York, 2015, 93–116.

Michon, Émile. *Un peu de l'âme de bandits: Étude de psychologie criminelle*. N.p., 1913.

Miller, Paul B. *From Revolutionaries to Citizens: Anti-Militarism in France, 1870–1914*. Durham, NC, 2002.

Morand, Paul. *1900*. Paris, 1931.

Nemeth, Luc. "Victor Serge, marqué, par son passé," in Rirette Maîtrejean, *Souvenirs d'anarchie*. Quimperlé, 2005.

Néris, Philippe. *La Bande à Bonnot*. Paris, 1925.

Nye, Robert. *Crime, Madness, and Politics in Modern France*. Princeton, 1984.

Pacaud, Serge. *Vie quotidienne des français à la Belle Époque*. Romorantin, 2008.

Parry, Richard. *The Bonnot Gang*. London, 1987.

Pécherot, Patrick. *L'Homme à la Carabine*. Paris, 2011.

Michelle Perrot, "Dans la France de la Belle Époque, les 'Apaches,' premières bandes de jeunes," in Les Marginaux et les exclus dans l'histoire, Cahiers Jussieu no. 5 (1979).

Porot, Jacques. *Louis Lépine: Préfet de Police, Témoin de sons temps (1846–1933)*. Paris, 1994.

Prost, Antoine. *Si nous vivions en 1913*. Paris, 2014.

Rearick, Charles. *Paris Dreams, Paris Memories: The City and Its Mystique*. Stanford, 2011.

Rearick, Charles. *Pleasures of the Belle Epoque: Entertainment and Festivity in Turn-of-the-Century France*. New Haven, CT: Yale University Press, 1985.

Rière, Jean. *Cahiers Henry Poulaille, Hommage à Victor Serge (1890–1947) pour le centenaire de sa naissance*, Éditions Plein Chant, mars 1991, no. 4 et 5. (Présentation par Jean Rière). Bassac, 1990.

Roe, Sue. *In Montmartre: Picasso, Matisse and the Birth of Modernist Art*. New York, 2014.

Rustenholz, Alain. *Paris ouvrier: Des sublimes aux camarades*. Paris, 2003.

Salmon, André. *La Terreur noire*. Paris, 2008.

Sante, Luc. *The Other Paris*. New York, 2015.

Schwartz, Vanessa. *Spectacular Realities: Early Mass Culture in Fin-de-Siècle Paris*. Berkeley, 1998.

Serge, Victor. *Les hommes dans le prison*. Preface by Richard Greeman. Paris, 2011.

Serge, Victor. "Méditation sur l'anarchie," *Esprit*, 55, April 1, 1937.

Serge, Victor. *Mémoires d'un révolutionnaire, 1901–1941*. Edited by Jean Rière. Paris, 1978.

Serge, Victor. *Memoirs of a Revolutionary*. Forward by Adam Hochschild. New York, 2012.

Serge, Victor. *Le Rétif: Articles parus dans "L'Anarchie" 1909–1912*. Edited by Yves Pagès. Paris, 1989.

Shattuck, Roger. *The Banquet Years: The Origins of the Avant-Garde in France 1885 to World War I*. New York, 1958.

Steiner, Anne. *Les En-dehors: anarchistes individualistes et illégalistes dans la Belle Époque*. Montreuil, 2008.

Steiner, Anne. *Le gout de l'émeute: manifestations et violences de rue dans Paris et sa banlieue à la "Belle Époque."* Paris, 2012.

Steiner, Anne. *Rirette l'insoumise*. Tulle, 2013.

Texier, Robert Le. *De Ravachol à la bande à Bonnot*. Paris, 1989.

Thomazo, Renaud. *Mort aux bourgeois! Sur les traces de la bande à Bonnot*. Paris, 2009.

Weber, Eugen. *France, Fin-de-Siècle*. Cambridge, MA: Harvard University Press, 1986.

Weissman, Susan, ed. *The Ideas of Victor Serge: A Life as a Work of Art*. Critique Books, 1997.

Weissman, Susan. *Victor Serge: The Course Is Set on Hope*. London: Verso 2001.

Winock, Michel. *La Belle Epoque*. Paris, 2002.

Winock, Michel. *Les derniers feux de la Belle Époque*. Paris, 2014.

ACKNOWLEDGMENTS

Most books are inevitably long solo flights, but in fact one of the nice things about writing is the assistance that friends and colleagues provide along the way. At Fletcher and Company, I would like to thank Don Lamm, as well as Melissa Chinchillo and Erin McFadden. In conceptualizing and researching this book, I have benefited greatly from conversations with and advice from Dominique Kalifa and Quentin Deluermoz. Sven Wanegffelen joined me on a fascinating trek to the Parisian suburb of Choisy-le-Roi to find what is left of the garage where police and soldiers surrounded and then killed Jules Bonnot, and then to Thiais to find where stood the house in which several members of the Bonnot Gang massacred two elderly people. Thanks also to Jean-Claude Petilon and Jean Mpaka, who took me to the viaduct over the Marne that loomed over the "villa" in which Octave Garnier and René Valet met their fate. Cory Browning, Ken Loiselle, and Steve Harp provided helpful suggestions. The staff of the Archives de la préfecture de police was unfailingly professional in facilitating my research there.

For the research for this project, I received support from the MacMillan Center and the Whitney Griswold Faculty Research fund. I was kindly invited to present talks based on the research for this book at the Sorbonne, as a plenary talk at the Western Society of French History in San Antonio and another at the United Kingdom Society for the Study of French History in Glasgow, and at the University of Oregon, Central Michigan University, and Southern Methodist University.

I am extremely fortunate to have been able to work for the second time with Katy O'Donnell, now at Nation Books. She is an absolutely remarkable editor. Jennifer Crane provided splendid copyediting. Thanks also to Brooke Parsons who worked on publicity for the book.

I dedicate this book to my great friend Peter McPhee, a terrific historian of modern France, one of the very best anywhere. We became friends in the early 1970s, when he was working in and on the Pyrénées-Orientales and I was still researching in Limoges. We share a love of French Catalonia, particularly Collioure. Thanks to Peter, I enjoyed two wonderful trips to Australia and began to follow Australian Footy (Australian Rules Football).

★★★★★

Carol Merriman passed away suddenly in December 2016. Carol and I were married more than thirty-six years. The two greatest gifts she gave us both are Laura and Chris Merriman. The final stages of the preparation of this book occurred during a time of great sadness for the three of us. We have been fortunate to have the friendship and support of Victoria Johnson, Bruno and Flora Cabanes, Mark Lawrence, Charles Keith, Steve Pincus and Sue Stokes, Richard and Sandy Simon, Dave Bushnell, Joe and Nancy Malloure, Don and Jean Lamm, Steve Shirley, Mike Johnson, Jeanne Innes, Jim Read, Ben Kiernan and Glenda Gilmore, Jim Collins, Gil Joseph, Endre Sashalmi, Peter Kracht, Andrzej Kamiński, Thomas Forster, Dominique Kalifa, Jean-Claude Petilon, Sylvain Venayre, Nancy Green, Sven Wangelffelen, Phil Kalberer, and Peter McPhee.

ACKNOWLEDGMENTS

And in Balazuc, Hervé and Françoise Parain, Élodie Parain, Lucien and Catherine Mollier, Eric Fruleux, Mathieu Fruleux, William and Ng Claveyrolat, and so many others. Laura, Chris, and I owe much to many people, above all, to Carol.

Balazuc, July 9, 2017

NOTES

_____

Prologue

1   EA 141, officer de la paix, Paris XVIIIe, December 21, 1911; JA 15; JA 20, October 21, 1912.

2   Rirette Maîtrejean, *Souvenirs d'anarchie* (Paris, 2005), pp. 85–86.

Chapter 1: The Good Old Days in Paris

1   Vanessa R. Schwartz, *Spectacular Realities: Early Mass Culture in Fin-de-Siècle Paris* (Berkeley, 1998), pp. 13–16, 20. Schwartz controversially suggests (pp. 201–204) that the new consumerism and Parisian crowds rushing to see what turned up in the morgue, going to the Musée Grévin, participating in the O'Rama craze, or going to the cinema transformed potentially revolutionary crowds into contented participants in the spectacle of consumption, an "urban culture of spectatorship." In my view, if Paris seemed less revolutionary, this had far more to do with the increasing bourgeoisification of the city and the enhanced presence of the "forces of order."

2   Jean-Pierre Bernard, *Les deux Paris: les représentations de Paris dans le seconde moitié du xixe siècle* (Seyssel, 2001), p. 241.

3   Mark S. Micale, "France," in Michael Saler, ed., *The Fin-de-Siècle World* (New York, 2015), p. 99.

4   Charles Rearick, *Paris Dreams, Paris Memories: The City and Its Mystique* (Redwood City, 2011), pp. 13–14; Frédéric Lavignette, *La bande à Bonnot à travers la presse de l'époque* (Lyon, 2008), p. 229, January 8, 1912.

5   Eugen Weber, *France Fin de Siècle* (Cambridge, MA, 1986), pp. 4, 70–73; James Laux, *In First Gear: The French Automobile Industry to 1914* (Montréal, 1976), pp. 201–202; Vanessa R. Schwartz, *Spectacular Realities: Early Mass Culture in Fin-de-Siècle Paris* (Berkeley, 1998), p. 21.

6   Patrice Higonnet, *Paris, Capital of the World* (Cambridge, MA, 2002), p. 422.

7   Roger Shattuck, *The Banquet Years: The Origins of the Avant-Garde in France 1885 to World War I* (New York, 1958), p. 21.

8   Micale, "France," pp. 101–103.

9   Shattuck, *The Banquet Years*; Mary McAuliffe, *Twilight of the Belle Epoque: The Paris of Picasso, Stravinsky, Proust, Renault, Marie Curie, Gertrude Stein, and Their Friends Through the Great War* (Lanham, MD, 2014), p. 111.

10   Paul Morand, *1900* (Paris, 1931), p. 205, adding "*Au style-nouille en architecture et en littérature correspond la morale-nouille*"; Micale, "France," p. 101.

11   Hubert Juin, *Le Livre de Paris 1900* (Paris, 1994), pp. 104–105; Bernard Marchand, *Paris, histoire d'une ville, xixe–xxe siècle* (Paris, 1993), p. 173.

12   Jean-Pierre Bernard, *Les deux Paris: les représentations de Paris dans le seconde moitié du xixe siècle* (Paris, 2001), pp. 240–241.

13   John Merriman, *Massacre: The Life and Death of the Paris Commune* (New York, 2014).

14   Higonnet, *Paris, Capital of the World*, p. 315. Goncourt used the term with a sarcasm that would not have pleased the Parisian elite thirty to forty years later: "Tonight, illustrious Tout Paris gathered at the Italiens for a private performance. Well, the reflection to which this gathering gives rise is the following: French aristocratic high society is dead. There is nobody left nowadays but financiers and tarts, or women who look like tarts."

15   Lenard Berlanstein, *The Working People of Paris, 1871–1914* (Baltimore, 1984), pp. 6–7, 21, noting that "To distinguish definitively between the 'workshop' and the 'factory' is an impossible task." Berlanstein emphasizes the gradual "embourgeoisement" of Paris and the growing significance of service work.

16   Marie-Claire Bancquart, *Paris "Belle Époque" par ses écrivains* (Paris, 1997), p. 95; Juin, *Le Livre de Paris 1900*, pp. 54–55.

17   Higonnet, *Paris, Capital of the World*, pp. 249. 291, 310; Bancquart, *Paris "Belle Époque" par ses écrivains*, p. 59; Elections for the Chamber of Deputies in 1902 confirmed the political geography of the capital; socialists were defeated in central Paris and the Latin Quarter. In the municipal elections two years later, the more prosperous western and central districts returned conservative representatives [Michel Winock, *La Belle Époque* (Paris, 2002), pp. 288, 366; Marchand, *Paris, histoire d'une ville, xixe–xxe siècle*, p. 160; Pierre Castelle, *Paris Républicain 1871–1914* (Abbeville, 2003), pp. 35, 103, although the legislative elections brought better results for the left.

18   Rearick, *Pleasures of the Belle Epoque: Entertainment and Festivity in Turn-of-the-Century France* (New Haven, 1985), pp. 95–97.

19   Rearick, *Paris Dreams, Paris Memories*, pp. 61–62; Winock, *La Belle Époque*, p. 110; McAuliffe, *Twilight of the Belle Epoque*, p. 244.

20   Michel Winock, *Les derniers feux à la Belle Époque* (Paris, 2014), p. 132; Winock, *La Belle Époque*, pp. 347–348, 370; Colin Jones, *Paris: Biography of a City* (London, 2004), p. 429; Rearick, *Pleasures of the Belle Epoque*, p. 192; Castelle, *Paris Républicain 1871–1914*, p. 415.

21   Weber, *France, Fin-de-Siècle*, p. 162; Higonnet, *Paris, Capital of the World*, p. 304; Morand, *1900*, pp. 9, 205, 209; Shattuck, *The Banquet Years*, pp. 3–5. Shattuck focuses on four avant-garde symbols of the age: Guillaume Apollinaire, Erik

Satie, Alfred Jarry, and the *Douanier* Rousseau, identifying four traits that the four shared: youth, humor, a sense of dreaming, and ambiguity (Chapter 2 and pp. 198–199 and 275). The four "did not seek courage in numbers; they found it in themselves. We see them variously as children and determined humorists, as dreamers and mystifiers, and they played all these roles. But their ultimate virtue lies deeper, lodged beneath all their vices. They had the wisdom, already rare, to know themselves, and the courage, which is far rarer, to be themselves."

22   Marchand, *Paris, histoire d'une ville, xixe–xxe siècle*, p. 208; Rearick, *Paris Dreams, Paris Memories*, p. 41.

23   Weber, *France, Fin-de-Siècle*, pp. 90–91, 102–104; McAuliffe, *Twilight of the Belle Epoque*, pp. 151–152.

24   Shattuck, *The Banquet Years*, p. 5.

25   Morand, *1900*, pp. 190–191.

26   Christophe Charle, *La crise des sociétés impériales (1900–1940)* (Paris, 2001), p. 107.

27   Charle, *La crise des sociétés impériales (1900–1940)*, pp. 112, 116.

28   This arguably provided a surprising stability that allowed the regime to survive right-wing challengers who wanted to destroy the Republic, notably the followers of General Georges Boulanger, who in 1889 wanted to overthrow the Republic, and the opponents of Captain Alfred Dreyfus during that monumental crisis that lasted from 1894 to 1906. Dreyfus, who was Jewish, was falsely accused in 1894 of handing over military secrets to Germany. The Dreyfus Affair divided France, pitting the army, much of the French right wing, and some conservative Catholics against Dreyfus's defenders, who notably included Émile Zola. The great novelist published a shot across the bow with his newspaper article that memorably began "*J'Accuse*," accurately denouncing the General Staff for lying and using blatant forgeries in the attempt to convict Dreyfus. The Jewish captain was convicted, formally humiliated, and sent to Devil's Island before finally being pardoned in 1897.

29   Winock, *La Belle Époque*, p. 21.

30   The politics of the Third Republic during this period have been described as having "found a surprisingly stable balance between corruption, passionate conviction, and low comedy" (Shattuck, *The Banquet Years*, p. 3).

31   Dominque Kalifa, *L'Encre et du sang* (Paris, 1995), p. 56.

Chapter 2: Victor Kibaltchiche

1   Victor Serge, *Mémoires d'un révolutionnaire 1901–1941*, edited by Jean Rière (Paris, 2010), 7–9, 14.

2   Victor Serge, *Memoirs of a Revolutionary* (New York, 2012), pp. 7–8.

3   Serge, *Mémoires d'un révolutionnaire*, pp. 10–12; Rirette Maîtrejean, *Souvenirs d'anarchie*, p. 82; Victor Serge, *Le Rétif: Articles parus dans "L'Anarchie," 1909–1912*, edited by Yves Pagès (Paris, 1989), 215–216; Victor Serge, "Méditation sur l'anarchie," *Esprit*, 55, April 1, 1937, p. 29.

4   Serge, *Mémoires d'un révolutionnaire*, pp. 12–14; Steiner, *Rirette l'insoumise*, p. 39; J(ean) Maitron, "De Kibaltchiche à Victor Serge. Le Rétif (1909–1919)," *Mouvement social*, 47, avril–juin 1964, p. 45; Serge, "Méditation sur l'anarchie," p. 29.

5   JA 17, dossier Callemin, report of July 3, 1913; Serge, "Méditation sur l'anarchie,"
        p. 30; Émile Michon, *Un peu de l'âme de bandits: étude de psychologie criminelle* (1913),
        pp. 190–193.

6   Serge, *Memoirs of a Revolutionary*, p. 9.

7   Serge, *Mémoires d'un révolutionnaire*, pp. 10–17; Serge, "Méditation sur l'anarchie,"
        pp. 30–31.

8   Victor Méric, *Les bandits tragiques* (Paris, 1926), p. 54.

9   JA16, "Mes Mémoires: (Callemin dit Raymond la Science): Pourquoi j'ai cambriolé
        Pourquoi j'ai tué"; Méric, *Les bandits tragiques* (Paris, 1926), p. 65; Maîtrejean, *Souve-
        nirs d'anarchie*, p. 28.

10   JA16, "Mes Mémoires: (Callemin dit Raymond la Science): Pourquoi j'ai cambriolé
        Pourquoi j'ai tué."

11   Serge, ibid.; Serge, *Le Rétif: Articles parus dans "L'Anarchie," 1909–1912*, p. 216; Susan
        Weissman, *Victor Serge: The Course Is Set on Hope* (London: Verso, 2001), pp. 15–16.

12   Serge, *Memoires d'un révolutionnaire*, pp. 15–19; Maîtrejean, *Souvenirs d'anarchie*,
        p. 82; Serge, "Méditation sur l'anarchie," pp. 31–35, adding in retrospect that revo-
        lution did not appear possible "*dans ce grand calme d'avant-guerre.*"

13   Serge, *Mémoires d'un révolutionnaire*, pp. 14–15.

14   J(ean) Maitron, "De Kibaltchiche à Victor Serge. Le Rétif (1909–1919)," *Mouvement
        social*, 47, avril–juin 1964, pp. 48–49.

15   JA16, "Mes Mémoires: (Callemin dit Raymond la Science): Pourquoi j'ai cambriolé
        Pourquoi j'ai tué."

16   Victor Serge, *Le Rétif: Articles parus dans "L'Anarchie," 1909–1912* (Paris, 1989),
        including "Notice autobiographique," p. 216.

17   Serge, "Méditation sur l'anarchie," p. 30.

18   Steiner, *Les En-dehors*, pp. 68–70.

19   Serge, "Méditation sur l'anarchie," pp. 35–37; Serge, *Mémoires d'un révolutionnaire*,
        pp. 19–21.

20   Serge, "Méditation sur l'anarchie," pp. 35–37; Serge, *Mémoires d'un révolutionnaire*,
        pp. 19–21; Serge, *Le Rétif: Articles parus dans "L'Anarchie," 1909–1912*, pp. 9–10.
        Victor noted accurately that such colonies "*périclitaient de coutume assez vite, faute
        de ressources*" and that even though jealousy was formally forbidden, "*les histoires de
        femmes*" posed considerable problems.

21   Serge, *Mémoires d'un révolutionnaire*, pp. 24–25.

22   Serge, *Mémoires d'un révolutionnaire*, pp. 21–22; Richard Parry, *The Bonnot Gang*
        (London, 1987), p. 37.

23   Susan Weissman, *Victor Serge: The Course Is Set on Hope* (London, 2001), p. 16, writes
        that Victor was expelled from Belgium, but I find no confirmation of this.

24   Serge, *Mémoires d'un révolutionnaire*, pp. 22–23.

Chapter 3: Another Paris

1   Francis Carco, *La Belle Époque au temps de Bruant* (Paris, 1954), p. 18.

2   Dominique Depond, *Jules Bonnot et sa bande: Le tourbillon sanglant* (Paris, 2009), p. 31.

3   Louis Chevalier, *Montmartre du plaisir et du crime* (Paris, 1995), pp. 303–304; Victor Serge, *Memoirs of a Revolutionary* (New York, 2012), p. 27.

4   Mary McAuliffe, *Twilight of the Belle Epoque: The Paris of Picasso, Stravinsky, Proust, Renault, Marie Curie, Gertrude Stein, and Their Friends Through the Great War* (New York, 2014), p. 25.

5   Charles Rearick, *Paris Dreams, Paris Memories: The City and Its Mystique* (Stanford, 2011), pp. 29–34; Alexander Varias, *Paris and the Anarchists: Aesthetes and Subversives during the Fin-de-Siècle* (New York, 2002); Chevalier, *Montmartre du plaisir et du crime*, p. 269; Carco, *La Belle Époque au temps de Bruant*, p. 154.

6   The first Browning pistols were manufactured in the United States in the mid-1890s and were used by American troops during the Spanish-American war.

7   Rearick, *Paris Dreams, Paris Memories*, pp. 29–34; Varias, *Paris and the Anarchists*; Chevalier, *Montmartre du plaisir et du crime*, p. 269; Carco, *La Belle Époque au temps de Bruant*, p. 154; McAuliffe, *Twilight of the Belle Epoque*, pp. 98–99, 105–106, 147, 178. See Sue Row's recent *In Montmartre: Picasso, Matisse and the Birth of Modernist Art* (New York, 2014). *Excelsior*, October 20, 1911: *"Le browning, malheuresement, joit aujourd'hui d'une égale faveur dans tous les classes de société. Il est adapté à tous les usages. Une élégante jeune femme le manie aussi bien qu'un cambrioleur"* (Frédéric Lavignette, *La bande à Bonnot à travers la presse de l'époque*, p. 47).

8   Roger Shattuck, *The Banquet Years: The Origins of the Avant-Garde in France 1885 to World War I* (New York, 1958), p. 33.

9   As described by Chevalier, *Montmartre du plaisir et du crime*, p. 301. Chevalier argues that there was little difference between poets and artists who became anarchists and *"voyous"* who became anarchists.

10 Chevalier, *Montmartre du plaisir et du crime*, pp. 271–272.

11 Chevalier, *Montmartre du plaisir et du crime*, pp. 245, 271–277.

12 Dominique Kalifa, "Belle Époque: invention et usages d'un chrononyme," *Revue d'histoire du XIXe siècle*, 52 (2016/1), pp. 119–132; Kalifa, *La Véritable Histoire de la "Belle Époque"* (Paris, 2017). Octave Mirbeau referred to *"une belle époque"* in 1892, but not *"la belle époque"* when France never had seemed before *"aussi forte, assui grande, aussi respecté."* But the expression was not used in the 1920s. The 1930s represented the *"protohistoire de la Belle Époque,"* initiated by *1900* (1931), Paul Morand's diatribe against the alleged pretentiousness of the period. The retrospective embrace of the period was launched, but not yet the nostalgic concept of *"la Belle Époque,"* except with reference of specific trends, such as symbolism or style. That would come at the end of the 1930s. Abel Gance's *Le paradis perdu* filmed in 1939 and released in 1940, the same year as the Radio-Paris program, "Ah la Belle Époque." During the German occupation, amid the frenzy of seeking distractions, echoes of a much better time were required in the turn of the century, a vision of a Belle Époque of French rural life, music, theater, and luxury goods in a then-European power in the pre-Communist era. And after the horrors of World War II, Nicole Vedère's 1946 film *Paris 1900* offered a *"document authentique et sensationnel de la Belle Époque 1900–1914."* Jean Gourguet's film *Sur des airs d'autrefois* appeared the same year. With the United States joining the Soviet Union as the other great world power, the 1950s kept alive the importance of the memory of a "Belle Époque"

when France and its empire were still strong. Beginning in the 1970s, another wave of nostalgia gripped France, centering on the collection of old postcards from the turn of the century, carrying the nostalgia for the "Belle Époque" beyond Paris into every corner of France, urban and rural.

13   Chevalier, *Montmartre du plaisir et du crime*, p. 302.

14   Victor Serge, *Mémoires d'un révolutionnaire 1901–1941*, edited by Jean Rière (Paris, 1978), p. 28.

15   Pierre Castelle, *Paris Républicain 1871–1914* (Abbeville, 2003), pp. 135–136; Nancy Green, *The Pletzl of Paris* (New York, 1986).

16   Colin Jones, *Paris: Biography of a City* (London, 2004), pp. 411–412.

17   Bernard Marchand, *Paris, histoire d'une ville, xixe–xxe siècle* (Paris, 1993), pp. 163, 194–204.

18   Lenard Berlanstein, *The Working People of Paris, 1871–1914* (Baltimore, 1984), pp. 23–27.

19   Michelle Perrot, "The Three Ages of Industrial Discipline in France," in John M. Merriman, ed., *Consciousness and Class Experience in Nineteenth-Century France* (New York, 1979); Berlanstein, *The Working People of Paris, 1871–1914*, pp. 74–87, 97, 200–201.

20   Michel Winock, *La Belle Époque* (Paris, 2002), pp. 56–59, 68, 138; Castelle, *Paris Républicain 1871–1914*, pp. 191, 195, 203, 210; Christophe Charle, *La crise des sociétés impériales (1900–1940)* (Paris, 2001), p. 83.

21   Berlanstein, *The Working People of Paris, 1871–1914*, pp. 7–9, 71–73, 107–110; Jones, *Paris*, p. 413.

22   Berlanstein, *The Working People of Paris, 1871–1914*, pp. 104–105.

23   Jones, *Paris*, p. 413; Berlanstein, *The Working People of Paris, 1871–1914*, p. 44.

24   Serge Pacaud, *Vie quotidienne des français à la Belle Époque* (Romorantin-Lanthenay, 2008), pp. 50–54, 68; Castelle, *Paris Républicain 1871–1914*, pp. 192–197.

25   Winock, *La Belle Époque*, pp. 138–141. At the turn of the century, a working family of four consumed two kilos of bread a day [Antoine Prost, *Si nous vivions en 1913* (Paris, 2014), pp. 33–34]; Pierre Castelle, *Paris Républicain*, pp. 153–155, drawing on the work of Adeline Daumard's study of inheritance.

26   Winock, *La Belle Époque*, pp. 56–59, 68, 138; Pierre Castelle, *Paris Républicain 1871–1914* (2003), pp. 191, 195, 203, 210; Charle, *La crise des sociétés impériales (1900–1940)*, p. 83.

27   Winock, *La Belle Époque*, pp. 56–59, 68, 138; Castelle, *Paris Républicain 1871–1914*, pp. 191, 195, 203, 210; Charle, *La crise des sociétés impériales (1900–1940)*, p. 83.

28   Berlanstein, *The Working People of Paris, 1871–1914*, p. 49; Marchand, *Paris, histoire d'une ville, xixe–xxe siècle*, p. 227; Pacaud, *Vie quotidienne des français à la Belle Époque*, p. 89; Eugen Weber, *France, Fin-de-Siècle* (Cambridge, MA, 1986), pp. 65–66; Castelle, *Paris Républicain*, , pp. 192–194; Charle, *La crise des sociétés impériales (1900–1940)*, pp. 106–107; Frédéric Lavignette, *La bande à Bonnot à travers la presse de l'époque* (Lyon, 2008) p. 34.

29   Lavignette, *La bande à Bonnot à travers la presse de l'époque*, p. 35.

30   Berlanstein, *The Working People of Paris, 1871–1914*, p. 58.

31   Winock, *La Belle Époque*, p. 367; Weber, *France, Fin-de-Siècle*, p. 58; Jones, *Paris*, pp. 416–419; Marchand, *Paris, histoire d'une ville, xixe–xxe siècle*, p. 228; Castelle, *Paris Républicain*, pp. 145–146; Frédéric Lavignette, p. 36, from *Le Petit Parisien*, May 22, 1912, and p. 38, from *Lectures pour tous*, April 1913; James Cannon, *The Paris Zone: A*

Cultural History, 1840–1944 (Farnham, UK, 2015), pp. 108–109. Tuberculosis struck 39,477 of 77,149 Parisian residential buildings.

32 Cannon, *The Paris Zone: A Cultural History, 1840–1944*, pp. 89, 95–99, 112–116.

33 Berlanstein, *The Working People of Paris, 1871–1914*, p. 137.

34 Antoine Prost, *Si nous vivions en 1913* (Paris, 1914), p. 23.

35 Berlanstein, *The Working People of Paris, 1871–1914*, p. 141; Castelle, *Paris Républicain*, p. 139; Prost, *Si nous vivions en 1913*, pp. 12, 16; Frédéric Lavignette, *La bande à Bonnot à travers la presse de l'époque*, p. 53.

36 Marchand, *Paris, histoire d'une ville, xixe–xxe siècle*, p. 194.

Chapter 4: Anarchists in Conflict

1   Ian Birchall, "Proletarian Culture," in Susan Weissman, ed., *The Ideas of Victor Serge: A Life as a Work of Art* (Glasgow, 1997), pp. 76–77; Anne Steiner, *Les En-dehors: anarchistes individualistes et illégalistes à la "Belle Époque"* (Paris, 2008), pp. 68–73; Victor Serge, *Memoirs of a Revolutionary* (New York, 2012), p. 32.

2   Serge, *Memoirs of a Revolutionary*, pp. 30–32; see Dominique Kalifa, *Les Bas-fonds; l'histoire d'un imaginaire* (Paris, 2013).

3   Victor's article carried the title "L'Ouvrièrisme."

4   Dominique Depond, *Jules Bonnot et sa bande* (Paris, 2009), pp. 31–32; Rirette Maîtrejean, *Souvenirs d'anarchie* (Paris, 2005), p. 20. Victor never met Libertad, who died before Victor arrived in Paris.

5   BA 928, commissaire de police, September 5, 1907; Maîtrejean, *Souvenirs d'anarchie*, pp. 20–21.

6   BA 928, report of October 34, 1904; Maîtrejean, *Souvenirs d'anarchie*, pp. 72–73.

7   Maîtrejean, *Souvenirs d'anarchie*, pp. 22, 72–73; Victor Serge, "Méditation sur l'anarchie," *Esprit*, 55, April 1, 1937, pp. 36–37; Anne Steiner, *Rirette l'insoumise* (Tulle, 2013), pp. 13–15; André Salmon, *La Terreur noir* (Paris, 2008), pp. 267, 302.

8   Serge, *Mémoires d'un révolutionnaire*, pp. 28–29; Serge, "Méditation sur l'anarchie," pp. 36–37; Louis Chevalier, *Montmartre du plaisir et du crime* (Paris, 1995), pp. 303–304; Maîtrejean, *Souvenirs d'anarchie*, pp. 20–22, 74–76; JA 16, report of June 3, 1912; Steiner, *Rirette l'insoumise,* pp. 136–138. The influence of Victor Méric in *Le Libertaire* could be seen. For his part, Lorulut accepted the idea of anarchist "*organisation cellulaire*" (Vivien Bouhey and Philippe Levillain, *Les anarchistes contre la République: contributions à l'histoire des reseaux sous la Troisiène République [1880–1914]* [Rennes, 2008], pp. 381–386). Just before the war, *Le Libertaire* accepted the federative model of organization. *Les Temps Nouveaux* adopted a middle line between the two.

9   BA 928, June 26, 1905; Victor Méric, *Les bandits tragiques* (Paris, 1926), p. 82.

10 BA 928, January 1, 1908; BA 928, August 17 and November 16, 1907, January 1, 1908.

11 BA 928, April 10, 1908.

12 Steiner, *Rirette l'insoumise*, pp. 13–18.

13 Victor Serge (Le Rétif), "Les Pauvres," October 21, 1909, *L'Anarchie*, pp. 99–101, 173; and *L'Anarchie*, July 20, 1911.

14 Cited in Steiner, *Rirette l'insoumise*, p. 99, published in *L'Anarchie*, August 19, 1909.

15   Hubert Juin, *Le Livre de Paris 1900* (Paris, 1994), pp. 9–13.

16   Serge, *Memoirs of a Revolutionary*, p. 32.

17   Eugen Weber, *France Fin de Siècle* (Cambridge, MA, 1986), p. 119.

18   *L'Anarchie,* September 7, 1911 and July 25, 1912; André Girard, *Anarchistes et bandits* (Paris, 1914), p. 19; Serge, *Memoirs of a Revolutionary*, p. 23.

19   Gaetano Manfredonia, *Anarchisme et changement social: Insurrectionnalisme, syndicalisme, éducationnisme-réalisateur* (Loriol, 2007), pp. 346–347; Anne Steiner, *Le gout de l'émeute: manifestations et violences de rue dans Paris et sa banlieue à la "Belle Époque"* (Paris, 2012), p. 114.

20   Serge, *Mémoires d'un révolutionnaire*, pp. 24–25.

21   Serge, *Mémoires d'un révolutionnaire,* pp. 38–39; Victor Serge (Le Rétif), "Révolutionnaires? oui. Mais Comment?," *L'Anarchie,* December 14, 1911, pp. 64–67; Susan Weissman, *Victor Serge: The Course Is Set on Hope* (London: Verso, 2001), p. 16.

22   Serge, *Le Retif,* "Les Épaves," p. 36.

23   Serge, *Le Rétif,* "Les Épaves," pp. 36–37; *L'Anarchie,* June 2, 1910, p. 49; *L'Anarchie,* March 9, 1911.

24   Steiner, *Rirette l'insoumise*, pp. 19–20; Jean Maitron, ed., *Le mouvement anarchiste en France.* Vol. 1, *Des origines à 1914* (Paris, 1975), pp. 423–424.

25   Victor Serge, *Le Rétif,* pp. 36–37, 58–59, 63, 77, from *L'Anarchie,* April 28, 1910, March 9, 1911, and December 6, 1911.

26   Serge, *Le Rétif,* pp. 102, 105. *L'Anarchie,* March 24, 1910. "*Organiser la classe ouvrière en vue d'une transformation sociale, c'est perdre du temps et de l'énergie. . . . Par conséquent: il n'est qu'une besogne urgente, utile, indispensable—celle qui en créant des individus enfin dignes du titre d'hommes amérliore petit à petit le milieu—la besogne d'éducation et de combat anarchiste*" (p. 110, February 24, 1910). In Brussels, Victor had already become acutely aware of the bitter division developing at *Le Révolté* between more traditional, intellectual anarchists and those espousing pure "individualism."

27   F7 13053, "Notes sur l'Anarchie en France," April 25, 1913, and BA 1499, report of April 12, 1913; Victor Serge, *Le Rétif,* pp. 26, 125; *L'Anarchie,* September 7, 1911; Steiner, *Rirette l'insoumise,* p. 18; Vivien Bouhey and Philippe Levillain, *Les anarchistes contre la République*, pp. 373–379 (June 17, 1908), 420; Victor Serge, "Méditation sur l'anarchie," *Esprit,* 55, April 1, 1937, pp. 36–37; Émile Michon, *Un peu de l'âme de bandits: étude de psychologie criminelle* (Paris, 1913), p. 197; Gaetano Manfredonia, *Anarchisme et changement social: Insurrectionnalisme, syndicalisme, éducationnisme-réalisateur* (Loriol, 2007), p. 341. The thirty-nine goups were counted in 1913.

28   Jean Maitron, *Le mouvement anarchiste.* Vol. 1, *Des origines à 1914,* pp. 414–423, citing *Le Libertaire,* August 7–13, 1898; Robert Le Texier, *De Ravachol à la bande à Bonnot* (Paris, 1989), p. 143.

29   Jacob may have been the inspiration for Maurice Leblanc's *Arsène Lupin, gentleman cambrioleur*, which had considerable success after its publication in 1907, and *L'Arrestation de Arsène Lupin* (1913) [Michel Winock, *Les derniers feux de la Belle Époque* (Paris, 2014), pp. 62–67]. Lupin's thefts were from bankers, financiers, and German barons, thus acceptable to a sizeable public.

30   BA 1499, report of July 9, 1907.

31   Maîtrejean, *Souvenirs d'anarchie*, p. 18.

32   Vivien Bouhey, *Les anarchistes contre la République*, pp. 363–424, 442–459; *L'Anarchie*, April 18, 1912.

33   Maitron, *Le mouvement anarchiste*. Vol. 1, *Des origines à 1914*, pp. 423–424; Luc Nemeth, "On Anarchism," in Susan Weissman, ed., *The Ideas of Victor Serge: A Life as a Work of Art* (N.p., 1997), p. 121.

34   Victor Méric, *Les bandits tragiques* (Paris, 1926), pp. 83–84.

35   Victor Serge, *Le Rétif: Articles parus dans "L'Anarchie," 1909–1912*, edited by Yves Pagès (Paris, 1989), pp. 7, 23: *"Rétif, ive, adj, se dit d'un cheval ou autre bête de monture qui refuse d'obéir. Fig. Se dit des choses qui n'obéissent pas,"* Dictionary *Littré*.

36   Yves Pagès, in Victor Serge, *Le Rétif*, p. 26; Serge, *Memoirs of a Revolutionary*, p. 29.

Chapter 5: Rirette Maîtrejean

1   Anne Steiner, *Rirette l'insoumise* (Paris, 2013), pp. 7–11.

2   Rirette Maîtrejean, *Souvenirs d'anarchie*, pp. 72–73; Steiner, *Rirette l'insoumise*, pp. 10–11; Anne Steiner, *Les En-dehors: anarchistes individualistes et illégalistes à la "Belle Époque"* (Paris, 2008), pp. 15–18; see Judith Coffin, *The Politics of Women's Work: The Paris Clothing Trades, 1750–1915* (Princeton, 1996).

3   Maîtrejean, *Souvenirs d'anarchie*, pp. 72–73.

4   Steiner, *Rirette l'insoumise*, p. 11.

5   Maîtrejean, *Souvenirs d'anarchie*, p. 15.

6   Maîtrejean, *Souvenirs d'anarchie*, p. 16.

7   Maîtrejean, *Souvenirs d'anarchie*, p. 26.

8   Maîtrejean, *Souvenirs d'anarchie*, p. 15; Steiner, *Les En-dehors*, pp. 23 25.

9   Céline Beaudet, *Les milieux libres. Vivre en anarchie à la Belle Époque* (Paris, 2006), p. 185; Steiner, *Les En-dehors*, pp. 25–27; Gaetano Manfredonia, *La chanson anarchiste en France des origines à 1914* (Paris, 1997), pp. 239–250.

10   Maîtrejean, *Souvenirs d'anarchie*, p. 73; Steiner, *Les En-dehors*, pp. 30–34.

11   JA 16, report of June 3, 1912; Gérard Jacquemet, "La violence à Belleville au début du xxe siècle," *Bulletin de la Société de l'histoire de Paris et de l'Île-de-France*, 1978, pp. 150–163. Jacquemet argues that Belleville's reputation for crime and delinquency was unjustified in that its rate of criminality at this time was slightly less than Paris as a whole and that arrests of young people did not increase. Yet he admits that arrest for *coups et blessures* and drunkenness did increase, at least until 1911. Moreover, the number of murders rose from sixty-two between 1904 and 1908 to eighty between 1909 and 1913.

12   Steiner, *Rirette l'insoumise*, pp. 24–25.

13   Steiner, *Les En-dehors*, pp. 38–40.

14   Steiner, *Les En-dehors*, pp. 44–50; Steiner, *Rirette l'insoumise*, pp. 25–31.

15   EA 141 *L'Aurore*, June 17, 1968; Maîtrejean, *Souvenirs d'anarchie*, pp. 14–15; Steiner, *Rirette l'insoumise*, pp. 23–27, 34–35.

16   BA 928, November 23, 1907, and April 11, 1908.

17   BA 928, May 5, 14, and 25, 1908. Yet Libertad remained resilient. On May 25 he and thirty young men and women took the train from Gare Saint-Lazare to Garches,

where they distributed copies of *L'Anarchie* and *papillons anarchists*, before a *déjeuné sur l'herbe* with provisions they had brought along.

18   BA 928, February 8, 18, and 20 and March 10, 17, and 24, 1908.

19   William Caruchet, *Ils ont tué Bonnot: Les révélations des archives policières* (Paris, 1990), pp. 21, 38–39. See Charles Tilly, *The Contentious French* (Cambridge, MA, 1986).

20   Anne Steiner, *Le gout de l'émeute: manifestations et violences de rue dans Paris et sa banlieue à la "Belle Époque"* (Paris, 2012), pp. 9–16.

21   Jacques Julliard, *Clemenceau briseur de grèves* (Paris, 1965), p. 23.

22   Céline Beaudet, *Les milieux libres. Vivre en anarchie à la Belle Époque* (Paris, 2006), pp. 171–172, 183–185, 191, 199–208; Castelle, *Paris Républicain*, p. 199. Yet in 1913, only 13 percent of the work force had joined unions (Michel Winock, *La Belle Époque*, p. 150).

23   Eugen Weber, *France, Fin-de-Siècle* (Cambridge, MA, 1986), p. 139.

24   Michel Winock, *La Belle Époque* (Paris, 2002), pp. 336–337.

25   Steiner, *Le gout de l'émeute*, pp. 25–56.

26   Steiner, *Le gout de l'émeute*, pp. 9–17.

27   Maîtrejean, *Souvenirs d'anarchie*, pp. 75–76.

28   Maîtrejean, *Souvenirs d'anarchie*, pp. 74–76; Steiner, *Les En-dehors*, pp. 60–61; Steiner, *Le gout de l'émeute*, pp. 25–56; Jacques Julliard, *Clemenceau briseur de grèves* (Paris, 1965), pp. 21–23, 47–48; Steiner, *Les En-dehors*, pp. 58–63.

29   Julliard, *Clemenceau briseur de grèves*, pp. 9–10, 99.

30   BA 928, reports of November 14 and 15, 1908; Maîtrejean, *Souvenirs d'anarchie*, p. 22. Suspicion abounded in anarchist circles that he died as a result of police blows on a Montmartre stairway (Victor Méric, p. 58, quoting André Colomer).

Chapter 6: A Love Story

1   Anne Steiner, *Les En-dehors: anarchistes individualistes et illégalistes à la "Belle Époque"* (Paris, 2008), p. 67; Rirette Maîtrejean, *Souvenirs d'anarchie*, p. 27.

2   Alain Rustenholz, *Paris ouvrier: des sublimes aux camarades* (Paris, 2003), p. 325; Maîtrejean, *Souvenirs d'anarchie*, pp. 27–28; Anne Steiner, *Rirette l'insoumise* (Tulle, 2013), pp. 35–36; Steiner, *Les En-dehors*, pp. 64–65. Belgian police indicated in a letter to their French counterparts that Rirette had gone to Belgium in 1909 (EA 141, interrogation of Femme Maîtrejean), presumably early in the year, with Mauricius or with Victor. Rirette notes that another anarchist had entered Belgium with her papers, and then had been kicked out because of her efforts in diffusing anarchist propaganda.

3   Rirette Maîtrejean, "De Paris à Barcelone," *Témoins*, no. 21, February 1959, pp. 37–38.

4   Maîtrejean, *Souvenirs d'anarchie*, pp. 30–31.

5   Victor Serge, *Memoirs of a Revolutionary* (New York, 2012), pp. 25–26.

6   JA 19 report of January 26 and May 21, 1912, and n.d.; JA 24, accountant of company, September 29, 1911; Maîtrejean, *Souvenirs d'anarchie,* pp. 29–31, 85; Robert Le Texier, *De Ravachol à la bande à Bonnot* (Paris, 1989), p. 158.

7   Steiner, *Rirette l'insoumise*, pp. 28, 37–39; Serge, *Memoirs of a Revolutionary*, p. 23.

8   Anne Steiner, *Le gout de l'émeute: manifestations et violences de rue dans Paris et sa banlieue à la "Belle Époque"* (Paris, 2012), pp. 21–22, 101–106, 198–199; Serge, *Memoirs of a Revolutionary*, pp. 33–34. A police report indicates that Victor was expelled in August 1909, along with Rirette, but this seems unlikely (J[ean] Maitron, "De Kibaltchiche à Victor Serge. Le Rétif [1909–1919]," *Mouvement social*, 47, avril–juin 1964, p. 47).

9   Steiner, *Les En-dehors*, pp. 78–79.

10 Victor Serge, *Mémoires d'un révolutionnaire*, pp. 33–37; Serge, *Memoirs of a Revolutionary*, p. 35; Victor Serge, *Le Rétif*, pp. 118–119, *L'Anarchie*, October 20, 1910; Steiner, *Le gout de l'émeute*, pp. 120–145, 199.

Chapter 7: A Bitter Split

1   Rirette Maîtrejean, *Souvenirs d'anarchie* (Quimperlé, 2005), pp. 28, 78.

2   Maîtrejean, *Souvenirs d'anarchie*, p. 28; Anne Steiner, *Les En-dehors: anarchistes individualistes et illégalistes à la "Belle Époque"* (Paris, 2008), p. 75.

3   JA 17, dossier Callemin, especially report of July 3, 1912; JA16, "Mes Mémoires: (Callemin dit Raymond la Science): Pourquoi j'ai cambriolé Pourquoi j'ai tué"; Céline Beaudet, *Les milieux libres. Vivre en anarchie à la Belle Époque* (Saint-Georges-d'Oléron, 2006), pp. 101, 187: "*Telle est la définition même de l'anarchisme, que le melieu libre reprend au sens propre: ni domination, ni hiérarchie, ni structure figée*"; Victor Serge, *Le Rétif: Articles parus dans "L'Anarchie," 1909–1912*, p. 10; Maîtrejean, *Souvenirs d'anarchie*, p. 93. The account of his life that he provided Émile Michon in 1913 (*Un peu de l'âme de bandits: étude de psychologie criminelle*, pp. 197–201) differs somewhat, having Callemin arriving in Paris with his girlfriend in 1910. He describes this as the beginning of his "nomadic" period, followed by work in Lausanne (where his friend met him), the best time of his life with her and two French friends. Unemployment in Paris followed, and then it was back to Lausanne, and then to Marseille, where Callemin and his girlfriend apparently briefly explored possibilities of going to Algeria or Cairo, but with no work assured there and confronted by police, he was forced to return to Paris, using up all his money to get there. He claimed his girlfriend ended up in Paris. Given Raymond's reputation for misogyny, it seems possible that he invented this girlfriend.

4   Émile Michon, *Un peu de l'âme de bandits: étude de psychologie criminelle* (Paris, 1913), pp. 197–201.

5   Victor Méric, *Les bandits tragiques*, p. 67.

6   JA 16, dossier Carouy, report of July 5, 1912; EA 141, *Le Temps*, June 2, 1912.

7   Maîtrejean, *Souvenirs d'anarchie*, pp. 17, 83; Dominique Depond, *Jules Bonnot et sa bande*, pp. 47–48, Victor's description; Émile Becker, *La "Bande à Bonnot,"* pp. 65–66. Later, Jeanne became Lorulot's lover. A police report had his father being a well-respected customs employee (JA 16, report of July 5, 1912).

8   JA 15, "Anarchistes signalés comme étant en rapport avec le Né Carouy Édouard," September 22, 1911.

9   Victor Serge, *Memoirs of a Revolutionary* (New York, 2012), p. 40.

10   Maîtrejean, *Souvenirs d'anarchie*, pp. 32–33, 78; Victor Serge, *Memoirs of a Revolutionary*, pp. 40–41.

11   JA 18, report of June 13, 1912.

12   JA 19, report of June 13, 1912; Steiner, *Les En-dehors*, pp. 97–98, 219–220; Maîtrejean, *Souvenirs d'anarchie*, pp. 31–34, 78–79; Victor Serge, *Mémoires d'un révolutionnaire, 1901–1941* (Paris, 1978), p. 41; Frédéric Lavignette, *La bande à Bonnot à travers la presse de l'époque*, pp. 224–225, 484; *Le Petit Parisien*, April 1, 1912; *Excelsior*, May 29, 1912; Serge, *Memoirs of a Revolutionary*, pp. 41–41.

13   Victor Méric, *Les bandis tragiques*, pp. 68–69.

14   JA 19, dossier Lorulot, report of August 11, 1912; André Lorulot, *Chez les loups: Moeurs anarchistes* (Paris, 1922), while remaining loyal to anarchism: "*L'anarchie . . . solutionne définitivement le problème sociale: elle met l'homme à sa place dans la nature.*" *Chez les loups* is a supposedly fictional account but obviously closely follows the events in prewar Paris.

15   *L'Anarchie,* July 6, 1911.

16   Steiner, *Les En-dehors*, p. 81; Beaudet, *Les milieux libres*, p. 101, noting that Émile Armand frequently used this expression. The walls of Paris had long since lost any military value. The city of Paris and military authorities went back and forth following a law in 1898 that took away any control by the city in the military declassification of the fortifications. Finally, in 1904 the army abandoned any plan to consider the circumference of Paris as militarily useful and built more defenses on the edge of Paris, after refusing the city's demand that the entire circumference be declassified and sold to the city in 1913. Thereafter, the exterior forts were considered the defense of Paris (Pierre Castelle, *Paris Républicain*, pp. 250–253). The remaining walls around Paris were scheduled for demolition in 1913, but that would have to await the end of the Great War.

17   JA 18, report of May 23, 1913; Steiner, *Les En-dehors*, pp. 81–82; Maîtrejean, *Souvenirs d'anarchie*, pp. 38–44.

18   Serge, *Memoirs of a Revolutionary*, p. 38; Émile Michon, *Un peu de l'âme de bandits: étude de psychologie criminelle* (1913), pp. 197–198; Victor Méric, *Les bandits tragiques*, p. 71.

19   Richard Parry, *The Bonnot Gang* (London, 1987), pp. 40–41.

20   JA 19, dossier Vuillemin, *femme Schoofs*, p.v. January 24, 1912, interrogation of Madame Jouin (coincidence); Serge, *Memoirs of a Revolutionary*, p. 38.

21   JA 19, reports of January 2, 22, 25, 1912, p.v. of interrogation of Delinotte, Florine, who then admitted she was Marie *femme* Schoofs, Jouin, n.d., and p.v., May 24 and report of July 13, 1912.

22   JA 19, p.v. January 24, 1912.

23   Serge, *Mémoires d'un révolutionnaire*, p. 39; Victor Méric, *Les bandits tragiques*, pp. 70–71.

24   Serge, *Mémoires d'un révolutionnaire*, p. 38–39; Méric, *Les bandits tragiques*, pp. 70–71.

25   Steiner, *Les En-dehors*, pp. 30–38; Maîtrejean, *Souvenirs d'anarchie*, pp. 23–26, 38–39.

26   Maîtrejean, *Souvenirs d'anarchie*, pp. 41–42.

27   Maîtrejean, *Souvenirs d'anarchie*, pp. 23–26.

28   Maîtrejean, *Souvenirs d'anarchie*, p. 39.

29   JA 19, report of July 15, 1912; reports of August 27 and September 20, 1911, *mandat d'amener*; report of April 26, 1912.

30   Maîtrejean, *Souvenirs d'anarchie*, pp. 35–36, 78.

31   JA 17, report of June 20, 1911. "Mistral," 20 to 22 years of age, 1 meter 64 in height, black hair, round face, *teint mat*, moustache noire, black eyes, *"regard fuyant,"* with *"un nez large et aplati"*; Gros, 28–30 Edouard, rather fat, chestnut hair, and a mustache.

32   KC 19, dossier Louis Jouin: "travail d'épreuve," February 16, 1898; personnel report, May 2, 1895; general secretary of the Prefecture of the Seine, July 2, 1895; "note de service 1902," etc. The dossier included a letter from a commissaire in Puteaux (July 22, 1900) claiming that Jouin had *"une sensibilité maladive. M. Jourin pleure à la plus petit contrarité."*

33   KC 19, dossier Louis Jouin, report of April 25, 1912, etc.; Marcel Guillaume, *Mes Grandes Enquêtes criminelles: De la Bande à Bonnot à l'Affaire Stavisky* (Mayenne, 2005), pp. 51–53.

34   Steiner, *Les En-dehors*, pp. 81–82, 89–92; Steiner, *Rirette l'insoumise*, pp. 18, 43; Serge, *Mémoires d'un révolutionnaire*, pp. 29–30.

35   Maîtrejean, *Souvenirs d'anarchie*, p. 40; Steiner, *Les En-dehors*, pp. 83–89, 216–217; Victor Serge, *Le Rétif,* "Vie de Victor Kibaltchiche, dit le Rétif, *alias* Victor Serge," p. 12.

36   Maîtrejean, *Souvenirs d'anarchie*, p. 40; Steiner, *Les En-dehors*, pp. 83–89, 216–217; Victor Serge, *Le Rétif,* "Vie de Victor Kibaltchiche, dit le Rétif," p. 12.

37   BA 1499, report of April 12, 1913; Rirette Maîtrejean, *Souvenirs d'anarchie*, p. 82.

38   Serge, *Memoirs of a Revolutionary*, p. 38; Maîtrejean, *Souvenirs d'anarchie*, pp. 37, 44; Steiner, *Rirette l'insoumise*, pp. 40–41.

39   Victor Méric, *Les bandits tragiques*, p. 64; Luc Nemeth, "Victor Serge, marqué par son passé," in Rirette Maîtrejean, *Souvenirs d'anarchie*, pp. 110–111.

40   Maîtrejean, *Souvenirs d'anarchie*, pp. 40, 82–84; Parry, *The Bonnot Gang*, p. 61.

41   JA 19, report of July 15, 1912; Parry, *The Bonnot Gang*, pp. 57–58, adding that Carouy feared being extradited back to Belgium for the attempted murder of a policeman in Charleroi.

42   Maîtrejean, *Souvenirs d'anarchie,* pp. 38–44; JA 16, "Mes Mémoires: (Callemin dit Raymond la Science): Pourquoi j'ai cambriolé Pourquoi j'ai tué."

43   Maîtrejean, *Souvenirs d'anarchie*, p. 43; Parry, *The Bonnot Gang*, p. 58.

44   Maîtrejean, *Souvenirs d'anarchie*, p. 44; Méric, *Les bandits tragiques*, pp. 68–69.

45   Maîtrejean, *Souvenirs d'anarchie*, p. 44.

46   Serge, *Mémoires d'un révolutionnaire*, p. 39; Maîtrejean, *Souvenirs d'anarchie*, p. 44; Steiner, *Les En-dehors*, pp. 95–96; Luc Nemeth, "On Anarchism," p. 123, from "The Unlawful," *Le Communiste*, June 10, 1908; Victor Serge, *Le Rétif,* "Le Révolté," February 6, 1909, p. 204.

47   The number of Bretons living in Paris had increased from 88,000 in 1891 to 119,000 a decade later.

48   JA 18, mayor of Le Faouët, April 9, 1911, reports of prefect of police March 28 and police reports of March 25 and 28, April 27, July 13, October 24 and 25, 1912, and January 31, 1913. See Leslie Page Moch, *Pariahs of Yesterday: Breton Migrants in Paris* (Durham, NC, 2012).

49   JA 24, October 19, 1911; January 9 and October 18, 1912; JA 18, dossier Lecot. Metge was a suspect in a theft from a factory on rue de Metz in Romainville the night of March 7, 1911.

50   Renaud Thomazo, *Mort au bourgeois!* (Paris, 2009), pp. 23–24, 116–117.

51   Steiner, *Les En-dehors*, pp. 99–100; Émile Becker, *La "Bande à Bonnot"* (Paris, 1968), pp. 56–58.

Chapter 8: Jules Bonnot

1   JA 16, "Mes Mémoires: (Callemin dit Raymond la Science): Pourquoi j'ai cambriolé Pourquoi j'ai tué"; Marcel Guillaume, *Mes Grandes Enquêtes criminelles: De la Bande à Bonnot à l'Affaire Stavisky* (Mayenne, 2005), p. 56; Richard Parry, *The Bonnot Gang* (London, 1987), pp. 73–75.

2   Michel Chomarat, *Les Amants tragiques. Histoire du bandit Jules Bonnot et de sa maîtresse Judith Thollon* (Lyon, 1978), p. 2.

3   Dominique Depond, *Jules Bonnot et sa bande* (Paris, 2009), pp. 52–56. In 1913 Berliet employed 2,000 workers and turned out 3,000 vehicles.

4   William Caruchet, *Ils ont tué Bonnot: Les revelations des archives policières* (Paris, 1990), pp. 20–21; Chomarat, *Les Amants tragiques*, pp. 5–6, referring to *"des traitements inhumains infligés par Bonnot à son fils et à son épouse."* The *Tribunal civil* of Lyon officially granted the divorce in April 1912 (Émile Becker, p. 47).

5   EA 140.

6   Chomarat, *Les Amants tragiques*, p. 49, letter sent by Mercier to Monsieur le chef de la Sûreté, March 30, 1912: "I knew Bonnot very well, although it was more than three years ago when I quarreled with him. I know how anxious he becomes when he is alone and although he seems ready for anything, he has a terrible fear of being hit." He offered his services to help arrest him.

7   Parry, *The Bonnot Gang*, p. 69.

8   Chomarat, *Les Amants tragiques*, pp. 7–9.

9   Frédéric Delacourt, *L'Affaire bande à Bonnot* (Paris, 2006), pp. 18–20; Caruchet, *Ils ont tué Bonnot*, pp. 24–26; Maîtrejean, *Souvenirs d'anarchie*, pp. 34, 42; Dominique Depond, *Jules Bonnot et sa bande* (Paris, 2009); Caruchet, *Ils ont tué Bonnot*, pp. 56–57; Guillaume, *Mes Grandes Enquêtes criminelles*, p. 57. Guillaume relates the story of Platano's response to Bonnot having run over a dog and a chicken.

10   JA 24, *signalement* and n.d.; Frédéric Lavignette, *La bande à Bonnot à travers la presse de l'époque* (Lyon, 2008), p. 19.

11   Caruchet, *Ils ont tué Bonnot*, pp. 27–28; Maîtrejean, *Souvenirs d'anarchie*, pp. 34, 85; Anne Steiner, *Les En-dehors: anarchistes individualistes et illégalistes à la "Belle Époque"* (Paris, 2008), pp. 100–101, 214; Victor Serge, *Memoirs of a Revolutionary*, p. 39; Depond, *Jules Bonnot et sa bande* (Paris, 2009), p. 56. Platano was allegedly carrying with him 27,000 francs, his part of the loot, and that same amount later turned up during a police search in the home of the Thollons, adding to the confusion. Judith Thollon was convicted in May 1912 in Lyon and sentenced to four years in prison. She died after one year (Depond, *Jules Bonnot et sa bande*, p. 114).

12   Caruchet, *Ils ont tué Bonnot*, pp. 15–17, 28; Chomarat, *Les Amants tragiques*, pp. 19–21, 25–31, 41–42; Frédéric Lavignette, *La bande à Bonnot à travers la presse de l'époque* (Lyon, 2008), pp. 159–160, *Le Petit Parisien*, March 15, 1912. Judith Thollon said she was not sure if this had been in the hand of Bonnot, claiming it was part of a

collection for the newspaper, to which Bonnot subscribed and which arrived at the Thollon residence.

13 Caruchet, *Ils ont tué Bonnot*, p. 44; Chomarat, *Les Amants tragiques*, p. 17; Lavignette, *La bande à Bonnot*, p. 23.

14 Caruchet, *Ils ont tué Bonnot*, pp. 85–88; JA 15, dossier Bélonie, suggests that David Bélonie noted to Bonnot that he could find a room there.

15 André Salmon, *La Terreur noir* (Paris, 2008), p. 275: The poet, art critic, and journalist André Salmon recalled being introduced to Bonnot. Salmon was on boulevard Saint-Michel, at the corner of rue Soufflot, on a warm day. He ran into Victor Méric (Henri Coudon), an anarchist journalist. Méric was sitting in the Café Mahieu with a man, whom he introduced as "my pal Bonnot, an *anar*." Bonnot mumbled something to Salmon about being pleased to meet him, and that was it.

16 JA 19, report of January 26, 1912; Maîtrejean, *Souvenirs d'anarchie*, p. 85; Pierre Castelle, pp. 129–130; EA 141, *L'Aurore*, June 17, 1968; Caruchet, *Ils ont tué Bonnot*, p. 22; Marie-Joseph Dhavernas, "La surveillance des anarchistes individualistes (1894–1914)," in Philippe Vigier, Alain Faure, et al., *Maintien de l'ordre et polices en France et en Europe au XIXe siècle* (Montrouge, 1987), pp. 354–356. Victor relates in his memoirs, speaking of the attack on rue Ordener, that he did not actually know Bonnot, but this could mean that he had only seen him at *causeries* when Bonnot was attacking Victor and Rirette on behalf of the illegalists in the relatively brief time between Bonnot's arrival in Paris and the bank robbery on rue Ordener.

Chapter 9: The Bonnot Gang Strikes

1 JA 16, "Mes Mémoires: (Callemin dit Raymond la Science): Pourquoi j'ai cambriolé Pourquoi j'ai tué"; JA 24, report of December 14, 1911; James M. Laux, *In First Gear: The French Automobile Industry to 1914* (Montréal, 1976), pp. 154–155. Between 1904 and 1914, the company produced 7,576 automobiles in forty different models, half of them of the six-cylinder variety. Yet most owners did not actually drive their Delaunay-Belleville: "No owner *ever* drives his Delaunay. It just isn't done." Chauffeurs did the job. Delaunay-Belleville was one of the elite manufacturers of automobiles in the early years of the industry. Tsar Nicholas II of Russia owned one.

2 Frédéric Lavignette, *La bande à Bonnot à travers la presse de l'époque* (Lyon, 2008), p. 75, and *Le Petit Parisien*, December 25, 1911.

3 JA 17, report of November 28, 1911; Marcel Guillaume, *Mes Grandes Enquêtes criminelles: De la Bande à Bonnot à l'Affaire Stavisky* (Mayenne, 2005), p. 63.

4 Guillaume, *Mes Grandes Enquêtes criminelles*, pp. 59–61; Anne Steiner, *Les En-dehors: Anarchistes inidividualistes et illégalistes à la "Belle Époque"* (Paris, 2008), pp. 102–103, 108; William Caruchet, *Ils ont tué Bonnot: Les révélations des archives policières* (Paris, 1990), pp. 51–56; Renaud Thomazo, *Mort aux bourgeois! Sur les traces de la bande à Bonnot* (Paris, 2009), p. 25.

5 EA 141, officer de la paix, Paris eighteenth arrondissement December 21, 1911; JA 15; JA 20, October 21, 1912.

6 JA 15.

7   EA 141, officer de la paix, Paris, eighteenth arrondissement, report of December 21–22, 1911; JA 15.

8   JA 16, "Mes Mémoires: (Callemin dit Raymond la Science): Pourquoi j'ai cambriolé pourquoi j'ai tué."

9   Lavignette, *La bande à Bonnot*, p. 93, *L'Humanité*, January 2, 1912; Steiner, *Les En-dehors*, pp. 107–108; Victor Méric, *Les bandits tragiques* (Paris, 1926),p. 11.

10   JA 15, report of December 29, 1911; Dominique Depond, *Jules Bonnot et sa bande: Le tourbillon sanglant* (Paris, 2009), pp. 9–12; Steiner, *Les En-dehors*, pp. 102–105; Caruchet, *Ils ont tué Bonnot*, pp. 61–62.

11   JA 24, p.v., January 10, February 12, and March 28, 1912.

12   *Le Petit Journal*, December 22, 1911; Méric, *Les bandits tragiques*, p. 9; Philippe Néris, *La Bande à Bonnot* (1925), p. 8; Frédéric Lavignette, p. 66, *L'Intransigeant*, December 22, 1911. The Bonnot Gang appear in the last chapter in the recent *The Other Paris*, by Luc Sante (New York, 2015).

13   Jean-Marc Berlière, *Le Préfet Lépine: Vers la naissance de la police modern* (Paris, 1993), pp. 53–58; Depond, *Jules Bonnot et sa bande*, p. 13; Mary McAuliffe, *Twilight of the Belle Epoque: The Paris of Picasso, Stravinsky, Proust, Renault, Marie Curie, Gertrude Stein, and Their Friends Through the Great War* (New York, 2014), p. 214.

14   Jean-Marc Berlière, *Le monde des polices en France* (Paris, 1996), pp. 62–91, 117–120, and Chapter 3.

15   Berlière, *Le Préfet Lépine*, pp. 23–52 (especially 24–26). On the history of state-municipal conflict over the police, see John Merriman, *Police Stories* (New York, 2005).Laurent López, *La guerre des polices n'a pas eu lieu: Gendarmes et policiers, co-acteurs de la sécurité publique sous la Troisième République (1870–1914)* (Paris, 2014), pp. 371–374.

16   Thomazo, *Mort aux bourgeois!*, pp. 42–43; Pierre Castelle, *Paris Républicain 1871–1914* (Abbeville, 2003), pp. 81–95.

17   Victor Serge, *Memoirs of a Revolutionary* (New York, 2012), p. 40.

18   Victor Serge, *Mémoires d'un révolutionnaire 1901–1941*, edited by Jean Rière (Paris, 2010), pp. 38–39; Maîtrejean, *Souvenirs d'anarchie*, pp. 85–86.

19   Maîtrejean, *Souvenirs d'anarchie*, pp. 45–49, 78, 85–88; Guillaume Davranche, *Trop jeunes pour mourir* (Paris, 2014), p. 213; Méric, *Les bandits tragiques*, pp. 72–74.

20   JA 17, dossier Dettweiller, report of December 21, 1912.

21   Guillaume Davranche, *Trop jeunes pour mourir: ouvriers et révolutionnaires face à la guerre (1909–1914)* (Paris, 2014), p. 212. Marcel Guillaume would later relate that an anarchist met the police at École Militaire, fearing to be killed for revealing information to the police, and said that the car could be found in Bobigny (Marcel Guillaume, *Mes Grandes Enquêtes criminelles: De la Bande à Bonnot à l'Affaire Stavisky* [Mayenne, 2005], p. 67).

22   JA 17, p.v. December 29 and 30, 1911, report of December 12, 1913, report of December 1911; director of school, July 10, 1912. Arthur Bernède, *Bonnot, Garnier et Cie* (Paris, 1930), p. 29, has Jeanne leaving Carouy.

23   JA 17, p.v., and p.v. of Octave Hamard, December 29, 1911.

24   JA 17, n.d., December 1911, report of December 28 and p.v., and p.v. of Octave Hamard, December 29, 1911.

25   Steiner, *Les En-dehors*, pp. 109–110, noting that Dettweiller's spouse dreamed of setting up a laundry, but this clashed with anarchist ideals.

26 Steiner, *Les En-dehors*, p. 110; Caruchet, *Ils ont tué Bonnot*, pp. 65–66. Marie-Joseph Dhavernas, "La surveillance des anarchistes individualistes (1894–1914)," in Philippe Vigier, Alain Faure, et al., *Maintien de l'ordre et polices en France et en Europe au XIXe siècle* (Montrouge, 1987), p. 357, relates that the police path to Carouy's involvement passed through agents following up a message in *L'Anarchie*, "François, une lettre pour toi à Lens," leading to Carouy, who had been born in Montignies-les-Lens in Belgium, whose presence in France had been related by Belgian authorities in 1910.

27 JA 24, n.d.

28 Caruchet, *Ils ont tué Bonnot*, pp. 71–74, 97–98.

29 JA 20, report of February 15 and June 3, 1912; JA 20, p.v., January 13, 1912; Davranche, *Trop jeunes pour mourir*, p. 213; EA 141, Rapport, n.d, Bertillon; Berlière, *Les monde des polices*, p. 45; Martine Kaluszynski, "Alphonse Bertillon et l'anthropométir," in Philippe Vigier, Alain Faure, et al., *Maintien de l'ordre et polices en France et en Europe au XIXe siècle* (Montrouge, 1987), pp. 269–285. Bertillon also took a plaster imprint of a footstep in the garden and tried to match up finger-prints the police had of Callemin, Carouy, and Soudy. The *fille* Froment, when interrogated by the police, claimed that she was present at 11 bis rue Kléber when Carouy, Metge, Callemin, and one or two other men divided up the 8,000 francs and various securities that had been stolen, and that they said they would kill her if she said anything. She had been arrested on May 8 as an accomplice of one of the men, Forget, for counterfeiting, although she was released the same day (JA 16, report of July 5, 1912).

Chapter 10: The Bonnot Gang at Bay

1 JA 18, dossier of Louis Rimbault, reports of February 13 and 23, March 21, and p.v. January 8 and February 13 and 23 and March 21, 1912, 6 a.m.; JA 19, report of January 29, 1912; Renaud Thomazo, pp. 51–52, 77–78.

2 JA 19, report of January 26, 1912; JA 24, reports of November 18, 1911, and March 13, 1912; Dominque Depond, pp. 61–63; Anne Steiner, *Les En-dehors: anarchistes individualistes et illégalistes dans la Belle Époque* (Montreuil, 2008), pp. 110–111; Renaud Thomazo, *Mort aux bourgeois! Sur les traces de la bande à Bonnot* (Paris, 2009), p. 134.

3 JA 15, dossier Caby; Thomazo, *Mort aux bourgeois!*, p. 31. Caby first said that the man who shot him had blue eyes and was wearing a long raincoat and wearing a British-style cap.

4 KA 74, dossier Paul Eugène Xavier Guichard (born in 1870), beginning as an inspec-teur à la Recherche, report of October 17, 1896, Guichard's "Travail d'épreuve, August 19, 1895," etc.; DOSS. FOL-LN1-232 (11228), *Paris-Midi*, December 25, 1935. Guichard retired from the police in 1934.

5 In 1905, France had begun obligatory two-year military service for young men, and until 1909 Belgium retained a system of drawing lots for a term in the army, although universal military conscription was not established until 1913.

6 Arthur Bernéde, *Bonnot, Garnier et Cie* (Paris, 1930), pp. 25–26, 37–38.

7 JA 16, February 3, 1912; Richard Parry, *The Bonnot Gang* (London, 1987), p. 94; William Caruchet, *Ils ont tué Bonnot: Les révélations des archives policières Ils ont tué Bonnot: Les révélations des archives policières* (Paris, 1990), p. 85.

8   JA 17, report of March 30, 1912; *Le Petit Parisien*, January 23, 1912; Police found there some furniture that had belonged to Dieudonné.

9   JA 19, p.v. January 24, 1912.

10   JA 19, reports of January 21, 22, and July 13, 1912; JA 17, surveillance reports; Thomazo, *Mort aux bourgeois!*, p. 134; Dominique Depond, *Jules Bonnot et sa bande* (Paris, 2009), p. 97. Several police reports confused passage de Clichy with passage Saint-Pierre.

11   JA 19, report of January 22, 1912; Thomazo, *Mort aux bourgeois!*, p. 134; Steiner, *Les En-dehors*, p. 112.

Chapter 11: How to Unload Stolen Securities

1   JA 16, "Mes Mémoires: (Callemin dit Raymond la Science): Pourquoi j'ai cambriolé Pourquoi j'ai tué."

2   JA 16, "Mes Mémoires: (Callemin dit Raymond la Science): Pourquoi j'ai cambriolé Pourquoi j'ai tué"; William Caruchet, *Ils ont tué Bonnot: Les révélations des archives policières* (Paris, 1990), pp. 84. A list of the securities can be found in JA 15, including "*ville de Paris*," 1898, 500 francs, and 4,000 francs; 1871, 400 francs; "*chemin de fer Rosaria Belgrano*," 500 francs, etc.

3   JA 15, "Vol de titres au prejudice de la Société Générale rue Ordener," report of May 5, 1912.

4   EA 141; JA 24, January 24, 1912, and Albert van der Straeten, March 1, 1912; Émile Becker, pp. 70–71; JA 16, "Mes Mémoires: (Callemin dit Raymond la Science): Pourquoi j'ai cambriolé Pourquoi j'ai tué"; Renaud Thomazo, *Mort aux bourgeois! Sur les traces de la bande à Bonnot* (Paris, 2009), pp. 128–130.

5   JA 19, report of July 15, 1912; Dominique Depond, *Jules Bonnot et sa bande: Le tourbillon sanglant* (Paris, 2009), pp. 60–61.

6   Guillaume Davranche, *Trop jeune pour mourir* (Paris, 2014), pp. 219–220; Jean Maitron, *Le mouvement anarchiste*. Vol. 1, *Des origines à 1914*, p. 436.

7   Victor Serge, *Le Rétif*, "Les Bandits," pp. 162–164; "Expedients," p. 166; *L'Anarchie*, January 4 and 18, 1912, June 20, 1908; Anne Steiner, *Rirette l'insoumise* (Tulle, 2013), pp. 51–53, *L'Anarchie*, January 4 and 11, 1912. On January 25, Victor offered another provocative take on the bandits: "Remember the number of workers with tuberculosis, which reaches 65% in some industries. All the thousand franc notes stolen in advance from the thankless labor of the suffering—calculate what they cost in ruined liveas, in lost lives" (Luc Nemeth, "On Anarchism," in Susan Weissman, ed., *The Ideas of Victor Serge: A Life as a Work of Art* (N.p., 1997), p. 124).

8   Victor Méric, *Les bandits tragiques* (Paris, 1926), pp. 75–77; Rirette Maîtrejean, *Souvenirs d'anarchie* (Quimperlé, 2005), pp. 50–51, 88–89.

Chapter 12: The Police in Action

1   Rirette Maîtrejean, *Souvenirs d'anarchie* (Quimperlé, 2005), pp. 48–49, 89. In "Commissaire Guillaume, Ne réveillez pas les morts!," published in 1937 and included in

Souvenirs d'anarchie. Rirette says she purchased a pistol from Soudy *"par goût de Romanesque,"* learning later that it had been taken from the gunstore on rue Lafayette.

2   Victor Serge, *Mémoires d'un révolutionnaire, 1901–1941,* edited by Jean Rière (Paris, 1978), pp. 41–42; Maîtrejean, *Souvenirs d'anarchie,* p. 122; Steiner, *Les En-dehors,* pp. 114–116.

3   Jean-Pierre Machelon, *La République contre les libertés?* (Paris, 1976), pp. 449–457. Robert A. Nye, *Crime, Madness, and Politics in Modern France* (Princeton, 1984), pp. 171–182. Nye writes, "By the period 1905–1908, a language of national pathology which regarded crime, mental illness, or alcoholism as signs of national debility was no longer a monopoly of medical specialists" (p. 172). He compares the social fear of anarchists to that of the "laboring and dangerous classes" in Paris during the July Monarchy (the Orleanist monarchy, 1830–1848).

4   Machelon, *La République contre les libertés?,* pp. 426–439. Anarchist propaganda *"fut somise à un régime pénal aggravé par rapport au droit commun."*

5   Machelon, *La République contre les libertés?,* pp. 407–410, 415–419, 445; Roger Shattuck, *The Banquet Years* (New York, 1958), pp. 188–189.

6   Steiner, *Les En-dehors,* p. 117.

7   Maîtrejean, *Souvenirs d'anarchie,* pp. 51–52, 89; EA 141, interrogation of *femme* Maîtrejean.

8   Guillaume Davranche, *Trop jeune pour mourir* (Paris, 2014), p. 214.

9   F7 13053, "Anarchistes possesseurs ou chauffeurs d'automobiles," minister of the interior to prefects, February 4, 1912; JA 21, "automobiles signalées et garages inconnus."

10   JA 21, January 6, 1912, to Monsieur le Chef de la Sûreté and report of February 5, 1912.

11   F7 13053, February 14, 1914, *"listes des écoles d'aviation actuellement connues"*; February 17, 1912, minister of the interior, note for *commissaire special* of Amiens; report of May 14, 1912; report of M. Caudron, *constructeur-aviateur,* April 19, 1912; February 14, 1914, *"listes des écoles d'aviation actuellement connues."*

12   JA 23; *Le Libertaire,* February 3, 1912; *Bataille Syndicaliste,* February 4, 1912.

13   Davranche, *Trop jeune pour mourir,* p. 213.

14   JA 16.

15   JA 24, report of February 28, 1912; JA 23, dossier, "Meurtre du gardien de la Paix Garnier François, commis place du Havre le 27 février 1912"; report of March 1, 1912; Frédéric Lavignette, pp. 125, 131, *Action Française,* February 2, 1912.

16   Richard Parry, *The Bonnot Gang* (Paris, 1987), pp. 95–96.

17   Frédéric Delacourt, *L'Affaire Bande à Bonnot* (Paris, 2006), p. 111; Arthur Bernède, *Bonnot, Garnier et Cie* (Paris, 1930), pp. 44–46. Monicr had been arrested in Alès on January 19, but then released.

18   JA 16, p.v. March 14 and March 18 and report of June 8, 1912; Dominique Depond, *Jules Bonnot et sa bande: Le tourbillon sanglant* (Paris, 2009), pp. 51–52; William Caruchet, *Ils ont tué Bonnot: Les révélations des archives policières* (Paris, 1990), pp. 42–43.

19   JA 16, report of June 8, 1912.

20   Caruchet, *Ils ont tué Bonnot,* p. 42.

21   JA 15, dossier Bélonie; JA 16, p.v. March 14 and 18, and dossier Dieudonné; JA 17, p.v. Jouin, February 28, and reports of June 8 and July 11, 1912; *L'Excelsior*, March 12, 1912.

22   *Le Petit Parisien*, March 1, 1912; Arthur Bernède, pp. 69–73, who has David Bélonie recommending *chez Rollet* to "M. Comtesse."

23   Frédéric Lavignette, *La bande à Bonnot à travers la presse de l'époque* (Lyon, 2008), pp. 14, 144, *Excelsior*, March 1, 1912.

24   EA 141; JA 24, report of February 29, 1912; William Caruchet, *Ils ont tué Bonnot: Les révélations des archives policières* (Paris, 1990), pp. 100–101.

25   Becker, *La "Bande à Bonnot"* (Paris, 1968), p. 58.

26   EA 141, Ordre de service, March 1, 1912.

27   JA 17, report of February 2, 1912.

28   Laurent López, *La guerre des polices n'a pas eu lieu: Gendarmes et policiers, co-acteurs de la sécurité publique sous la Troisième République (1870–1914)* (Paris, 2014), p. 372; André Salmon, *La Terreur noir* (Paris, 2008), p. 285; Davranche, *Trop jeune pour mourir*, pp. 215–116; Lavignette, *La bande à Bonnot à travers la presse de l'époque*, p. 241; *Excelsior*, April 4, 1912.

29   JA 16, dossier Dieudonné, report of June 8, 1912; Émile Becker, *La "Bande à Bonnot"* (Paris, 1968), pp. 21–22; Steiner, *Les En-dehors*, pp. 118–119; Caruchet, *Ils ont tué Bonnot*, pp. 85–88, 94; Renaud Thomazo, *Mort au bourgeois! Sur les traces de la bande à Bonnot* (Paris, 2009), pp. 136–138; Lavignette, *La bande à Bonnot à travers la presse de l'époque*, p. 151. Dieudonné admitted recommending the place on the rue Nollet to a *compagnon* named Jules, but claimed that he had no idea that it was Bonnot. Rollet and his wife insisted that Bélonie sent Comtesse/Bonnot to their establishment.

30   JA 20, police report of June 8, 1912; Frédéric Lavignette, pp. 167–168, *Le Petit Parisien*, March 20 and June 26, 1912, *Le Matin*, March 20, 1912.

31   Becker, *La "Bande à Bonnot,"* pp. 25–26; Thomazo, *Mort au bourgeois!*, pp. 152–154; Lavignette, p. 166, *Le Petit Parisien*, March 14, 1912; Caruchet, *Ils ont tué Bonnot*, pp. 90–94, claiming that 500 francs that ended up with Bonnot, representing the value of securities left in the *consigne,* had been given to an informer named Georges Taquard, a usurer.

32   JA 20, report of June 8, 1912; Becker, *La "Bande à Bonnot,"* pp. 26–28; Depond, *Jules Bonnot et sa bande*, pp. 72–73; Thomazo, *Mort au bourgeois!*, pp. 154–144. They claimed that a banker had agreed to purchase half of the securities there available for 2,500 francs but had only 500 francs with him—this on a Paris street—and that he would pay the remainder the next morning. However, the man was no banker; rather, he was Georges Tacquart, a fence.

33   Caruchet, *Ils ont tué Bonnot*, pp. 95–96; EA 141; *Le Petit Parisien*, May 6, 1912; Bill joined the army during the war under a false name, but in 1918 he was recognized by another soldier and imprisoned, dying in March 1918.

34   JA 15, report of March 19, 1912, 4 p.m.

35   Lavignette, *La bande à Bonnot à travers la presse de l'époque*, pp. 206–207; *Excelsior*, March 29, and *Le Petit Parisien*, March 27, 1912.

36   *L'Anarchie*, March 21, 1912.

37   *Le Petit Parisien,* March 26, 27, and 28; *L'Excelsior*, March 28.

38 Last quote from JA 17, report of April 3, 1912. Thomazo, *Mort aux bourgeois!*, p. 121; André Salmon, *La Terreur noir* (Paris, 2008), pp. 275, 298. One letter from Ixelles by Clément Vander Cammen, an administrative employee there, related that he knew Callemin and wanted to take the liberty of reporting that "he had always given good advice to his comrades in the office, and that he followed it himself."

39 Steiner, *Les En-dehors*, pp. 117–118; Thomazo, *Mort aux bourgeois!*, pp. 121–122.

40 JA 16, report of June 3, 1912; Lavignette, *La bande à Bonnot à travers la presse de l'époque*, p. 217; *Le Petit Parisien*, March 30, 1912; Steiner, *Les En-dehors*, pp. 123–124.

41 Victor Serge, *Memoirs of a Revolutionary* (New York, 2012), pp. 41–42; Maîtrejean, *Souvenirs d'anarchie*, pp. 52–55, 90; Steiner, *Rirette l'insoumise*, pp. 56–57; Steiner, *Les En-dehors*, pp. 124–125.

42 *L'Anarchie,* February 28 and April 11, 1912.

43 Steiner, *Les En-dehors*, p. 155.

Chapter 13: The Bonnot Gang's Murder Spree

1 Richard Parry, *The Bonnot Gang* (London, 1987), p. 113.

2 Dominique Depond, *Jules Bonnot et sa bande: Le tourbillon sanglant* (Paris, 2009), pp. 79–80; Anne Steiner, *Les En-dehors anarchistes individualistes et illégalistes dans la Belle Époque* (Montreuil, 2008), pp. 125–126; Frédéric Lavignette, *La bande à Bonnot à travers la presse de l'époque* (Lyon, 2008), p. 183; *L'Excelsior*, March 26, 1912.

3 Victor Serge, *Mémoires d'un révolutionnaire, 1901–1941,* edited by Jean Rière (Paris, 1978), pp. 42–43; Émile Becker, *La "Bande à Bonnot"* (Paris, 1968), pp. 30–33; Steiner, *Les En-dehors,* pp. 125–126; William Caruchet, *Ils ont tué Bonnot: Les révélations des archives policières* (Paris, 1990), pp. 105–110; Lavignette, *La bande à Bonnot à travers la presse de l'époque*, pp. 188, 194; *Le Petit Parisien*, March 26, 1912.

4 EA 140; *Le Matin*, March 18, 1912; André Salmon, *La Terreur noir* (Paris, 2008), p. 77.

5 *Le Petit Parisien*, March 27, 1912; *Action Française*, March 28, 1912.

6 Victor Serge, *Memoirs of a Revolutionary* (New York, 2012), pp. 40–42.

7 JA 19, report of March 28, 1912; JA 20, report of June 8, 1912, Rodriguez from the prison de la Santé, March 26 and 28, 1912; Lavignette, *La bande à Bonnot à travers la presse* de l'époque, p. 210; *Action Française*, March 29, 1912.

8 Rirette Maîtrejean, *Souvenirs d'anarchie* (Quimperlé, 2005), pp. 88–89.

7 JA 19, report of April 25, 1912. A poem by Aristide Bruant captures the atmosphere surrounding Deibler: "*L'aut' matin Deibler, d'un seul coup / Place d'la Roquette y a cou / -pé la tête.*" (Francis Carco, *La Belle Époque au temps de Bruant* [Paris, 1954], p. 144).

8 Rirette Maîtrejean, *Souvenirs d'anarchie*, p. 88; Caruchet, *Ils ont tué Bonnot*, pp. 114–116. Baraille was not prosecuted, although possibly he knew about Soudy's alleged crimes (EA 141, *procureur*, n.d.). The unidentified anarchist may have been Napoléon Jacob, a specialist in counterfeit money, who probably was a *mouchard* (Jean Grave, *Mémoires d'un anarchiste*, p. 371).

9 JA 19, letter from a *gardien de paix*, Paris, fourteenth arrondissement, sent from the Sanatorium d'Angicourt, Liancourt, Oise, March 31, 1912; report of April 13, 1912; Maîtrejean, *Souvenirs d'anarchie*, p. 79; Steiner, *Les En-dehors*, pp. 127–129.

10   JA 19, letter from a gardien de paix, Paris, fourteenth arrondissement, sent from the Sanatorium d'Angicourt, par Liancourt, Oise, March 31, 1912; report of April 13, 1912; Rirette Maîtrejean, *Souvenirs d'anarchie*, p. 79; Anne Steiner, *Les En-Dehors*, pp. 127–129.

11   Ibid.

12   Victor Méric, pp. 108–110; Émile Becker, pp. 39–40; Émile Michon, *Un peu de l'âme de bandits: étude de psychologie criminelle* (1913), p. 278; Frédéric Lavignette, p. 246, *Le Petit Parisien*, April 5, 1912.

13   JA 24, report of April 27, 1912; JA 16, report of April 4, 1912 (relating that he had somehow got a pair of scissors); Rirette Maîtrejean, *Souvenirs d'anarchie*, p. 49; Dominique Depond, pp. 8, 83–84; Anne Steiner, *Les En-Dehors*, pp. 129–30.

14   JA 19, police report April 5 and procès-verbal April 6, 1912.

15   JA 18, reports April 15, June 11, 14, and July 10, 1912; JA 19, report of April 5 and p.v. April 6, 1912; Frédéric Lavignette, pp. 213–214, *Le Matin* March 20, 1912.

16   JA 16, "note" on Anna Dondon; Frédéric Delacourt, p. 84; JA 19, reports of May 1 and July 13, 1912.

Chapter 14: Panic in Paris

1   Frédéric Lavignette, *La bande à Bonnot à travers la presse de l'époque* (Lyon, 2008), pp. 197–198; *L'Humanité*, March 27, 1912. See Aaron Freundschuh, "Colonial War Veterans as Police Investigators: La Sûreté de Paris in the early Third Republic," paper presented at the Western Society for French History, Chicago, November 2015, noting that gendarmerie posts had been cut in half in Paris by 1887, to about 3,000, while the number of *gardiens de la paix* had increased to about 8,000.

2   Louis Lépine, *Mes souvenirs* (Paris: Payot, 1929), p. 266; EA 140, telegram 3:00, March 25, 1912; JA 15, "Recherches et vérification dans les cafés de Montmontre"; Louis Chevalier, *Montmartre du plaisir et du crime* (Paris: Payot, 1995), pp. 304–305. Chevalier differentiates between "*haut*" Montmartre, where anarchist ideas thrived, "lower Montmartre" of pleasure adn treason," and eastern Montmartre, where "*plaisir*" combined with violence. He sees the two as essentially part of the same phenomenon.

3   Mark S. Micale, "France," in Michael Saler, ed., *The Fin-de-Siècle World* (New York, 2015), pp. 110–111; Robert A. Nye, *Crime, Madness, and Politics in Modern France: The Medical Concept of National Decline* (Princeton, 1984).

4   Marie-Claire Bancquart, *Paris "Belle Époque" par ses écrivains* (Paris, 1997), p. 53; Lavignette, *La bande à Bonnot à travers la presse de l'époque*, p. 48; *L'Humanité*, October 13, 1911.

5   Newspaper coverage of the Bonnot Gang clearly reflected the role that crime played in contemporary editorial strategies; Dominque Kalifa, *L'Encre et du sang* (Paris, 1995), pp. 27, 44, 82, 123; Michel Winock, *Les derniers feux à la Belle Époque* (Paris, 2014), pp. 148–154; Frédéric Lavignette, *La bande à Bonnot à travers la presse de l'époque* (Lyon, 2008), p. 11.

6   Winock, *La Belle Époque*, pp. 176–179, 187–188; Kalifa, *L'Encre et du sang*, p. 354. James Cannon notes that "zone" comes from the Greek for *zôné*, in this case the belt or girdle around Paris (p. 114). In the zone there were 79, 53, 43, and 42 murders, compared with but 3 in the sixteenth arrondissement and 5 in the seventh arrondissement.

7   Kalifa, *L'Encre et du sang*, pp. 151–163; Gérard Jacquemet, "La violence à Belleville au début du xxe siècle," *Bulletin de la Société de l'histoire de Paris et de l'Île-de-France*,

Michelle Perrot, "Dans la France de la Belle Époque, les 'Apaches', premières bandes de jeunes," in *Les Marginaux et les exclus dans l'histoire, Cahiers Jussieu* no. 5 (1979); Louis Chevalier, *Montmartre du plaisir et du crime* (Paris: Payot, 1995), pp. 298–300; Pierre Castelle, *Paris Républicain 1871–1914* (Abbeville, 2003), p. 184; Lavignette, *La bande à Bonnot à travers la presse de l'époque*, p. 41; *L'Excelsior*, September 1912. On March 13, 1913, an *apache* wounded two policemen with a Browning, although knives remained the weapon of choice in La Chapelle. A journalist came up with the term *apache* (Nye, *Crime, Madness, and Politics*, pp. 197–198.)

8   Francis Carco, *La Belle Époque au temps de Bruant* (Paris, 1954), pp. 55–56.

9   James Cannon, *The Paris Zone: A Cultural History, 1840–1944* (Farnham, UK, 2015), pp. 83–88, quoting Soulier's "*Le Zonier*," December 1, 1897, "Think of your safety and carry a gun when you walk through the *zone*."

10   *Fantômas* was the creation of Marcel Allain and Pierre Souvestre.

11   Kalifa, *L'Encre et du sang*, pp. 152–163, especially p. 153; Gérard Jacquemet, "La violence à Belleville au début du xxe siècle," *Bulletin de la Société de l'histoire de Paris et de l'Île-de-France*, 1978, pp. 141–144; Bernard Marchand, *Paris, histoire d'une ville, xixe–xxe siècle* (Paris, 1993), pp. 210–211; Lavignette, *La bande à Bonnot à travers la presse de l'époque*, p. 47; Jean-Marc Berlière, *Le Préfet Lépine: Vers la naissance de la police moderne* (Paris, 1993), pp. 212–218.

12   Jacquemet, "La violence à Belleville au début du xxe siècle," p. 164; Nye, *Crime, Madness, and Politics*, p. 212.

13   EA 140, April 28, 1912.

14   Émile Michon, *Un peu de l'âme de bandits: étude de psychologie criminelle* (Paris, 1913), pp. 20–21; Laurent López, *La guerre des polices n'a pas eu lieu: Gendarmes et policiers, co-acteurs de la sécurité publique sous la Troisième République (1870–1914)* (Paris, 2014), p. 393, from an article in the *Revue pénitentiaire et de droit penal* (juillet–octobre 1913), p. 1081.

15   Kalifa, *L'Encre et du sang*, pp. 49, 227; Michel Winock, *Les derniers feux à la Belle Époque* (Paris, 2014), pp. 133–137.

16   James Laux, *In First Gear: The French Automobile Industry to 1914* (Montréal, 1976), pp. 169–171; Eugen Weber, *France, Fin-de-Siècle* (Cambridge, MA, 1986), p. 207; Michel Winock, *Les derniers feux à la Belle Époque*, p. 61; Paul Morand, *1900* (Paris, 1931), p. 118; James Laux, pp. 195–202, 212; Winock, *La Belle Époque*, p. 61. In 1913, Peugeot turned out 5,000 automobiles, Rochet-Schneider 4,704, Berliet 3,000, Dion-Bouton 2,800, and Delauney-Belleville 1,500; Pierre Castelle, *Paris Républicain 1871–1914* (2003), p. 344.

17   Weber, *France, Fin-de-Siècle*, pp. 208–209; Winock, *La Belle Époque*, pp. 326–327.

18   Stephen L. Harp, *Michelin: Publicité et identité culturelle dans la France du XXe siècle* (Paris, 2008), pp. 245–246, 256–257; Steiner, *En-dehors*, p. 103; Mary McAuliffe, *Twilight of the Belle Epoque: The Paris of Picasso, Stravinsky, Proust, Renault, Marie Curie, Gertrude Stein, and Their Friends Through the Great War* (New York, 2014), p. 94.

19   Harp, *Michelin: Publicité et identité culturelle dans la France du XXe siècle*, pp. 12–13, 55–64, 89–90, 97–104, 109, referring to "a certain kind of national consciousness in la bourgeoisie française."

20   William Caruchet, *Ils ont tué Bonnot: Les révélations des archives policières* (Paris, 1990), pp. 59–60. Caruchet's book, although unfootnoted, is the best of the many journalistic accounts of the Bonnot Gang.

21   Paul Morand, *1900* (Paris, 1931), pp. 116–117; McAuliffe, *Twilight of the Belle Epoque*, p. 44.

22   Jean-Pierre Bernard, *Les deux Paris: les représentations de Paris dans le seconde moitié du xixe siècle* (Paris, 2001), p. 191. There were about 98,000 horses in Paris in 1900, more than at any time in the previous century. Omnibuses drove at 8 km per hour, but automobiles sped by at 10 km an hour. *Bateaux-mouche* could go even faster—15 km per hour.

23   Émile Becker, *La "Bande à Bonnot" 1911–1912* (Paris, 1968), pp. 9–10.

24   Kalifa, *L'Encre et du sang*, pp. 235–245; Renaud Thomazo, *Mort aux bourgeois! Sur les traces de la bande à Bonnot* (Paris, 2009), pp. 163–166.

Chapter 15: Police Dragnet

1   Renaud Thomazo, *Mort aux bourgeois! Sur les traces de la bande à Bonnot* (Paris, 2009), pp. 164–166.

2   Jean Grave, *Mémoires d'un anarchiste (1854–1920)* (Paris, 2009), p. 377; *L'Anarchie*, March 14, 1912.

3   Guillaume Davranche, *Trop jeune pour mourir* (Paris, 2014), pp. 220–222; André Salmon, *La Terreur noir* (Paris, 2008), p. 279.

4   F7 13053, "Notes sur l'Anarchie en France," April 25, 1913.

5   F7 13053, "Notes sur les menées anarchistes," March 30, 1912.

6   Émile Becker, *La "Bande à Bonnot"* (Paris, 1968), p. 19; Renaud Thomazo, *Mort aux bourgeois! Sur les traces de la bande à Bonnot*, pp. 166–168.

7   JA 15, A. Rivat, Lyon, March 27, 1912; February 28, 1912; JA 25, n.d. and May 2, 1912; March 21, 1912.

8   JA 15, dossier "Assassinat de M. Jouin," report of April 24, 1912.

9   William Caruchet, *Ils ont tué Bonnot: Les révélations des archives policières* (Paris, 1990), pp. 111–12; André Salmon, *La Terreur noir*, p. 291; Frédéric Lavignette, *La bande à Bonnot à travers la presse de l'époque* (Lyon, 2008), p. 204; *Le Petit Parisien*, March 28, 1912.

10   Lavignette, *La bande à Bonnot à travers la presse* de l'époque, p. 277; *L'Humanité*, April 24, 1912, poem of A.M. Maurel.

11   Émile Michon, *Un peu de l'âme de bandits: étude de psychologie criminelle* (Paris, 1913), pp. 266–274; Lavignette, *La bande à Bonnot à travers la presse* de l'époque, p. 300, *Le Petit Parisien*, April 27, 1912.

12   Rirette Maîtrejean, *Souvenirs d'anarchie* (Quimperlé, 2005), p. 57.

13   JA 18, January 7, April 7 and 11, July 10, 1912, and March 13, 1913.

14   JA 17, dossier Clément *femme* Hutteaux; reports of April 7 and July 3, 1912.

15   EA 141, prefect of police, April 7, 1912; JA 17, dossier Callemin, p.v. Louis Jouin, April 5, 1912; report of July 3, 1912; Maîtrejean, *Souvenirs d'anarchie*, pp. 57, 78; Depond, *Jules Bonnot et sa bande*, pp. 84–86; Lavignette, *La bande à Bonnot à travers la presse de l'époque*, pp. 253, 269, *Le Matin*, April 8, and *Action Française*, April 12, 1912. In 1913, Louise Hutteaux would be condemned to prison for five years for helping a young woman obtain an abortion.

16   JA 17, report April 27, 1912.

17   EA 141, Interrogation of Callemin; Lavignette, *La bande à Bonnot à travers la presse de l'époque*, p. 269; *Le Petit Parisien*, April 12, 1912.

18   Caruchet, *Ils ont tué Bonnot*, pp. 117–119.

19   *Le Petit Parisien*, April 8, 1912; *Le Matin*, April 10, 1912.

20   Becker, *La "Bande à Bonnot,"* pp. 35–36. *L'Anarchie* argued on May 2, 1912, that the sinking of the *Titantic* demonstrated that nature is more powerful than civilization.

Chapter 16: Antoine Gauzy's Variety Store

1   JA 16, dossier Pierre Cardi, report of September 3, 1912.

2   JA 16, dossier Pierre Cardi, reports of April 25 and September 3, 1912.

3   Louis Chevalier, *Montmartre du Plaisir et du crime* (Paris: Payot, 1995), p. 279.

4   JA 15, police report April 24, 1912; JA 24, April 19 and May 25, 1912; JA 19, report, n.d., April 1912; Renaud Thomazo, *Mort aux bourgeois! Sur les traces de la bande à Bonnot* (Paris, 2009), pp. 182–87; Anne Steiner, *Les En-dehors: anarchistes individualistes et illégalistes dans la Belle Époque* (Montreuil, 2008), p. 131.

5   JA 19, dossier Monier *dit* Simentoff, p.v. April 24 and report of July 15, 1912.

6   Monier had met Bonnot at place de la République on the morning of April 22.

7   JA 18, p.v. April 25, Xavier Guichard, and reports of n.d., April 25, n.d., and May 23, 1912; JA 19, report of June 10, 1912.

8   Frédéric Lavignette, *La bande à Bonnot à travers la presse de l'époque* (Lyon, 2008), p. 283; *L'Excelsior*, April 25, 1912.

9   JA 19, p.v.; KA 74, prefect of police, February 17, 1913 (remembering that he was *"fort capable"* of striking Gauzy following the death of Jouin but that *"il n'est pas possible que j'ai frappé Gauzy"*); Émile Becker, *La "Bande à Bonnot"* (Paris, 1968), pp. 37–40; Dominique Depond, *Jules Bonnot et sa bande* (Paris, 2009), pp. 67–69, 86–88, 141–42; William Caruchet, *Ils ont tué Bonnot: Les révélations des archives policières* (Paris, 1990), pp. 135–37.

10   JA 18, p.v. April 25, Xavier Guichard, and reports of April 25, n.d., and May 23, 1912.

11   KC 19, "discours de M. Lépine, préfet de police"; Émile Michon, *Un peu de l'âme de bandits: étude de psychologie criminelle* (Paris, 1913), p. 266.

12   *Le Matin*, April 26, 1912.

13   JA 22; Victor Serge, *Memoirs of a Revolutionary* (New York, 2012), pp. 42–43; Guillaume Davranche, *Trop jeune pour mourir: ouvriers et révolutionnaires face à la guerre (1909–1914)* (Paris, 2014), p. 218.

Chapter 17: Besieged in Choisy-le-Roi

1   EA 141, interrogation of *femme* Maîtrejean; Dominique Depond, *Jules Bonnot et sa bande* (Paris, 2009), pp. 80–81.

2   Anne Steiner, *Les En-dehors: anarchistes individualistes et illégalistes dans la Belle Époque* (Montreuil, 2008), pp. 226–227; Dominique Depond, *Jules Bonnot et sa bande* (Paris, 2009), pp. 93–94; Frédéric Lavignette, *La bande à Bonnot à travers la presse de l'époque* (Lyon, 2008), pp. 296–297; *Excelsior*, April 29, 1912.

3   Depond, *Jules Bonnot et sa bande*, pp. 93–94; Lavignette, *La bande à Bonnot à travers la presse de l'époque*, pp. 296–297; *L'Excelsior*, April 29, 1912.

4   Steiner, *Les En-dehors*, pp. 139–140.

5   Steiner, *Les En-dehors*, pp. 226–227.

6   Robert Le Texier, *De Ravachol à la bande à Bonnot* (Paris, 1989), p. 171.

7   Lavignette, *La bande à Bonnot à travers la presse de l'époque*, p. 329; *La Bataille syndicaliste*, April 29, 1912.

8   KA 77, dossier Paul Guichard.

9   JA 20, "Affaire de Choisy-le-Roi," p.v. April 28, 1912, 7:45 a.m., Xavier Guichard; JA 15m, dossier Jules Joseph Bonnot, report of April 28, 1912; Lavignette, *La bande à Bonnot à travers la presse de l'époque*, p. 348, *Excelsior*, April 29, 1912; Renaud Thomazo, *Mort aux bourgeois! Sur les traces de la bande à Bonnot* (Paris, 2009), provides a graphic account of the siege (pp. 202–215).

10   Richard Parry writes that Bonnot had written his testament on rue Saint-Ouen, thus before the siege in Choisy-le-Roi (*The Bonnot Gang* [London, 1987], pp. 125–126).

11   JA 15, dossier Bonnot; Steiner, *Les En-dehors*, pp. 140–143; Émile Becker, *La "Bande à Bonnot"* (Paris, 1968), pp. 41–46. In May 1912 the Tribunal civil condemned Judith Thollon to four years in prison, despite her constant denials that she had been aware of Bonnot's criminal activities or that she had been his lover, and her husband to one year, but a suspended sentence (Michel Chomarat, *Les Amants tragiques. Histoire du bandit Jules Bonnot et de sa maîtresse Judith Thollon* [Lyon, 1978], pp. 36–47). During the trial, an allegation was made that Garnier had been there, as well, but these seems improbable. Petit-Demange faced a year in prison.

12   Serge Pacaud, *Vie quotidienne des français à la Belle Époque* (Romorantin, 2008), p. 195; Lavignette, *La bande à Bonnot à travers la presse de l'époque*, p. 12.

13   EA 141, prefecture of police report, May 2, 1912; William Caruchet, *Ils ont tué Bonnot: Les révélations des archives policières* (Paris, 1990), pp. 157–158. The success of Maurice Leblanc's Arsène Lupin novels also indicate publication fascination with "anarchist" bandits [Michel Winock, *Les derniers feux de la Belle Époque* (Paris, 2014), pp. 62–67].

14   KC 19, dossier Louis Jouin; EA 141, *L'Excelsior*, May 15, 1912.

15   KA 74, dossier Xavier Guichard; Becker, *La "Bande à Bonnot,"* p. 45; Lavignette, *La bande à Bonnot à travers la presse de l'époque*, p. 412; *Le Petit Parisien*, May 13, 1912, *La Dépêche*, Région du Nord, May 14, 1912. Fortan would be killed in World War I (Richard Parry, *The Bonnot Gang* [London, 1987], p. 176).

16   KC 19, dossier Louis Jouin; *Bulletin Municipal Officiel de la Ville de Paris*, May 10, 1912.

17   Lavignette, *La bande à Bonnot à travers la presse de l'époque*, p. 354; *Le Matin*, March 9, 1912 and *Le Petit Parisien*, April 14, 1912.

18   Frédéric Delacourt, *L'Affaire bande à Bonnot* (Paris, 2006), p. 80; Anne Steiner, *Rirette l'insoumise* (Tulle, 2013), pp. 60–61. Mauricius was condemned to five years in prison for "*d'apologie de crimes*" but fled and the conviction was overturned on appeal in 1913. By then he had taken over directorship of *L'Anarchie*.

19   Steiner, *Les En-dehors*, pp. 150–151; William Caruchet, *Ils ont tué Bonnot*, pp. 160–161. In 1974, shortly before his death, Mauricius related that many anarchists

rejected the crimes of Bonnot and the others but believed they should continue to support them because contemporary society inflicted twenty times the damage every day.

20 Michel Winock, *Les derniers feux de la Belle Époque*, p. 98.

Chapter 18: Spectacle in Nogent-sur-Marne

1 Rumors later would have Marie *la Belge* as having revealed the residence of Garnier, although she would always deny this.

2 Dominique Depond, *Jules Bonnot et sa bande* (Paris, 2009), pp. 97–98. See also Jacques Porot, *Louis Lépine: Préfet de Police, Témoin de sons temps (1846–1933)* (Paris, 1994), pp. 269–272. Richard Parry relates (without citing a source) that a letter arrived at the prefecture of police on Monday from a man who claimed to have recognized Garnier on the tramway to Nogent, sitting with a younger man (p. 142).

3 JA 15, report of March 19, 1912, 4 p.m.; Rirette Maîtrejean, *Souvenirs d'anarchie* (Quimperlé, 2005), p. 78; Depond, *Jules Bonnot et sa bande*, pp. 98–99.

4 Marcel Guillaume, *Mes grandes enquêtes criminelles. De la bande à Bonnot à l'affaire Stavisky* (Paris, 2005), p. 103; Frédéric Lavignette, *La bande à Bonnot à travers la presse de l'époque* (Lyon, 2008), p. 422, *L'Excelsior*, May 15, 1912. Anna Dondon, Valet's girlfriend, had left the "villa" before the police arrived and was never accused of a crime (Frédéric Delacourt, *L'Affaire bande à Bonnot* [Paris, 2006], pp. 144–146; Anne Steiner, *Les En-dehors: anarchistes individualistes et illégalistes dans la Belle Époque* [Montreuil, 2008], p. 226).

5 Guillaume, *Mes Grandes Enquêtes criminelles*, pp. 101–104; EA 141, prefecture of police, May 15, 1912.

6 André Salmon, *La Terreur noir* (Paris, 2008), pp. 294–295; Lavignette, *La bande à Bonnot à travers la presse de l'époque*, p. 427; *Le Temps,* May 16, 1912.

7 JA 20, report May 14 and 15, 1912.

8 EA 141, Rapport, commissaire divisionnaire, chef du service, de sûreté, to Directeur de police, May 16, 1912; report of Paul Guillebaud, May 14, 1912; report of *gardien de la paix* Mametz; Émile Becker, *La "Bande à Bonnot"* (Paris, 1968), pp. 52–54; Maîtrejean, *Souvenirs d'anarchie*, p. 78; Depond, *Jules Bonnot et sa bande*, pp. 102–103; William Caruchet, *Ils ont tué Bonnot: Les révélations des archives policières* (Paris, 1990), pp. 172–177; Lavignette, *La bande à Bonnot à travers la presse de l'époque*, p. 438; *L'Excelsior*, May 15, 1912. Valet's father was denied the right to see and to take away his son's corpse. Rumors circulated that Garnier had been alive when he was killed—needlessly—by a policeman. Authorities refused to deliver the bodies of Garnier and Valet to their families, which compounded questions about their deaths.

9 Depond, *Jules Bonnot et sa bande*, p. 102.

10 Renaud Thomazo, *Mort aux bourgeois! Sur les traces de la bande à Bonnot* (Paris, 2009), pp. 238–241.

11 Laurent López, *La guerre des polices n'a pas eu lieu: Gendarmes et policiers, co-acteurs de la sécurité publique sous la Troisième République (1870–1914)* (Paris, 2014), pp. 382–391.

12 López, *La guerre des polices n'a pas eu lieu*, pp. 399–400.

13   López, *La guerre des polices n'a pas eu lieu*, p. 394; Jean-Marc Berlière, *Le monde des polices en France* (Paris, 1996), pp. 94, 107; Jean-Marc Berlière, *Le Préfet Lépine: Vers la naissance de la police moderne* (Paris, 1993), pp. 249–250.

14   *L'Anarchie*, September 5, 1912; Guillaume Davranche, *Trop jeune pour mourir: ouvriers et révolutionnaires face à la guerre (1909–1914)* (Paris, 2014), p. 223.

15   EA 141, *L'Humanité*, May 16, 1912.

16   Steiner, *Les En-dehors*, p. 149; Thomazo, *Mort aux bourgeois!*, pp. 246–247.

17   JA 22.

18   JA 22, April 28, 1912.

19   JA 20, report of February 16, 1912; *Le mouvement anarchiste*. Vol. 1, *Des origines à 1914*, pp. 431–432; Thomazo, *Mort aux bourgeois!*, pp. 255–256.

Chapter 19: On Trial

1   Émile Becker, *La "Bande à Bonnot"* (Paris, 1968), pp. 61–62.

2   Becker, *La "Bande à Bonnot,"* pp. 64–65.

3   Becker, *La "Bande à Bonnot,"* pp. 66–67.

4   Rirette Maîtrejean, *Souvenirs d'anarchie* (Quimperlé, 2005), p. 58; Victor Serge, *Mémoires d'un révolutionnaire, 1901–1941*, edited by Jean Rière (Paris, 1978), pp. 45–46.

5   J(ean) Maitron, "De Kibaltchiche à Victor Serge. Le Rétif (1909–1919)," *Mouvement social*, 47, avril–juin 1964, pp. 51–54, from a letter January 22, 1913, to Émile Armand; Victor Serge, *Memoirs of a Revolutionary* (New York, 2012), p. 46.

6   JA 18, reports of October 24–25, 1912; Frédéric Delacourt, *L'Affaire bande à Bonnot* (Paris, 2006), p. 101; *Le Petit Parisien*, February 4, 1912; Serge, *Memoirs of a Revolutionary*, p. 48.

7   Frédéric Delacourt, *L'Affaire bande à Bonnot* (Paris, 2006), pp. 99–100; Richard Parry, *The Bonnot Gang* (London, 1987), p. 7. Two of the accused were not present: Gorodsky, on the run, and Rimbault, in a mental institution.

8   *L'Anarchie*, February 6, 1913. The original forty included three *propriétaires*, four *commerçants*, four *rentiers*, one *officier supérieur en retraite*, three *agents de change* and *clercs de notaires*, nine *patrons* and *entrepreneurs*, and nine *employés*. Of the twelve jurors and two alternates, there were two engineers, a *rentier*, a *fabricant de voitures*, a *clerc de notaire*, a *propriétaire*, *commis d'agent de change*, *commerçant*, *employée*, *entrepreneur de ciments retraité, docteur en médecin*. One *propriétaire* and one *rentier* served as alternates.

9   *L'Anarchie*, February 6, 1913.

10   Marius Boucabelle, *A propos de l'affaire Bonnot* (Paris, 1912), p. 4.

11   Rirette Maîtrejean, *Souvenirs d'anarchie* (Quimperlé, 2005), p. 90; Victor Méric, *Les bandits tragiques*. (Paris, 1926), p. 105.

12   Maîtrejean, *Souvenirs d'anarchie*, p. 59; Victor Méric, *Les bandits tragiques* (1926), p. 95; Frédéric Lavignette, *Action Française*, February 4, 1913, p. 510.

13   Robert Le Texier, *De Ravachol à la bande à Bonnot* (Paris, 1989), p. 189; *Le Matin*, February 23, 1913.

14   Becker, *La "Bande à Bonnot,"* pp. 94–95, 129; Luc Nemeth, "Victor Serge, marqué, par son passé," in Rirette Maîtrejean, *Souvenirs d'anarchie,* p. 102; Frédéric Delacourt, *L'Affaire bande à Bonnot* (Paris, 2006), p. 107; Lavignette, *La bande à Bonnot à travers la presse de l'époque*, p. 510; *Le Matin,* February 23, 1913.

15   Serge, *Memoirs of a Revolutionary*, p. 46.

16   EA 141; Delacourt, *L'Affaire bande à Bonnot*, pp. 108–118, 151.

17   *Le Petit Parisien*, February 5, 1913.

18   Maîtrejean, *Souvenirs d'anarchie*, p. 59: Becker, *La "Bande à Bonnot,"* pp. 95–97; Delacourt, *L'Affaire bande à Bonnot*, pp. 110, 118–22; Arthur Bernède, *Bonnot, Garnier et Cie* (Paris, 1930), pp. 175–176.

19   JA 17, report of August 8, 1912.

20   Méric, *Les bandits tragiques*, p. 69; Depond, *Jules Bonnot et sa bande*, pp. 109–11; Becker, *La "Bande à Bonnot,"* pp. 98–100; Lavignette, *La bande à Bonnot à travers la presse de l'époque*, pp. 235, 513; *L'Humanité*, March 31, 1912; Robert Le Texier, *De Ravachol à la bande à Bonnot* (Paris, 1989), p. 187; *Le Petit Parisien*, February 6, 1912.

21   Frédéric Delacourt, *L'Affaire bande à Bonnot*, pp. 122–125.

22   Becker, *La "Bande à Bonnot,"* p. 100; Delacourt, *L'Affaire bande à Bonnot*, pp. 128–133.

23   Delacourt, *L'Affaire bande à Bonnot*, pp. 133–135.

24   JA 20, report of April 27, 1912; Delacourt, *L'Affaire bande à Bonnot*, pp. 137–143.

25   When Huc, the gardener at Romainville, testified, his head shaved for whatever reason, he related that he had promised to denounce his *"copains"* because he had been promised a pardon. He had changed his mind: *"Monsieur le president, parce que j'ai été lâche, je ne veux pas devenir un salaud."*

26   Depond, *Jules Bonnot et sa bande*, pp. 103–111; Caruchet, *Ils ont tué Bonnot*, pp. 184–185.

27   Maîtrejean, *Souvenirs d'anarchie*, pp. 55–61; Delacourt, *L'Affaire bande à Bonnot*, p. 160. Rirette noted that she and Victor had largely renounced *tu-to*ing each other because in the anarchist world everyone *tu-to*ied everyone.

28   *Le Petit Parisian*, February 20, 1913.

29   Becker, *La "Bande à Bonnot,"* pp. 135–137; Delacourt, *L'Affaire bande à Bonnot*, pp. 137–143, 160–161; Lavignette, *La bande à Bonnot à travers la presse de l'époque*, pp. 548–549, 554; *Le Petit Parisien*, February 25 and 27, 1913.

30   Maîtrejean, *Souvenirs d'anarchie*, p. 60; Victor Serge, *Mémoires d'un révolutionaire*, p. 48.

31   Rodriguez then was transferred to Lille to face charges of fencing stolen goods and counterfeit money (Delacourt, p. 180). He claimed that Dieudonné had not shot Caby, but had been in the car—indeed, was the mystery person. Rodriguez, of course, was not there, and his claim should be taken with a grain of salt. The identity of the mystery person remains unknown. Barbe Le Clerch was not convicted of any crime and was still living in Paris in 1913 under an assumed name (JA 18, report of January 31, 1913). Anna Dondon told police that she did not know where the *Bretonne* was to be found.

32   Anne Steiner, *Les En-dehors: anarchistes individualistes et illegalistes dans la Belle Époque* (Montreuil, 2008), p. 161; Caruchet, *Ils ont tué Bonnot*, p. 198. Others who knew or sympathized or had helped gang members in any way also received prison sentences: Jean-Marcel Poyer to five years and Kléber Bénard to six years, both for having been go-betweens in stolen guns that ended up in the hands of the Bonnot Gang. Henri Joseph Crozat de Fleury, denounced by his wife, received five years for having sold stolen securities. Jourdan received eighteen months in prison (to which *le conseil de guerre* subsequently added six more). Charles Reinert went to prison for having concocted a false alibi for poor Dieudonné.

33   Eugène Dieudonné, *La vie des forçats* (Paris, 2014), pp. 21–25.

34   Victor Serge, *Memoirs of a Revolutionary*, p. 49.

35   Maîtrejean, *Souvenirs d'anarchie*, pp. 62–63; Serge, *Mémoires d'un révolutionnaire*, p. 48; Méric, *Les bandits tragiques*, pp. 109–110; Becker, *La "Bande à Bonnot,"* pp. 146–147;Lavignette, *La bande à Bonnot à travers la presse de l'époque*, p. 564; *Le Petit Parisien*, February 28, 1913.

36   Luc Nemeth, "Victor Serge, marqué, par son passé," in Rirette Maîtrejean, *Souvenirs d'anarchie*, p. 103.

37   *L'Anarchie* March 6, 1913.

38   André Salmon, *La Terreur noir* (Paris, 2008), p. 302; Guillaume Davranche, *Trop jeune pour mourir: ouvriers et révolutionnaires face à la guerre (1909–1914)* (Paris, 2014), pp. 304–306, 312. The former indicates that Raymond Callemin wrote a letter from his cell to *L'Anarchie* for it to stop making "*apologies stupides*" for acts that had no "*aspect d'anarchisme ou de revendication sociale.*" *L'Anarchie* devoted a column to "*le droit d'asile*" on January 2, 1913.

Chapter 20: The Widow

1   Émile Michon, *Un peu de l'âme de bandits: étude de psychologie criminelle* (N.p., 1913), pp. 45–51, 70–72. Michon concluded that if the bandits had been born into a different milieu, their lives could have turned out very differently. He noted that often the fathers were "not beyond reproach," as in the case of Callemin. Another was brutal. Yet in several cases grandparents or aunts had played a positive role. While their level of intelligence varied, none had more than basic primary schooling. Those who read were essentially autodidacts. Besides Dostoevsky, Kropotkin, and Tolstoy (from whom they had taken ideas not of charity and kindness but only of violence and revolutionary instincts), a few had read Darwin, Lamarck, and Le Dantec, who viewed the ego as the basis of society. This, in Michon's view, pointed at least several of them toward their obsession with the individual and "*vivre sa vie!*" The *causeries* pushed them toward individualism and then illegalism. Many had vowed revenge against society for their poverty. Carouy had been in Thiais but had not wielded a knife. Yet he tried to justify the killing of Monsieur Moreau and his aged maid because the securities stored in a chest of drawers had been built on the suffering of the poor. Strangely, he insisted that it was a good deed to put the securities back in circulation and benefit from them. Michon concluded that all of them were in some ways violent.

2   Michon, *Un peu de l'âme de bandits*, pp. 186–187.

3   Michon, *Un peu de l'âme de bandits*, pp. 65–66.

4   Michon, *Un peu de l'âme de bandits*, pp. 20–21, 34–38.

5   Victor Serge, "Méditation sur l'anarchie," *Esprit*, 55, April 1, 1937, pp. 38–39.

6   JA 16, "Mes Mémoires: (Callemin dit Raymond la Science): Pourquoi j'ai cambriolé Pourquoi j'ai tué." He added that "*l'attentat contre la vie humaine*" was a crime, but seemed to excuse it with the corollary, "*perpétré dans certaines conditions*" (Victor Méric, p. 115).

7   William Caruchet, *Ils ont tué Bonnot: Les révélations des archives policières* (Paris, 1990), p. 59.

8   Rirette Maîtrejean, *Souvenirs d'anarchie* (Quimperlé, 2005), p. 58.

9   Patrick Pécherot, *L'Homme à la Carabine: Esquisse* (Paris, 2011), pp. 263–264.

10   JA 21, April 11, 1913; Renaud Thomazo, *Mort aux bourgeois! Sur les traces de la bande à Bonnot* (Paris, 2009), pp. 265–266.

11   EA 140, report of April 18, 1913.

12   Gaetano Manfredonia, *La chanson anarchiste en France des origines à 1914* (Paris, 1997), pp. 260–261.

13   JA 21, p.v. of executions, April 21, 1913; Serge, *Memoirs of a Revolutionary*, p. 50; André Salmon, *La Terreur noir* (Paris, 2008), p. 303; Maîtrejean, *Souvenirs d'anarchie*, pp. 79, 131–132 (Annex II, Alexandre Crois, *Crapouillot*, January 1938); Dominique Depond, *Jules Bonnot et sa bande* (Paris, 2009), p. 113; Philippe Néris, *La Bande à Bonnot* (Paris, 1925), p. 154; Émile Becker, *La "Bande à Bonnot"* (Paris, 1968), pp. 155–156. Depond notes that it was known for criminals to have tattooed on their neck *"Pour Deibler,"* or *"Réservé à Deibler"* (p. 186); Michon, *Un peu de l'âme de bandits*, pp. 221–291. On June 27, 1908, Doctor Paul Gleize in Beaugency had expressed in writing his opinion that André Soudy *"est attaint de troubles mentaux . . . il présente des idées d'homicide."* He recommended surveillance and perhaps admission to *"un asile d'aliénés"* (Michon, *Un peu de l'âme de bandits*, p. 337). Soudy was the subject of a novel published in 1911 by Patrick Pécherot, *L'Homme à la Carabine; Esquisse.* Marie Besse was shattered by Soudy's execution and died at age seventeen (Richard Parry, *The Bonnot Gang* [London, 1987], p. 175).

14   Becker, *La "Bande à Bonnot,"* pp. 163–164; Robert Le Texier, *De Ravachol à la bande à Bonnot* (Paris, 1989), p. 191; Eugène Dieudonné, *La vie des forçats* (Paris: Libertalia, 2014), p. 26. The writer and journalist Albert Londres launched a campaign asking for his release from prison, and Dieudonné died on August 21, 1944, in the hospital of Eaubonne in the suburbs of Paris. Metge spent the rest of his life in Guiana, dying of fever in 1931 several years after being freed [Frédéric Lavignette, *La Bande à Bonnot à travers la presse de l'époque* (Lyon, 2008), p. 591.] Gauzy benefited from a campaign on his behalf and went free in July 1913. He sold old clothes and textiles in markets of the suburbs of Paris until his death in 1963 at age 83. An article in *Paris-Jour* on June 16, 1963, noted the death of the last member [*sic*] of the Bonnot Gang (EA 141). Émile Michon contended that Dieudonné, whom he interviewed several times at La Santé, had come to see his "errors" and that little by little *"l'evidence a repris ses droits."* It had saddened him that many anarchists, who had evoked solidarity and the possibility of human happiness, had turned to individualism and egotism. Anarchists should return to the sincere sentiments of Kropotkin and others (Michon, *Un peu de l'âme de bandits*, pp. 279–285).

15   Rirette Maîtrejean, "Commissaire Guillaume, Ne réveillez pas les morts!," in *Confessions*, 15, March 11, 1937, in *Souvenirs d'anarchie*, p. 71.

16   Susan Weissman, *Victor Serge: The Course Is Set on Hope* (London, 2001), p. 17; Salmon, *La Terreur noir*, pp. 300–301. This came much later, as indicated by Victor's suggestion such values could be found in Russia.

17   BA 1499, report of April 18 and August 28, 1913.

18   André Girard, *Anarchistes et bandits* (Paris: Publications des Temps Nouveaux, 1914), pp. 3–9.

19   *La Société Nouvelle*, August, 1913.

20   See, above all, George Orwell, *Homage to Catalonia*, first published in 1938.

21   Anne Steiner, *Rirette l'insoumise* (Tulle, 2013), pp. 66–69, noting that Rirette was not consulted about the form that her memoirs would take in *Le Matin*; Maîtrejean, *Souvenirs d'anarchie*, p. 81, which first appeared in the series in *Le Matin*.

22   Victor Serge, "Méditation sur l'anarchie," *Esprit*, 55, April 1, 1937, p. 39; Victor Serge, *Les hommes dans la prison*. Preface by Richard Greeman (Paris, 2011), p. 10; Victor Serge, *Mémoires d'un révolutionnaire, 1901–1941,* edited by Jean Rière (Paris, 1978), pp. 44, 56.

23   Victor Serge, *Mémoires d'un révolutionnaire*, p. 50.

Chapter 21: The Violence of States; the Clouds of War

1   Paul B. Miller, *From Revolutionaries to Citizens: Anti-Militarism in France, 1870–1914* (Durham, NC: Duke University Press, 2002), pp. 161–167.

2   Victor Serge (Le Rétif), "La Guerre au service de la vie," *L'Anarchie*, November 2, 1911, p. 130.

3   See Vivien Bouhey, *Les anarchistes contre la République: Contribution à l'histoire des réseaux sous la Troisième République (1880–1914)* (Rennes, 2008), especially pp. 363–439.

4   Eugen Weber, *France Fin de Siècle* (Cambridge, MA, 1986), p. 120.

5   Vivien Bouhey, *Les anarchistes contre la République*, pp. 425–428.

6   Miller, *From Revolutionaries to Citizens*, pp. 161–167.

7   *L'Anarchie,* October 11, 1911.

8   *L'Anarchie,* March 30 and October 10, 1911.

9   Hubert Juin, *Le Livre de Paris 1900* (Paris, 1994), p. 52.

10   Charles Rearick, *Pleasures of the Belle Epoque: Entertainment and Festivity in Turn-of-the-Century France* (New Haven, CT: Yale University Press, 1985), pp. 208–213; Louis Chevalier, *Montmartre du plaisir et du crime* (Paris: Payot, 1995), pp. 295–297; Michel Winock, *Les derniers feux de la Belle Époque* (Paris, 2014), pp. 54–59; Mary McAuliffe, *Twilight of the Belle Epoque: The Paris of Picasso, Stravinsky, Proust, Renault, Marie Curie, Gertrude Stein, and Their Friends Through the Great War* (New York, 2014), p. 206.

11   Michel Winock, *Les derniers feux de la Belle Époque* (Paris, 2014), pp. 16–19, 38–42.

12   David Schoenbaum, *Zabern 1913: Consensus Politics in Imperial Germany* (Boston, 1982); Stephen L. Harp, *Michelin: Publicité et identité culturelle dans la France du XXe siècle* (Baltimore, 2008), p. 14; Winock, *Les derniers feux à la Belle Époque*, pp. 38–39.

13   Victor Serge, *Le Rétif*, pp. 132–133, *L'Anarchie*, April 6 and November 2, 1911.

14   BA 1499; Miller, *From Revolutionaries to Citizens*, pp. 153–154; F7 13053, *Le Libertaire*, June 29, 1912; Mary McAuliffe, *Twilight of the Belle Epoque*, p. 212.

15   *L'Anarchie*, December 12, 1912, and January 9 and March 20, 1913.

16   Antoine Prost, *Si nous vivions en 1913* (Paris, 1914), p. 123. James Cannon, *The Paris Zone: A Cultural History, 1840–1944* (Farnham, UK, 2015), pp. 102–105; Miller, *From Revolutionaries to Citizens*, pp. 150–151; Vivien Bouhey, *Les anarchistes contre la République*, pp. 426–432. Miller writes, "Antimilitarism had not become the 'self-standing' ideology that its leaders hoped it would. . . . But it succeeded brilliantly as a

rallying cry against social and political inequities on behalf of ordinary citizens" (p. 212).

18   Michel Winock, *Les derniers feux de la Belle Époque* (Paris, 2014), p. 278.

19   Mark S. Micale, "France," in Michael Saler, ed., *The Fin-de-Siècle World* (New York, 2015), p. 103; Winock, *Les derniers feux de la Belle Époque*, p. 110; Marie-Claire Bancquart, *Paris "Belle Époque" par ses écrivains* (Paris, 1997), pp. 41–43.

20   Winock, *Les derniers feux à la Belle Époque,* pp. 166–168; Edward Berenson, *The Trial of Madame Caillaux* (Berkeley, 1992), pp. 1–2, 241.

21   Miller, *From Revolutionaries to Citizens*, p. 207; Chevalier, *Montmartre du plaisir et du crime*, pp. 294–295, *"l'Europe tout entière entraînée vers la violence par le contraste entre l'écrasante richesse des uns et la misère des autres."*

22   Frédéric Lavignette, *La bande à Bonnot à travers la presse de l'époque*, p. 56, from *L'Excelsior*, May 5, 1912; F7 13053, "Mouvement anarchiste," 1913.

23   Louis Chevalier, *Montmartre du plaisir et du crime*, p. 309.

24   Michel Winock, *La Belle Époque* (Paris, 2002), pp. 278–279; Bouhey, *Les anarchistes contre la République,* pp. 458–459; Jean-Jacques Becker, *1914: Comment les Français sont entrés dans la guerre. Paris: presses de la foundation nationale des sciences politiques* (1977), pp. 190–192, 211, 338–339, 405–406, 574–575, 582–583.

25   Becker, *1914: Comment les Français sont entrés dans la guerre*, p. 588; Victor Serge, *Mémoires d'un révolutionnaire, 1901–1941,* edited by Jean Rière (Paris, 1978), p. 56.

26   Winock, *Les derniers feux de la Belle Époque* (Paris, 2014), pp. 30–34; Stephen Romer, *Times Literary Supplement*, February 6, 2015.

27   In January 1915 (in an account not published until 1922 for reasons of censorship), Lorulot denounced the Socialists and the CGT for supporting the war by placing it in the context of national defense against an imperial, autocratic regime: *"Allez, les brutes, laissez la bride à vos instincts. . . . La déclaration de guerre est officielle et dans les bars qui regorgent, l'absinthe coule à flots. Les faces alcoolisées suent la brutalité et la haine. . . . Á Berlin! . . . Ah! Les chauvins! Ils triomphent! Qui oserait leur résister? La rue est à eux."* André Lorulot, *Le crime de 1914* (Paris: Éditions de la Revue L'Idée Libre, 1922), pp. 5, 9, 15, 22, 25.

28   Michael Walzer, *Just and Unjust Wars* (New York, 1977), p. 29.

Chapter 22: Aftermath

1   Victor Serge, *Mémoires d'un révolutionnaire, 1901–1941,* edited by Jean Rière (Paris, 1978), pp. 52–54; Luc Nemeth, "Victor Serge, marqué, par son passé," in Rirette Maîtrejean, *Souvenirs d'anarchie* (Quimperlé, 2005), p. 103.

2   Maîtrejean, *Souvenirs d'anarchie*, p. 94.

3   Anne Steiner, *Rirette l'insoumise* (Tulle, 2013), pp. 72–73.

4   Serge, *Mémoires d'un révolutionnaire*, pp. 57–58; J(ean) Maitron, "De Kibaltchiche à Victor Serge. Le Rétif (1909–1919)," *Mouvement social*, 47, avril–juin 1964, p. 58, including letter of February 16.

5   Steiner, *Rirette l'insoumise*, pp. 73–74.

6   J(ean) Maitron, "De Kibaltchiche à Victor Serge. Le Rétif (1909–1919)," *Mouvement social*, 47, avril–juin 1964, pp. 62–63, letters of March 3, March 28, and April 13, 1917. As for the memoirs, *"J'y suis étranger. J'y reste étranger."*

7   Luc Nemeth, "Victor Serge, marqué, par son passé," in Rirette Maîtrejean, *Souve-nirs d'anarchie*, p. 104; Victor Serge, *Le Rétif*, p. 14; J(ean) Maitron, "De Kibaltchiche à Victor Serge. Le Rétif (1909–1919)," *Mouvement social*, 47, avril–juin 1964, p. 56; Steiner, *Les En-dehors,* p. 185; J(ean) Maitron, "De Kibaltchiche à Victor Serge. Le Rétif (1909–1919)," *Mouvement social*, 47, avril–juin 1964, pp. 45–80. While respond-ing to reproaches on his attitude during his time in Barcelona, Victor corresponded with Émile Armand over the criticism that had come his way from Lorulot over Victor's attitude toward illegalists during the trial. The latter had severely criti-cized his denunciation of illegalists. Raymond now insisted "*que j'étais écoeuré de voir nos idées, si belles et si riches, aboutir à tel gaspillage crapuleux de jeunes forces dans la boue et le sang*" and that he had asked to be judged not on what others did "*mais pour mes propres actes et mes propres idées*"; (J(ean) Maitron, "De Kibaltchiche à Victor Serge. Le Rétif (1909–1919)," *Mouvement social*, 47, avril–juin 1964, p. 61, letter of March 28, 1917.

8   Victor Serge, "Méditation sur l'anarchie," *Esprit* 55, April 1, 1937, p. 41.

9   Maîtrejean, *Souvenirs d'anarchie*, p. 95; Richard Greeman, "The Novel of the Revo-lution," in Susan Weissman, ed., *The Ideas of Victor Serge: A Life as a Work of Art* (Critique Books, 1997), p. 49. He would write in his memoirs, "Poets and novelists are not political beings because they are not essentially rational. Political intelli-gence, based though it is in the revolutionary's case upon a deep idealism, demands a scientific and pragmatic armour, and subordinates itself to the pursuit of strictly defined social ends" (p. 63, from Greeman).

10   J(ean) Maitron, "De Kibaltchiche à Victor Serge. Le Rétif (1909–1919)," *Mouve-ment social*, 47, avril–juin 1964, pp. 56–57 and 73, the latter letter of May 6, 1917, in which he wrote "*Je suis, en effet, beaucoup moins distant que toi des rév[olutionnaires'] et des comm[unistes] (quoique je m'abstienne absolument de poser la question soc[iété] future). Mais individualiste dans le sense liber[aire], éclectique, éducation[niste]—et surtout subjectif du moi.*"

11   Steiner, *Les En-dehors*, pp. 187–193; Steiner, *Rirette l'insoumise*, pp. 74–78, who suggests this interpretation.

12   Steiner, *Rirette l'insoumise*, pp. 77–78; Steiner, *Les En-dehors*, pp. 193–194.

13   Nemeth, "Victor Serge, marqué, par son passé," p. 105.

14   EA 141 *L'Aurore,* June 17, 1968.

15   Susan Weissman, ed., *Victor Serge: The Course Is Set on Hope* (London: Verso, 2001), p. 15.

16   Victor expressed such views in a 1921 pamphlet: "The anarchists and the experi-ence of the Russian Revolution."

17   Victor Serge, *Les Hommes dans la prison* (2011). Preface by Richard Greeman, pp. 22–23; "On the Leninist Tradition," in Susan Weissman, ed., *Victor Serge: The Course Is Set on Hope*, pp. 136–159; Steiner, *Rirette l'insoumise*, pp. 122–124. Victor refused to accept—from a Leninist perspective—the justifications put forward by Bolshevik leaders following the crushing of the Kronstadt rebellion (pp. 144–147). While opposing the repression as reflecting authoritarian tendencies within the Party, unlike anarchists and left-wing Socialist Revolutionaries, he did not accept the rebellion as "the harbinger of a necessary or new third revolution against the Party." Victor believed that the only alternative to Bolshevism at the time was the unthinkable horror of the White counter-revolution and inevitable military

dictatorship (p. 159); Victor Serge, "Thirty Years after the Russian Revolution," in Susan Weissman, ed., *Victor Serge, The Course Is Set on Hope* (London: Verso, 2001), p. 240. Serge remained impressed by the spontaneous nature of the February Revolution and remained convinced that the Bolsheviks in 1917 "had shown themselves to be the best equipped to express the aspirations of the masses in a coherent, clearsighted and determined fashion" (p. 242).

18   Victor Serge, *Les hommes dans la prison*. Preface by Richard Greeman (Paris, 2011), pp. 24, 42; Rachel Polonsky, "Review: *Victor Serge, Memoirs of a Revolutionary*," *Times Literary Supplement*, June 14, 2013.

19   Victor Serge, *Les hommes dans la prison*. Preface by Richard Greeman (Paris, 2011), pp. 12–13, 17, 117.

20   Polonsky, "Review: *Victor Serge, Memoirs of a Revolutionary*."

21   *Cahier Henry Poulaille, Hommage à Victor Serge (1890–1947) pour le centenaire de sa naissance* (Paris: Éditions Plein Chant, mars 1991, nos. 4 et 5), Présentation par Jean Rière, p. 135. The letter was sent to Henry Poulaille, the anarchist writer in Paris. In May 1939, Victor signed a contract for a history of anarchism, but this was never written. Victor's journal appeared in a monthly review of Jean-Paul Sartre, *Les Temps Modernes*, June and July of 1949 (77W 4255-487-689, report of June 13, 1950).

22   77W 4255-487-689, report of June 13, 1950.

23   Steiner, *Rirette l'insoumise*, pp. 81–83, 124–125; Caruchet, *Ils ont tué Bonnot*, pp. 198–199. Vlady became an influential artist and lived in Mexico until his death in 2005.

24   Nemeth, "Victor Serge, marqué, par son passé," in Maîtrejean, *Souvenirs d'anarchie*, p. 108; Victor Serge, *Le Rétif*, p. 14; "On the Leninist Tradition," p. 158; Guy Desolre, "On Leon Trotsky and the Fourth International," in Susan Weissman, ed., pp. 171, 182; Polonsky, "Review: *Victor Serge, Memoirs of a Revolutionary*."

25   Richard Greeman, "The Novel of the Revolution," p. 67; Victor Serge, "Thirty Years after the Russian Revolution," p. 253; 77W 4255-487-689, report of June 13, 1950; Polonsky, "Review: *Victor Serge, Memoirs of a Revolutionary*."

26   Greeman, pp. 32–33.

27   Victor Serge, "Thirty Years after the Revolution," p. 258.

28   I still find him that. Paul Gordon, *Vagabond Witness: Victor Serge and the Politics of Hope* (Washington, DC, 2013), p. 102. Gordon offers a particularly moving account.

29   Nemeth, "On Anarchism," p. 130. Victor assisted anarchists in the Soviet Union during the early 1930s. Although in 1927 Rirette received a letter from Victor: "*Madame, je ne puis que vous confirmer ce que vous savez. Je suis fixé en U.R.S.S. où ma vie s'est refaite. Il vous appartient désormais de déduire de ces faits toutes les conséquences légales et morales.*"

30   Steiner, *Rirette l'insoumise*, pp. 83–85; Caruchet, *Ils ont tué Bonnot*, pp. 201–202. Her daughters both married and moved to Pré-Saint-Gervais, where some of the first *logements sociaux* had been constructed. When Maud and her husband moved to Spain in 1936, Rirette moved into their apartment.

31   EA 141 *L'Aurore*, June 17, 1968. Ironically, Rirette passed away in the hospice right across the street from where, in the late 1880s and early 1890s, Émile Henry's mother had run a little bar and restaurant.

32   The film *La Bande à Bonnot*, directed by Philippe Fourastié, has Bonnot killing Jouin above Dubois's garage, not in Ivry-sur-Seine, and has Bonnot dying at the

siege in Nogent-sur-Marne, just after Garnier is shot dead after raising the black flag of anarchism on the roof of the "villa." The Thiais murders are not depicted, nor was René Valet. In the film, Jules Bonnot comes out as more of an anarchist than he probably was in reality. Victor is a minor presence, and Rirette was virtually absent. The film ends with the siege in Nogent-sur-Marne.

33   *Near the Société Génerale*
An auto starts up and in the terror,
The Bonnot Gang puts up its sails,
Carrying away the sack of the courier
In the Dion-Bouton which hides the thieves.
Octave counts the big bills and the securities
With Raymond-la-Science and the bandits in the auto
It's the Bonnot Gang. . . .
Dassin's song makes the gang seem like circus characters.

34   Florenci Clavé, *La bande à Bonnot* (Grenoble, 1978), paying particular attention to Bonnot's time with Judith Thollon and to the ultimate plight of Dieudonné, ending with (p. 48) "*Mais alors, qui était 'le quatrième homme' des 'bandits en auto'?*"

35   EA 141, Albert Philiponet from Poissy, September 8–9, 1973; December 8, 1972.

36   Victor Méric, *Les bandits tragiques*, pp. 112–113, 122–123.

INDEX

Italicized numbers indicate photographs or illustrations.

John Merriman is the Charles Seymour Professor of History at Yale University and the author of many books, including *Massacre: The Life and Death of the Paris Commune, The Dynamite Club: How a Bombing in Fin-de-Siècle Paris Ignited the Age of Modern Terror*, and the classic *A History of Modern Europe*. He is the recipient of Yale's Byrnes/Sewell Teaching Prize, a French Docteur Honoris Causa, and a frequent speaker at universities across the United States, the United Kingdom, France, and Australia.

The Nation Institute

Founded in 2000, **Nation Books** has become a leading voice in American independent publishing. The imprint's mission is to tell stories that inform and empower just as they inspire or entertain readers. We publish award-winning and bestselling journalists, thought leaders, whistleblowers, and truthtellers, and we are also committed to seeking out a new generation of emerging writers, particularly voices from underrepresented communities and writers from diverse backgrounds. As a publisher with a focused list, we work closely with all our authors to ensure that their books have broad and lasting impact. With each of our books we aim to constructively affect and amplify cultural and political discourse and to engender positive social change.

Nation Books is a project of The Nation Institute, a nonprofit media center established to extend the reach of democratic ideals and strengthen the independent press. The Nation Institute is home to a dynamic range of programs: the award-winning Investigative Fund, which supports groundbreaking investigative journalism; the widely read and syndicated website TomDispatch; journalism fellowships that support and cultivate over twenty-five emerging and high-profile reporters each year; and the Victor S. Navasky Internship Program.

For more information on Nation Books and The Nation Institute, please visit:

www.nationbooks.org
www.nationinstitute.org
www.facebook.com/nationbooks.ny
Twitter: @nationbooks